LOVE, LUST'

and the Longing for

G✦D

LOVE, LUST'
and the Longing for GOD

Justice Saint Rain

SPECIAL IDEAS

Special Ideas
511 Diamond Rd Heltonville IN 47436
1-800-326-1197

Love, Lust and the Longing for God
By Justice Saint Rain
© 2013 Justice Saint Rain All rights reserved.

Other books by Justice Saint Rain

Why Me? A Spiritual Guide to Growing Through Tests
The Secret of Happiness
A Spiritual Guide to Great Sex
Falling Into Grace
My Bahá'í Faith
The Hard Way – Lessons Learned
from the Economic Collapse
The Secret of Emotions
4 Tools of Emotional Healing
Longing for Love

Printed in the USA

ISBN 978-1888547-54-2

To all of the people who are
longing to call a truce
in the battle
between
the head
and the heart.

Contents:

Introduction

Part One:

The Secret of Emotions

Part Two:

4 Tools of Emotional Healing

Introduction:

If following your heart has repeatedly gotten you into trouble, but to follow your head feels like a kind of soul-death, then this book will open up a whole new world of possibilities for you. It will teach your head how to understand the language of your heart, and teach your heart how to speak the language of God.

It is not a mysterious as it sounds. The premise of this book is that emotions are our heart's response to the presence or absence of virtue. When I show people the list of emotions next to the list of virtues on page 54—and they are identical—they have an "ah-HA" moment, then wonder why no one ever noticed this before.

Associating emotions with virtues gives us clearer guidance than if we simply label them as "good emotions vs. bad emotions." It gives us an incredibly rich vocabulary to identify exactly what it is we are attracted to, or what quality seems to be missing in a situation. This gives us specific insights as to what we should do next.

Since most people make their life-choices based on their feelings rather than reason, understanding the meaning of our emotions is the *second*-most important lesson we can learn in this life.

The *most* important lesson is that *virtues are our path to the Transcendent.* Whether you call it God, Higher Power, Creative Spirit, or just your better self, we are all born with a longing to become more than we are right now—to demonstrate that we are, indeed, created in the image of the Divine.

So this book has the humble goal of helping you accurately identify your feelings so that you can develop the virtues that will help you become the best person possible. Along the way, you will heal old wounds, overcome shame, learn the true meaning of love, let go of compulsive behaviors, break unhealthy relationship patterns and develop new, healthy habits that will make future growth even easier.

If all of this seems too much to promise, I offer you this observation: simple awareness is often curative. Understanding the source and meaning of your emotions can literally change everything *in a heartbeat.*

ACKNOWLEDGEMENTS

Many thanks to the people who read early copies of this work and gave invaluable feedback: Phyllis Edgerly Ring, editor, and the author of *Life at First Sight – Finding the Divine in the Details*; Phyllis K. Peterson, author of **Remaining Faithful**; Kim Bowden-Kerby, whose advice was worth much more than I paid for it; and Jay Cardwell who found more in it than I put in.

Thanks, also, to all of the readers of my earlier works whose support and encouragement made the publication of this book possible. I am particularly grateful to the friends and strangers who have taken the time to write reviews of my books at GoodReads.com and at Amazon.com. You make all of the effort worthwhile.

I am particularly grateful to the friends and strangers who have taken the time to write reviews of my books at GoodReads.com and at Amazon.com. You make all of the effort worthwhile.

PART ONE

The Secret of Emotions

THE LANGUAGE OF THE *HEART*

We are all born with an innate longing for God—not a god with a long white beard who shakes his finger at us, but the Divine Creative Spirit that blessed the universe with breathtaking wonder and touched our hearts with limitless grace.

This God filled His creation with His most noble attributes—and then placed the potential for each of these qualities within the human heart. Our longing for God is not an intellectual longing. It is a *spiritual* longing. We approach God, not through theological study, but by being attracted to the attributes of God that are both reflected in creation and placed within our hearts. It is these attributes, then, such as love, beauty, honesty, forgiveness, patience, creativity and compassion that are the source of our longing for God.

Of all of the attributes that we long for, the one that pulls at our hearts most strongly is love. It is the one we sing songs about; the one we organize our lives around; the one that we are absolutely sure will solve all of our problems.

One would think, then, that over the course of thousands of years we would all have come to a clear understanding of what love is, how it feels in our hearts, and how true *spiritual* love differs from its more material counterparts of lust and passion. Yet we have not.

Almost no one has.

Our inability to understand and accurately identify love causes many of us to do things in the name of love that are anything but loving; things that take us further from our goals instead of nearer to them; things that make us feel ashamed instead of noble; things that convince us that we are failures instead of the radiant children of God that we are.

If we are ever going to satisfy our longing for love, and live the lives we were meant to live, then we will need to find a way to accurately identify spiritual love when we experience it so that we can create more of it in our lives.

This is the golden ring.
This is what we all want.

But it is bigger than that.

In order to learn how to recognize *one* of God's attributes, we must develop the understanding and skills needed to recognize *all of them*. God is not a grab-bag of isolated gifts, like faith, hope and love that you get to pick and choose. God is One. If you want to tap into God's love, you have to be prepared to accept *all* of God's bounties, and if you want to be able to recognize and create one virtue, you will need to develop the skills to recognize and create them all – not all at once, but as a lifelong process.

That process, I believe, begins by getting our hearts, our minds and our bodies all speaking the same language so that what we want, what we feel and what we know all fit together accurately and are in harmony with one another.

When our spiritual, physical and intellectual sides understand and respect each other, then we become whole. We are no longer divided against ourselves. We become the pilots of our own lives rather than being buffeted by needs, wants and sensations that confuse us, sabotage our best intentions and lead us astray.

You see, none of us wants a series of dysfunctional relationships. We don't want to destroy our marriages, sit alone in dark rooms watching videos, fantasize about people who will never love us, or do any of the other things that cause us shame. And yet if that is what we find in our lives, *that must be what we are pursuing*. Why is it, then, that we spend time and energy trying to acquire something that isn't what we really want?

What is it that we are looking for when we walk into that bar, pick up that phone, log onto that website, smile at that stranger or knock on that door?

The answer is…
The answer ALWAYS is…

God.

We are looking for God manifested in the world of creation.

We are looking for love, kindness, meaning, security, joy, hope, nobility, connection, and a myriad other virtues that God deposited within the human heart when He made it His home.

But if that is what we are looking for...

Why can't we find it?

The answer, if you think about it, is pretty obvious: Because we don't know what these qualities look like, or, more accurately, we don't know what these qualities FEEL like when we encounter them. How could we know how to accurately identify the signs of God's virtues, when everyone out there is as confused as we are? We mistake kindness for weakness, hope for naïveté, nobility for stuffiness, and love... well love is the most misidentified virtue of all. We have been given wildly inaccurate and misleading information about this most important of virtues by everyone – from our families, schools, and religious communities, to almost every single movie and pop song ever made. The feelings we mistake for love range from need and lust to pity, fear and shame.

I can say this because at different times in my life, I've mistaken each of these sensations for love, and I don't think I'm alone. If you have your doubts, let me describe a few experiences and see if they sound familiar. Then I'll describe what I have come to believe love really is and how it really feels. But first, the mistakes:

My Rosetta Stone

This is the story of how I became painfully aware that I had absolutely no idea of what my emotional sensations were trying to tell me.

During my last year of college, I was dating someone pretty seriously. She was an absolutely wonderful woman—one with whom I might have been happy my entire life. We had talked about marriage, but this was several years before her graduation so we hadn't become "officially" engaged or set a date.

One weekend, I went home to visit friends. While there, my best friend, who was married, told me about a wonderful single woman who had recently joined the community. He encouraged me to check her out before making any final commitments to my girlfriend.

I went to visit her, and had one of the strangest experiences of my entire life. Sitting in her room, my entire body began to tingle. I felt like I had electricity running through my veins. I remember that when she left the room for a minute, I paced back and forth, shaking my arms and fingers, trying to fling the excess energy out of my body. I was sure that if I touched her, sparks would fly between us.

Surely, this was a sign from God.

My heart was beating, my body tingled from head to toe; this must be what love was supposed to feel like.

Even though I knew almost nothing about this woman, I went back to my girlfriend and confessed that I would not be able to commit to getting married to her until I had explored this new relationship. She looked me in the eye and said, "Get out."

So I moved back home to see if I could turn sparks and tingles into a permanent relationship. As you might guess, over the next few months the sparks and tingles began to fade, and when I was offered a job in a different city, our relationship died a natural death.

I was befuddled. What had it all been about?

Fast forward almost exactly ten years. I am divorced, broke, depressed, alone and horny. I find myself in the middle of the night, standing in the parking lot of an adult video store. As I contemplate whether or not to go in, my body starts to tingle. I feel like I have electricity running through my veins. I start shaking my arms and fingers, trying to fling some of that excess energy out of my body.

I stop.

I remember this feeling.

But now it sure doesn't feel like love.

What was it all about?

I now had two data points for one sensation. What did they have in common? It wasn't love. It wasn't sex (I hadn't been contemplating sex with the woman I had just met). So what were my heart and body trying to tell my short-circuited brain?

Finally, after much time, prayer, journaling and therapy, I figured it out.

This is what intense shame feels like.

I was ashamed of myself for being untrue to my girlfriend.

I was ashamed of myself for thinking of buying pornography.

My body had been trying to tell me to turn around and run, and what I heard was, "This is really, really important. Stay and explore it."

If I could so completely misidentify a message of shame as a message of love, what *other* sensations had I misidentified over the years?

I began to listen, and watch, and correlate sensations with the experiences that went with them.

I discovered that when I got weak in the knees, it didn't mean I was in love. It meant that I was afraid that I would be blamed for breaking someone's heart.

I discovered that when my heart was moved by a woman's tears, it wasn't love, but a desire to rescue someone.

Over time, I began to identify sensations that were so subtle that I couldn't put a name to them, I could only identify them by the patterns they followed.

A certain tug on my heart let me know that women had been sexually abused.

A similar tug said that they were afraid of men.

Another told me that they were recently divorced with small children at home.

An uneasiness that at one time might have felt exciting now tells me that someone is not being completely honest.

At one point, all of these little emotional cues—whispers of the heart—would have been interpreted as, "God wants me to explore a relationship with this person." Now these messages simply say, "This person reflects some aspect of my relationship to my original God-figure. Resolve that relationship, don't enter into this one."

Recalibrating Our Inner Compass

Each of us is born with many wonderful capacities, but very little information, and even less understanding of how to make sense of that information. We have the capacity to see, for example, but it takes months for us to recognize faces, and years before we can make the distinction between pink and purple. We could say that parents and children work together to calibrate the child's visual perception so that the child not only sees, but understands what it sees and can distinguish between similar sensory cues.

We are also born with an inner compass. Instead of visual sensory input, we use spiritual emotional input to point us towards the many attributes of God in our environment. We learn to recognize love, kindness, joy, respect, compassion, security, patience, and a host of other qualities through our innate emotional attraction to their presence.

Just as our physical senses need to be trained, so do our spiritual senses. They need input, and that input needs to be calibrated against some kind of standard – a base against which all input is measured. For a baby, its inner compass is calibrated to point towards the god-figure in its life – its parents, particularly its mother. Just as we are born with the ability to see, but are taught to give names and meanings to the things we see, we are born with the ability to feel, but we are taught, mostly by our parents, how to give names and meanings to our feelings.

If your parent didn't know the difference between pink and any other random light color, you would have gone to kindergarten calling every pastel color "pink." Likewise, if your parent didn't know the difference between love and other strong spiritual sensations, then you would learn to look for love every time your heart or your body tried to send you a message, regardless of what that message was. This is how many of us come to interpret *any* intense sensation as a signal that we are falling in love.

It is also possible that your parents had a very clear image of what love is all about, but it just wasn't accurate. In this case, you would consciously or unconsciously, absorb your parent's expectations about love, and associate love with any number of unhealthy sensations.

If, for example, your parent said, "I love you" as they punished you, or ignored you, or laid guilt on you, or shamed you, or clung to you, or abused you, then *your* search for God will probably lead you towards people and activities that generate the sensations associated with these feelings. And when you find them, you will probably *think* that you are head-over-heels in love.

As children, we have an innate need to believe that our caregivers love us, and we will go to great lengths to reinterpret anything and everything they do as an expression of love. So *however* you were treated as a child, *that* is your core-level definition of love, no matter how many layers of intellectual calibrating you have done since then. It is important to change your conscious understanding of what love is. It is even more important to re-educate your subconscious emotional responses so that your heart doesn't drag you, kicking and screaming, where your head knows not to go.

Of course, this realization is not really anything new. Most people are aware that they learned about relationships from their parents. What is helpful about this framing of the idea is that it focuses not just on an abstract intellectual lesson learned, but on the *sensations* that we subconsciously learned to associate with God, love, and the goal of our desire. It then relates these sensations to the virtues that are the true goal of our search.

Understanding the relationship between virtues and emotions gives us a new and valuable tool in accurately identifying the meaning behind our emotional sensations. This tool can be used by both the mind *and* the heart and can help establish harmony between them.

So if we ask our original question again – "Why can't we find what we are looking for?" the answer is that we DO find what we are looking for, but what we are looking for is not what we really want. What we are looking for is things that remind us of the god of our childhood, but this god was not an accurate guide to the virtues and sensations that we really want.

If we want to start finding GOD, with a capital G, as manifested in holy virtues like love, kindness, patience, and serenity, then we will have to recalibrate our inner compass.

We will have to correlate the sensations we experience with a more accurate and objective assessment of the virtues we are experiencing. We will have to learn to distinguish between fool's gold and true gold, between lust, pity, need or fear, and *love*.

Then, finally, we will have to fall in love with the *real* virtues that are reflections of God and that reside in our own hearts. When we learn to love what is real and true, our obsessions with imitation love and the sensations surrounding it will fade.

The Importance of Emotions

"God conceals himself from the mind of man, but reveals himself to his heart."   — *African Proverb*

Most of us understand on a gut-level that emotions are important. They need to be listened to. But we don't understand *why*, and so we alternate between ignoring our emotions, and following them blindly.

In a piece called "The New Humanism," New York Times columnist David Brooks described the importance of combining reason and emotion and noted that: "…our emotions assign value to things and are the basis of reason."

That is a great phrase: *emotions assign value to things*, but there is no explanation as to how or why. When we figure out how and why emotions are important and how they assign value, then we will be in a better position to figure out *what* they are telling us, and *when* to listen to them.

This is what I believe: our emotions are spiritual sensations that tell us about the presence or absence of virtues in our lives, and virtues are the attributes of God expressed in the world of creation. Since our purpose in life is to develop these virtues within ourselves, it is only natural that we have been given the tools to recognize them when they are present.

Not only is it *natural* that we would be given this amazing ability to perceive our spiritual environment, but it is absolutely necessary. How else could we be expected to love the attributes of God in the world, if we were not given the ability to perceive them? If all we had to rely on was our intellectual capacity, then love, kindness, beauty, harmony, and joy would be dry intellectual or philosophical exercises – outside the experience of the vast majority of humanity.

We all know this is not how life works. The ability to recognize kindness, patience and fairness is not bestowed upon those with superior intellects. It is given to those with pure hearts.

It is the heart, then, that has been created with the capacity to recognize these divine qualities. And what tool does the heart have to communicate its recognition of a spiritual quality other than the spiritual emotions?

It is this innate awareness that our emotions are our means of recognizing and celebrating the attributes of God in the world that makes us choose to follow the promptings of our hearts – even when we don't understand them.

As we come to understand a little of what the heart is trying to communicate, we can begin to create an emotional glossary of terms that correlates the sensations that we feel with the virtues that we observe. Eventually, this glossary will be rich enough and complete enough to allow real communication between our heads and our hearts.

Physical Emotions and Spiritual Emotions

When the heart becomes whole, it will know the flavors of falsehood and truth.   — *Rumi*

One of the things that complicates our ability to identify our emotions accurately is the fact that our minds, hearts and bodies influence each other, but not always in a helpful way. We have physical emotions, which respond to physical threats and stimuli, and spiritual emotions that respond to our spiritual environment, and a mind that tries to figure out what these similar yet different sources of sensations are trying to say.

I like to compare the relationship between physical emotions and spiritual emotions to the relationship between taste and smell. When you combine the sensation of taste on your tongue with the sensation of smell through your nose, you experience a flavor. Likewise, when you combine your physical response to a situation with your spiritual response to a situation, you experience the "emotional flavor" of the situation. The two work together to give you a more complete and satisfying understanding of what is going on.

To appreciate this analogy, it helps to understand how taste and smell work together. This is how Wikipedia explains it:

Of the three chemical senses, smell is the main determinant of a food item's flavor. While the taste of food is limited to sweet, sour, bitter, salty, and savory – the basic tastes – the smells of a food are potentially limitless. [Our perception of] a food's flavor, therefore, can be easily altered by changing its smell while keeping its taste similar.

Comparing physical emotions to taste and spiritual emotions to smell offers several insights. First, it illustrates the fact that our bodies have a limited range of responses to any given situation, but our spirits have an almost unlimited capacity to distinguish between different virtues that may be present.

Second, when we think of a flavor, we prioritize the experience of its taste on our tongue, even though for most flavors, it is the smell that imparts the most pleasure and information. Likewise, when we think of emotions, we often focus on our physical reaction to a situation. This is why researchers often limit their study of emotions to the handful that can be measured biochemically. In doing this, they ignore the fact that it is our spiritual response that distinguishes between the similar sensations of excitement and fear, between patience and boredom, between feeling hungry and feeling empty.

When we over-emphasize the importance of our physical emotional responses, we minimize the role that our mind and heart play in generating emotions. What we *think* makes a big difference in what we *feel*.

If you were handed a piece of red candy and told it was strawberry – and if it smelled like strawberry, you would have a very difficult time determining whether the actual taste was grape, cherry, or even chocolate! What we see, smell and hear can change what we taste.

Likewise, if you are about to go on stage to give a talk and you tell yourself, "I'm so scared. I'm so scared!" you can easily work yourself into a full-blown panic attack. On the other hand, if you tell yourself, "This is so exciting. This is so exciting!" you can walk out on stage with confidence and enthusiasm. So one experience can generate two very different feelings depending on what we tell ourselves.

This is because the physical symptoms of fear and excitement are almost exactly the same. There is not enough information in the physical sensation to tell us what is really going on. All we know is that we need to wake up and pay attention.

It is what we *tell ourselves* about the sensation that points it in one direction or another. Once you define the sensation for yourself, your spirit and your body will create a reinforcing feedback loop.

I've already talked about how easy it is to convince ourselves that we are in love when we are really experiencing shame. The other strong physical sensation that we often tell ourselves is love is really *fear*. Fear tells our body to wake up. What we tell ourselves after that determines whether our bodies produce more adrenaline or more pheromones. If we tell ourselves we are attracted to someone, then our bodies will start generating arousal rather than a fight or flight response. Once that happens, it is easy to convince ourselves that what we felt from the very beginning was attraction. I will talk about this more after I describe what I believe true love really is.

Understanding Love

Love is metaphysical gravity.   — *R. Buckminster Fuller*
The power which moves, controls and attracts the hearts of men is
the love of God.   — *'Abdu'l-Bahá*

If we want to recognize true love instead of being fooled by shame, fear, pity, need, and all of the other imitations we have been taught to accept, then we probably ought to have an accurate working definition of the term.

I will start by explaining my understanding of what real love is, and then contrast that with the experience of *romantic* love, or being *in* love. I will discuss other sensations we mistake for love in a later chapter.

Real Love

Pieces of iron are innately attracted to a magnet. Flowers in a garden naturally turn towards the light of the sun. When we walk through that garden, we are instinctively drawn to bend down and smell the sweetness of a rose.

The heart is naturally attracted to the signs of God in the world.

This attraction – this innate tendency to turn towards beauty, kindness, enthusiasm and generosity – is the essence of love.

When we look around the world, the best reflections of these qualities can be found in the human soul.

Human love, then, is simply the recognition of, admiration for and attraction to the attributes of God in another person.

This attraction is felt in the heart. It is warm and pleasant, and grows with increased interaction. It is rarely overwhelming, and can be felt for people of any age, race or sex.

If we have learned to love such attributes as kindness, patience, responsibility, and joyfulness, then we will recognize, appreciate and be attracted to these qualities when we see them expressed in a human being — no matter who the person may be.

How much we love a person is determined by our ability to recognize virtues when we experience them, the strength of our attraction to those virtues, and the number and quality of virtues that the person expresses.

Take a look at that definition again. It is simple and universal, but it may contradict your long-held beliefs about love. You may, for example, want to separate love into several sub categories like romantic love, brotherly love and parental love. Or you may want to define love by the *things we do* as a result of feeling love – things like psychologist Erich Fromm's *care, responsibility, respect* and *knowledge* from his book *The Art of Loving*, or Scott Peck's *the will to extend oneself for the purpose of nurturing one's own or another's spiritual growth.* You might associate love with many of the intense feelings that masquerade as love, such as passion, attachment or need.

Rather than either wrestling with this definition now, or accepting it outright, I invite you to set your current understanding aside for a while and see where this approach takes you. You can always pick it back up later.

This definition of love focuses on a person's qualities rather than his or her personality, and on our attraction to those qualities rather than the actions that are the result of that attraction. What does it mean to be attracted to a *quality* rather than a person? Let's take as examples two of the qualities I've been mentioning: kindness and responsibility.

Experiencing someone's kindness generates a sensation. It feels good just to watch a person showing kindness, even if it is towards someone else. If we are attracted to kindness – if we see it as a sign of strength instead of weakness – then our *attraction* will *also* generate a sensation. It feels like the invisible pull of a magnet. When the sensation of attraction combines with the sensation of kindness, they reinforce one another to a point that it is impossible to ignore or dismiss. The strength of the combined sensation can spill over into a general positive regard for the person expressing this attractive virtue.

The virtue of responsibility also generates sensations. Watching a person make wise and thoughtful decisions in the face of temptations to do otherwise can be very uplifting, and yet not as many people are aware of these sensations because they have not been taught to recognize and be attracted to them. Without the attraction, the sensations go unnoticed and are not reinforced. They therefore do not spill over into a general appreciation for the person demonstrating responsibility. If we don't love the qualities a person demonstrates, it is difficult to feel that we love them, no matter how wonderful they may be.

It is our ability to be attracted to positive qualities, then, that expands our ability to love the people around us. This means that the more virtues we learn to recognize and be attracted to, the more people we will love, and the more rewarding our interaction with them will be.

If we learn to be attracted to even a *hint* of a virtue, or even just the *potential* for a virtue, then we can find a way to love almost anyone. The ability to love *potential* is what makes a parent's love for their children come so naturally.

Though virtues are universal, each individual has developed a unique collection of virtues and expresses them in their own way. I like to think of virtues as stars, and individuals have their own constellations of qualities that create the patterns of their lives. We don't just love the individual points of light; we take pleasure in discovering the patterns that they form as they blaze their arc across the heavens.

⌘

The Limitations of Love as a Sensation

It is a good thing that love feels good. When we discover the signs of God in another person—courage, wisdom, kindness, responsibility—then it is helpful that our hearts respond with a positive sensation that attracts us to this person and those qualities. The sensation is a message that says, "Look this way! Notice this person! Learn from these qualities!" The sensation makes us enjoy spending time with this person and lets us know that we have found someone worth investing time and attention in.

But a message is just a message. Once the message has been delivered, there is no need for it to stand around whispering in your ear. The sensations of love need not last forever.

Think of love as a fragrance. When you step into a person's life, you smell the fragrance and it pleases you. But in time, your ability to smell that particular fragrance fades. It is not that the fragrance has gone away, but your need to smell it, and therefore your *ability* to smell it has disappeared.

Now, if a completely *different* fragrance enters the room, then *that* is what you will notice. Perhaps the person you love smells like kindness, responsibility and patience, but now someone who smells like creativity and courage steps into your life. If you believe that the most important thing about love is its ability to generate sensations, then you will believe that you no longer love the first person and now only love the second.

The truth is, you may love them both. The question is, which have you made a commitment to? When you understand how love, sensations and virtues relate to one another, then you know that commitment trumps sensation almost every time.

Knowing that sensations fade over time, we can do two things: 1) minimize the importance we give to sensations, and 2) never lose interest in our partners. If we keep growing and keep exploring one another's character, then we will continue to discover new virtues, new potentials, new capacities that will awaken new sensations of appreciation and attraction.

Romantic Love

There are many sensations that we mistake for love, but there are only a few that create that intense, overwhelming feeling that we associate with *romantic* love. One is shame, which I've already mentioned and will discuss in detail later. Another is *fear*.

The sensations that are usually associated with feeling "in love" – nervousness, butterflies in the stomach, weak knees, obsessive thinking, or light headedness – have little or nothing to do with love. If you felt these sensations while sitting next to an 800 pound gorilla rather than an attractive person, then you would recognize them for the symptoms of *terror* that they really are.

Why, you ask, would you feel fear when in the presence of an attractive person, and how could you possibly mistake fear for love?

I'll start with the second question. We don't recognize fear because it makes no logical sense. It is not what we expect, so we can't recognize it. What we *expect* is what every movie, song, story and friend has told us about this feeling: a fluttering heart is a sign of true love. In the face of such overwhelming evidence, your mind overrides your intuition and you call the feeling love.

Many years ago, for example, I found myself getting weak in the knees while kissing a new girlfriend, so I called an old friend and asked what she thought it might mean. She said she still got weak in the knees sometimes when kissing her husband of 15 years. I took this as a good sign and entered the relationship with high hopes and great enthusiasm. Two months later, my new relationship ended because of serious trust issues. How could this be? My knees had told me I could have a romantic relationship like my friend's. As it turned out, I did. "Weak knees" did not save my friend's marriage either. It was their *belief* in the significance of weak knees that had kept them together, but they had been secretly unhappy for years.

The answer to the question of how we can mistake fear for love, then, is quite simple. Even our best friends will tell us that fear is really love – because almost everyone believes it.

❤

America's Classic Romance

Love is a light that never dwelleth in a heart possessed by fear.
— Bahá'u'lláh

Perhaps you have heard of this classic romance—one that has sold millions of books and sent mothers and daughters to theaters together to swoon over its depiction of true love. It is about Bella, a pretty, but klutzy and socially awkward girl who is literally swept off her feet by the handsome, charming, very strong and *very* mysterious Edward. The minor problem in their affair is that he, unfortunately, is a vampire.

Given this situation, what would be the appropriate sensation for Bella to feel? Fear, of course. But Edward also manages to save her life using his superhuman strength, which makes him her savior. Thus he is both the source of her fear and the source of her protection from fear at the same time. The more they are together, the more she needs his protection. We can certainly understand the intensity of her feelings in his presence, but who in their right mind would call this love? Well, actually, every Disney movie for the last 50 years has confused love with being rescued, and several, such as The Beauty and the Beast, include the element of danger to intensify the sensation.

Edward, on the other hand, gets to feel a host of complementary intense feelings around Bella. First, there is the obvious sense of power he gets from protecting her (she is such a klutz that she is *always* needing protection). But this savior role is countered by the guilt he feels for putting her in danger in the first place, and his shame over being a vampire. What seals the deal, however, is the fact that, though vampires can read human's minds, he is unable to read hers. This makes her the most mysterious human he's ever met.

How many other times have we seen men fall for the mysterious "other" or the vulnerable person they want to protect? These paths to love are depicted over and over in movies and literature. *Yes*, it feels good to take care of people, and it is convenient that our imaginations can fill in the spaces in the mysterious unknown with whatever we hope might be there. But what do these things have to do with love?

When we don't understand what our feelings are trying to tell us, all we have to go on is their intensity. We then equate intensity with *significance*, and cling to the intensity in the hope of making our relationships—and our lives—seem more significant.

Bella and Edward's relationship was written to elicit the maximum intensity of feelings, but nowhere in their interactions were there any indications that those feelings had anything to do with an attraction to each other's spiritual virtues. And yet, for millions of readers, this story was not about fear, vulnerability, salvation, guilt and mystery, it was about *love*.

Back to you...

But you aren't in love with a vampire, so why would *you* feel fear in the presence of an attractive person in the first place? What is it about the people you are attracted to that you fear, and why would your heart recognize someone as dangerous before your mind did? If emotions tell us about virtues, where are the virtues?

Emotions tell us about our spiritual environment, which includes the presence and the *absence* of virtues. Our eyes see light, but they can also experience darkness. Our skin feels warmth, but it must also be able to respond to cold. Our stomachs can tell us when they are full, but are most insistent when they are empty. Our hearts are filled by the presence of love and kindness and faithfulness, but when they are empty, they are saddened by the lack of these things and feel the loss.

Just as our stomachs growl when empty without us telling them to, and our eyes can see colors whether we know the name for them or not, our hearts often respond to our spiritual surroundings without our making a conscious choice or using intellectual cues. When we feel that we "know" something without knowing why or how we know it, we often call it intuition, but that doesn't mean it is magic. We are simply using a kind of spiritual perception that we didn't know we had.

When you meet a person, some part of you is capable of recognizing the presence or absence of key spiritual qualities in them almost instantly. When it recognizes wonderful, loving, nurturing qualities, then you naturally respond with the warm, pleasant, heart-centered feelings described in the first section on love.

When it recognizes qualities that have caused you pain in the past—ones expressed by parents, siblings, teachers or previous relationships—then it experiences fear. This is not to say that these people are *evil*, only that they are *familiar* in a way that feels unsafe. Perhaps they are simply needy, or shaming, or are afraid of commitment. Because of the close relationship between the heart and body, this fear interacts with the body to release adrenaline and other chemicals. These chemicals cause the heart to pound and the stomach to tighten. Physical senses become more focused and intense, *but higher reasoning functions become blurred.*

If this fight-or-flight response is redefined as love, then you are left in a very vulnerable position. Your mind is telling your heart to start looking for things to love, so your heart tells your body to gear up, not for running, but for flirting. Consequently, all of that adrenaline is redirected towards arousal. You are now more susceptible to sexual stimulation (sensual and hormonal), and are less able to reason your way out of obviously compromising situations. This is how most unhealthy relationships begin.

Why do we stay?

Once you are physically separated from this person, these sensations will naturally fade, so why doesn't your better judgment kick in and point you towards someone less scary? There are two reasons. First, as I've said, these are the people whom your mind tells you are exciting, stimulating and sexy. Everyone is looking for their Bella or Edward.

But there is a deeper reason.

The purpose of life is to learn and grow. We learn when we face challenges and overcome them. Challenges that we faced when we were very young sometimes overcame *us.* We did not have the mental, physical or spiritual resources we needed in order to successfully overcome certain recurring trauma. If, as adults, we do not *consciously* seek out and work through these issues, then we will *subconsciously* recognize and be attracted to them when we least expect it. If we are lucky, we will recognize these people as learning experiences instead of marrying them.

It is a truism that when the thrill of romance (adrenaline) wears off, most people discover that they have married one of their parents. This is because a disapproving parent is what our souls fear most, and therefore respond to most intensely. We call these relationships *dealing with unfinished business.*

Recently, an acquaintance came up to me at a conference, wanting to tell me why she absolutely *had* to marry her new husband. You see, it seems that the first time she hugged him, the heavens opened up and the angels sang – for both of them. So even though she didn't want to get married, and it made no sense, she could not go against the will of God and refuse his offer.

Since I have great respect for this person, I was willing to consider the possibility that in this one instance, this was a sign of true love.

Then she ended with the statement: "hugging him felt just like hugging my father."

Her father... who I knew to be a wonderful man, was also a manic depressive who had divorced her mother when she was young. He left a hole in her life that had not yet been filled.

Who am I to stand in the way of unfinished business?

Why We Marry Our Mothers

We don't always enter into unhealthy relationships because we have misidentified a sensation as love.

Sometimes we are drawn into unhealthy relationships because we are subconsciously attempting to *reenact* situations, failures, traumas and problems that caused us stress in the past.

Now this might sound like some really heavy psychological mumbo-jumbo, but it is really pretty basic and easy to demonstrate.

Have you ever been in a situation where someone insulted you or embarrassed you, and you couldn't think of the right thing to say or do to save face right at that moment? Physically, your heart probably started beating faster, your body released adrenaline, and you felt physically agitated. Soon afterwards, you started mentally reliving the experience, trying to think of the right thing to say, or imagining the right physical response to prevent or rescue the situation.

How *soon* after the experience did you start thinking of alternative scenarios? How *long* after the situation were you still running through alternative responses? Was it minutes? Hours? Days? Perhaps months or years?

Chances are that the more adrenaline your body released during the stressful situation, the more times you relived the scene in your mind. Also, the more helpless you felt in the face of the humiliation, the more important the mental reliving is, and the wilder the fantasized victory over the other person will be.

This reliving process is completely natural. It applies to sports, video games, business transactions, failed romances, marital battles, and any other situation in which the mental, "If only I had…" kicks in after the fact.

This is how we learn. We remember difficult situations or mistakes that we have made, try to imagine how we might respond differently, and mentally rehearse this response in preparation for our next encounter. When a similar situation does arise, our bodies will respond with the same fight-or-flight excitement, but our minds will be better prepared to handle the challenge effectively.

In most day-to-day activities, this process serves us well. We visualize ourselves catching the football we dropped, or double-checking our work before submitting an assignment, or making some clever comment in a social situation. Reliving, imagining and rehearsing works when we possess the capacity to make things work out better the next time.

But what if we don't?

When we were humiliated, abused, insulted, or placed in difficult situations as *children*, there was little we could do to make things better the next time. The details of the situation may have changed from day to day, but the core dynamic — powerful adult interacting with powerless child — remained the same for years at a time. When we were hurt, we didn't feel safe enough to challenge the situation, but that didn't mean we weren't reliving it over and over. Each time we would try to imagine what it would take to make things better. Did we need to become big, strong and powerful like Superman to protect ourselves, or beautiful and perfect like a princess so no one would want to hurt us? The possibilities were as endless as our imaginations.

Because, as children, we never felt safe enough or powerful enough to challenge the people who hurt us directly, the fantasy reenactment that we rehearsed never got acted out. Consequently, it will *stay* a fantasy until we grow up and find a safe substitute on which to try out our response.

That safe substitute can be anyone who reminds us of the original stressful situation, but who does not have as much power to hurt us as the original offender.

The right person might not appear in our lives until much of the original pain has been consciously forgotten. But *consciously* forgotten is not the same as gone.

Most events in our lives happen only once. The painful ones that we think we could have changed are recreated in our minds dozens, hundreds, perhaps thousands of times. Many become so painful that we tuck them below the surface of our memory until we meet a person that reminds us of our past.

The problem is that we don't consciously know that this person reminds us of anything. The remembering that takes place is not an intellectual remembering. It is an emotional recognition of the familiar. When our hearts recognize a familiar pattern of behavior, they generate the appropriate emotional sensations, which are then communicated to the body.

Those sensations, so often mistaken for love, are really trying to tell us that *something important is going on here.*

This is not mysterious. This is not magical. These are common, day-to-day thought processes that have been stretched out over a period of decades instead of days, because they never got resolved. The only strange thing is that, by the time we get a chance to practice what we rehearsed, we have forgotten how the story started. We are struggling to answer a question we forgot we had even asked: *how do I make things better?*

Children are not deaf-mutes. They feel pain, and they observe pain in others, both physical and emotional. They have no power, and they have a very limited understanding of the motivations and behaviors of the people around them. They do, however, have very creative imaginations. Children try to imagine ways of being, ways of responding, ways of feeling, that would protect themselves and others from the pain they feel.

Now, we don't have to be talking about child abuse, violence or cruelty. Other conditions such as loneliness, depression, mental illness, divorce, estrangement, poverty, substance abuse all create environments in which children might wish to fantasize about the things they might be able to do someday to make things better.

A child who had an alcoholic parent is likely to have fantasized about being able to use the power of love to convince that parent to give up drinking. A child whose mother suffered from abuse, or poverty or depression, surely has fantasies about rescuing that parent and making everything better.

It is impossible for a heart to live with a constellation of needs (spoken or unspoken, acknowledged or hidden) without being able to recognize those needs at a glance.

Do we imagine that our hearts are blind?
Our hearts see more than our eyes.
And then the heart whispers…

As children, we were powerless to change anything, but surely, surely now that we are grown we will be able to meet the need, fill the void, solve the problem and make the hurt go away. Please God, let it be so.

Perhaps you are like me.

I would do anything to have been able to ease my mother's pain, but I couldn't. So I was drawn like a moth to a flame to that *same* pain as reflected in dozens upon dozens of other women's hearts. I found women who were afraid, abandoned, lonely and abused. Each time I hoped that *this* time I could make a difference.

But I never did.

Each person is responsible to God to solve their own problems. We can offer each other love and support and guidance, but we can't fix anyone else. This is attested to by millions upon millions of broken hearts.

Sometimes our desire to fix old hurts is played out in ways that are laughably obvious. If you watch your own patterns, or those of your friends, you may see people being attracted to the same kinds of people over and over again. For example, my mother has red hair, so I tried to date every woman with red hair I met. Other men only date blonds, or skinny over-achievers. Some women only date athletes or men who drive fast cars. It would be funny if it weren't so painful.

Other times, the patterns we are repeating are not so obvious. It took me years to realize that most of the women to whom I was sexually attracted had been sexually abused as children, and most of the women with whom I wanted to be best friends were manic-depressive. This does not mean that they weren't also wonderful people, but it did mean that a good portion of our relationship wasn't about *us* at all. Part of me had one foot in the past, trying to heal the people in my family whom I loved. It wasn't fair to these current relationships, and it didn't change the old ones. I failed them both, and the guilt of that double failure ate me up inside.

Healing *Shame*

Shame leads us into unhealthy relationships.
Shame is what we feel at the end of them.
Shame is what we are taught to feel about ourselves.
Shame is what we beat ourselves up with for our failures.
Shame is what we try to hide from through our acting out.
Shame is what our acting out leads to.

If you are reading this book because you are struggling to control inappropriate behaviors, then shame is probably the dominating force in your life much of the time.
That's OK.
Don't be ashamed.
We can do something to change that.
The first step is to understand what healthy shame is.
The second step is to see how our cultural beliefs cause it
to become unhealthy.
The third step is to understand shame spirals.
The fourth step is to stop using shameful behaviors to numb
the shame.

There are alternative ways to escape shame that are much more fun than shameful behaviors.
I promise.

What is Shame?

First of all, we need to know what healthy shame is.* Shame is simply an emotional reaction to a flash of self-awareness in which we realize that we are not perfect, that we are, in fact, human. This is a good thing. Being human is a good thing. *Knowing* we are human is a good thing. Knowing that we are not perfect is a *very good thing*.

Shame is like a little alarm that buzzes when we make a mistake. It lets us know that we need to adjust our behavior. Without it, we cannot recognize or learn from mistakes. We cannot become better. Because it is generally an unpleasant sensation, it motivates us to avoid shameful situations and behaviors.

So, if healthy shame is a good thing, how does it become unhealthy? Shame becomes toxic when we combine it with two unhealthy beliefs that are almost universally accepted by our culture. The first is perfectionism. The second is black-and-white thinking (also known as *all-or-nothing* thinking).

When we do anything, what we are really doing is making a choice. Most choices are rarely earth-shattering; they simply involve an attempt to balance competing goals. When added together over the course of our lives, however, these choices define who we are and create our legacy. When we feel a twinge of shame, it is simply telling us that the decision we just made could have been better. This is a good thing, because it allows us to either change our decision, or make a different one in the future.

Our shame alarm is designed to sound only if the difference between our two choices is moderately significant. Like a smoke detector, it is designed to ignore household dust or even Chinese stir-fry cooking. It only sounds if we are in danger of doing something spiritually unhealthy.

---

*Note: different therapeutic systems use the words guilt and shame differently. Since there are no universally-accepted definitions, if you use the ones I give here, the rest of the book will make more sense.

If, however, we are perfectionists, then our internal alarm is set for zero tolerance. Since perfection is impossible, our shame response gets stuck in the on position permanently.

Likewise, black-and-white thinking—the belief that everything is either right or wrong, good or bad, saved or damned—locks our shame alarm on high volume. It doesn't matter whether we pretend that we are godly or unrepentant, there is always a part of us that knows that we aren't 100% right, so we secretly feel we must be 100% wrong.

While perfectionism tells us that we have to be perfect, black-and-white thinking tells us how dire the consequences of failure will be.

This attitude is reinforced by our culture's dominant religious beliefs. Even if we are not raised Christian, a belief in original sin and heaven and hell is infused into almost every aspect of our culture. As a result, we carry a saved/damned duality deep in our psyches. For centuries, Christianity has taught that we are in need of salvation and deserving of damnation. It has also described a stark, black-and-white division between the forces of good and the forces of evil.*

The last few decades have seen a shift in some denominations, with even the Pope himself saying that hell is not a place, but a state of being far from God. This is a wonderful realization. Unfortunately, few people have heard this statement, and fewer still have been able to believe it. Two-thousand years of self-loathing and fear of punishment do not disappear from our collective worldview that easily.

Knowing we are forgiven and feeling forgiven are two very different things. When we feel unforgivable we continue to punish ourselves with shame.

---

*I need to say a few words to my Christian readers because I don't want them to misunderstand me. Christ is a messenger of God. Christianity is good and true. But the leaders of the Christian Church have over-emphasized shame and guilt as a means of controlling people, and have misrepresented what Christ actually meant by salvation. If this is a subject that concerns you (or even if it isn't) I encourage you to read the appendix titled **An Alternate View of Salvation**.

We all know what people do with smoke detectors that have zero tolerance. If it goes off every time we cook a meal, light a candle, or smoke a cigarette, then pretty soon we decide to unplug the battery.

No one can live with a smoke alarm going off in his head every minute. Likewise, no one can be happy when tormented by shame. We have to find a way to escape the buzzing alarm, the flush of embarrassment, the pang of guilt and the wave of regret that we experience when shame comes to dominate our lives.

Given the fact that perfectionism and black-and-white thinking have dominated Western culture for thousands of years, it is understandable that many people have chosen to react to these influences by swinging 180 degrees in the opposite direction. Rather than fixing the shame alarm by developing reasonable personal expectations and learning to appreciate the full spectrum of moral choices, they have tried to simply pull the plug on shame.

They try to fool themselves into thinking that inappropriate behavior is perfectly fine. There are no "rules." Everything is relative and arbitrary. If it feels good, they should be able to do it, and shame is a prudish response to be ignored if at all possible.

Unfortunately, it is NOT possible to ignore shame. Unhealthy shame is unhealthy, but to have NO shame leads us to behave in ways that are not becoming to our nobility as reflections of the attributes and virtues of God. No matter what our heads tell us, our hearts know something different. Because of this, we need to find a way to turn off the screaming shame siren in our heads while leaving the healthy little warning tingles intact.

One tool for achieving this is to understand shame spirals.

The way we perceive right and wrong affects our ability to heal our shame.

HEALING SHAME

involves letting go of Perfectionism,
Black & White Thinking,
and Shamelessness.

Perfectionist: I should be here ⟶

WORST	BEST

Black & White: I have to be
at least here ⟶

BAD	GOOD

Black & White Perfectionist:
I have to be at least here ⟶

HERE THERE BE DEMONS

The Shameless:
I can't improve, so why try?

GOOD AND BAD ARE ARBITRARY ANYWAY

Healthy Shame:
I would rather be <u>here</u>
than here ⟶

WORSE	BETTER

Shame Spirals

My nephew, who is wise beyond his years, posted this on Facebook:

TO DO LIST:

Find a cookie.
Tell yourself that eating the cookie is a bad idea.
Eat the cookie anyway.
Regret eating the cookie.
Deal with guilt by looking for more cookies.

Since our hearts will not allow us to permanently pull the plug on shame, we are left to find other ways to silence the alarm. The world is full of short fixes. Drugs, alcohol, sex, pornography, over-eating, shopping, gambling, television, web-surfing, games, gossip, sleep, and even work can be used to temporarily numb or distract us from our feelings of shame. An over-eater feels great for the 20 minutes it takes to eat a pint of ice cream, and the TV-addict is dead to shame as long as the tube is on.

The problem is that when we stop our numbing behavior, the numbness starts to go away. Eventually, a part of us wakes up to the understanding that the behavior was not good for us.

It doesn't take long before we begin to feel even more gluttonous, horny, lazy, evil or sick than we did before. When this happens, it is even more tempting to start numbing ourselves again. This is how it becomes a shame spiral. The very behavior that numbs the shame also feeds the shame. People who are caught in this spiral are miserable, but are often too ashamed to ask for help.

There are probably almost as many kinds of shame spirals as there are people in the world, but there is one that is more common than most that I would like to use as an illustration before addressing the steps it takes to break one.

Love, Sex and Shame, the Universal Spiral

Humans have a universal need for love. Humans are also created with a biological desire for sex. Love and marriage, love and sex, love and belonging, these are the conscious associations we have between love and sex.

It is tragic, then, that before this sweet and positive association can be planted in our conscious minds, a much less pleasant association has already taken root in our subconscious minds. Before children have the foggiest idea of what the word sex actually means, they absorb the cultural attitude that it is somehow shameful and evil. Body parts, bodily functions, kissing, nakedness, sex, ewww, GROSS! I don't think anyone on the planet can escape the constant and highly-charged association of sex with shame.

Here's the problem. Associations go two ways. If we are constantly bombarded with SEX = SHAME, SEX = SHAME, SEX = SHAME, then it is impossible not to also respond with SHAME = SEX. In other words, if we associate sex with shame, then when something happens to us that causes us to suddenly feel ashamed – even if it is *healthy* shame, our subconscious minds will start thinking about sex. If we *consciously* start thinking about sex at inappropriate times or with inappropriate people, then this can generate even *more* shame.

Now throw love into the mix. We subconsciously associate sex with shame, but we consciously associate it with love. That means that we also associate love with shame. We have a legitimate and natural desire to find love, but because we associate this love with sex, we feel ashamed of our desire for love.

Now consider the fact that love, sex and shame all generate what *should* be unique physical and spiritual sensations. Because love, sex and shame are all tied into knots in our subconscious, the sensations that they generate also associate, interact, overlap and get confused, one with another. When we feel a strong reaction to a person or situation, our conscious mind has no way to decipher the feelings that are washing over it. Is it love, lust, shame, fear, confusion, or a combination of all of them? Which sensation should be exalted, and which should be numbed? Which is a sign from God, and which is a temptation from a lower nature?

Caught in the whirlwind of conflicting emotions, sensations and interpretations, we often choose the wrong course of action, only to realize hours, days, or years later that we zigged when we should have zagged, and what we thought we were pursuing was not what we snagged.

When that happens, then the shame rises to the surface, and the search begins for some way to numb it. Drugs, alcohol, flirtation, sex, sugar, shopping, pornography, gambling, there are dozens of ways to numb shame. If the substance or behavior that numbs the shame is something that can also *cause* shame, then a spiral has begun.

You can see from this that a shame spiral can be started by something *other* than the behavior that keeps it going. In fact, it is likely that it was. For many, the part of the shame spiral that keeps us numb is all that we can see. It becomes the *identified problem* that keeps us distracted from the deeper source of shame that hides behind it. Almost anyone in recovery will tell you that breaking the addiction is only the first step. It is what is *behind* the unhealthy behavior that takes the real work.

But then... maybe I shouldn't have told you that.

If you picked up this innocent looking book thinking that it would give you a quick fix for your identified problem and then let you go right on being the same person, you might not be very happy to learn that that is only the beginning. Before you are through, you may have to change your understanding of *who you are* from the bottom up. Not everyone is ready for that. For any solution to work, however, you have to really *want* to get at the source of your behaviors, or you will sabotage your efforts to change them and you will never get a chance to peek behind the curtain.

Do you *want* to become a happy, healthy, fully-present person? OK, good. Then let's break this shame spiral.

Breaking the Shame Spiral

In trying to find a way to break this spiral, it might be helpful to review the cookie analogy. It has five steps:

Find a cookie.
Tell yourself that eating the cookie is a bad idea.
Eat the cookie anyway.
Regret eating the cookie.
Deal with guilt by looking for more cookies.

This means that there are multiple points at which you can break the cycle. Most people focus on #3, and they think that if they work harder at #2 then they will break the cycle there. *Ha.* The more intensely you do #2, the more you set yourself up for #4. The whole cycle is designed to maximize shame so that you can justify keeping the cycle going.

What I recommend instead is to reduce the level of shame and guilt so that you aren't motivated to numb them with more acting out.

The way to do this is to:
1. Develop a more mature approach to perfectionism.
2. Be more "present" during the behavior so you can better understand your motivations and the payoff you are getting for continuing it.
3. *Replace* rather than *resist* unhealthy patterns.
4. Utilize a different kind of motivator, one based on your longing for God rather than shame over your mistakes.
5. Learn about and practice virtues, particularly the virtues of honesty, forgiveness and compassion.

While shame spirals involve a circular process of negative reinforcement, spiritual healing is a holistic process of positive reinforcement. Doing a little bit of any one of these things will make it easier to do all of the others. Start anywhere, take baby steps, and the incremental changes will create exponential progress.

Transforming Our Perfectionism

The first step in breaking our shame spirals is to deal with our perfectionism. Earlier I explained how perfectionism helps generate shame. Let's review that idea, and then explore how to transform perfectionism into something healthy.

Perfectionism turns every success into a failure. When you try to celebrate, it whispers in your ear that you should have done better. Though I have absolutely no idea of what specific things your personal demons are saying to you, I have a pretty good idea of the general themes of their chorus:

You will never be good enough.

Close to good enough is nowhere *near* good enough – you are either in or out, saved or damned, acceptable or unworthy.

These two closely-related attitudes, perfectionism and black-and-white thinking, pervade our culture and poison our beliefs about ourselves. The difference between them is that perfectionism says that you need to be perfect, but can imagine shades of grey leading up to that perfection. Black-and-white thinking says that there is no grey. If it is not perfect, it must be evil.

Combined, these two attitudes are deadly, and yet they form the foundation of much of our beliefs about ourselves and the world. Once we have acknowledged the damage that they can cause, we are still left with the dilemma of how to escape them. It would be nice if we could just tell ourselves to stop being such perfectionists, and did! Unfortunately, it is not that easy. Perfectionism carries with it a built-in catch-22, a kind of circular logic that is difficult to break away from.

If I need to be perfect, then to acknowledge that this need *itself* is unhealthy would violate my need to be perfect.

Before I can accept that I've been wrong to believe in perfectionism, I have to accept that it is all right to be wrong. But I can't allow myself to be wrong until *after* I accept that it is OK to not be perfect. Aargh!

It gets even more complicated.

Some of us are willing to accept that we have been wrong. After all, our shame comes from the fact that we believe we are *not* good enough. But then there is the question of *where we learned* our perfectionism. We did not wake up as infants and decide, "I think that if I am not perfect, I should be ashamed of myself."

No, we were *taught* to feel shame for being imperfect. We were taught by people who wanted us to believe that *they* were always right, because they also feared the shame of imperfection. The people who taught us perfectionism and black-and-white thinking were our parents, teachers and clergy.

Consciously trying to contradict these sources of inner authority can stir up all sorts of emotions, including even more shame. We are betraying people we love, contradicting people we are supposed to respect, and denying the teachings of those who claim to represent God Himself. That's a lot to fight against just to give yourself a little wiggle room in the area of perfection.

The answer to this dilemma, I believe, is that instead of denying perfectionism and labeling black-and-white thinking, *wrong* and a *mistake*, we can *transform* our old attitudes by listening to, respecting and educating them. Instead of doing battle with our inner demons, we can understand where they came from, the purpose they served, and how they can grow into something new.

In short, we can introduce the concept of *appropriate* to our world-view. This allows us to see perfectionism and black-and-white thinking as good, right, useful and *appropriate* for many times, places and situations, while not being helpful here and now.

Perfectionism is *appropriate* in a dangerous and competitive world where small mistakes can cost you your life. Black-and-white thinking is *natural and appropriate* for children who are trying to make sense of the world by clinging to rules and order. It is *understandable* that imperfect church leaders would interpret the perfect teachings of a loving religion based on their own fears and need for rules and order.

But now… *now,* a different, more mature attitude towards life, perfection and God are *more appropriate.* We can thank our parents, thank our leaders, thank the powers of earth and heaven that held civilization together long enough for us to be able to see things differently. And it is with this attitude of openness and forgiveness that we will be *able* to see things differently without sabotaging ourselves with shame and fear over our audacity to think something new.

We will talk about this attitude of openness and forgiveness again in book two, because perfectionism is not the only demon that needs to be stared straight in the eye and lovingly transformed rather than beaten down.

Once we have the right attitude to transform perfectionism, we can replace it with this: The understanding that good and bad, light and dark, are only meaningful when considered in relation to one another.

Life is a process of moving from darker grays to lighter grays. Where we stand is not as important as which direction we are moving in. We are not simply *loving.* We are either *more* or *less* loving than we were yesterday. We should not feel shame for being imperfect. We should only be alarmed if we do something that moves us backwards dramatically. A mature individual is able to recognize options as better and worse, rather than as good and bad. Adults should be able to see the consequences of their choices as reasonable successes or relative failures, rather than wins and losses.

Another important understanding is that God neither expects nor desires perfection. Our mistakes are learning experiences that bring us closer to achieving our spiritual potential. Recognizing that some of our most shameful qualities can be seen as *virtues in the rough* may allow us to love and forgive those aspects of ourselves that we try hardest to hide.

You may have noticed that there is a big difference between what I am describing and both the traditional religious view *and* the newer alternative perspectives.

As I've noted, mainstream religions often see good and evil as opposing forces. This leaves individuals feeling trapped in an internal battle. There is no middle ground, no shades of gray, so every slip from perfection is a fall into hell.

The modern attitude of moral relativism, on the other hand, often dismisses distinctions entirely. Instead of acknowledging the gray area between light and darkness, it ignores darkness entirely, claiming that all actions are equally good because we are the creators of our own reality. This approach is intended to reduce people's sense of shame, but it runs the danger of backfiring. By making no distinctions, it encourages unhealthy, inappropriate behavior. Inappropriate behaviors have real-world consequences that can destroy our lives whether we feel shame over them or not.

What we want is *healthy* shame, not toxic shame or no shame at all. Perhaps another analogy would be helpful: Guilt, shame and fear are like the guide rail in the middle of the track in a kiddie car ride. You can drift a few feet to the right or left and shame will pull you back on track, but if you ignore the scrapes and bumps and drive completely over the rail, it will be really hard to get back in line. The pain, shame and fear that you felt when you veered away from what was right lingers in your memory. You know that to get back on track, you will have to face that shame again. It is easier, sometimes, to drive off into the trackless wilderness than to acknowledge that you are not where you need to be. You will need to lower that barrier by reducing your shame, so that it is not too painful to admit that you've made a wrong turn.

Being Present

The second step in breaking our shame spirals is to focus on being present. Being "present" means that you continue to pay attention to your thoughts, feelings and sensations, monitoring all three — staying in the moment even as you participate in behaviors designed to keep you numb and distracted.

In the early stages of your healing, you might not be able to stop yourself from doing inappropriate things, but you *can* try to stay present before, during, and especially *after* you do something so that you can be open to hints of your true needs and motivations. Find ways to listen to and monitor the negative messages of your inner critic and private demons. If you are going to make mistakes, you might as well milk them for as much information as possible so that you can learn from them.

I once participated in a unique exercise called "The Cocktail Party." At a real cocktail party, people often stand around talking, but rarely actually listen to anyone else. People are sort of strutting back and forth presenting a mask, pretending to be someone they aren't.

In the cocktail party exercise, a dozen people were put in a small circle, with the lights turned down, and were told to let our "limiting characters" have their voice. We walked around for two hours yelling, crying, blaming, shaming, denying, arguing, accusing, and, in essence, letting our inner demons share their fears and concerns. No one listened to anyone else. We were all just props for each other. We would walk by one person and yell at them like they were a parent. Another would be ourselves. Another would be the whole damned world. We said things that we had not allowed ourselves to even acknowledge we had ever thought, and we brought up into the conscious world feelings that had lain hidden for lifetimes.

When we go directly from inappropriate behavior to shame, we close the door to any opportunity to learn from our mistakes. We are too busy shaming our inner motivations to even consider asking them what they are and where they came from. It would be helpful if we could, instead, hold our shame at bay long enough to discover what it is hiding from us.

On the way home from one inappropriate encounter, I allowed my limiting characters the opportunity to hold a mini-cocktail party. I gave voice to my inner critics, and they had a lot to say. "God was going to punish me, I was a criminal, a heart-breaker, an irresponsible male – just like my father. I would catch a disease, I would be blackmailed, I would go broke, everyone would hate me"… and on and on for half an hour.

Wow. So this was what went on in the back of my head every time I did something wrong? No wonder I tried to keep the voices quiet through more numbing behavior. But this time, instead of telling the voices to go away and shut up, I thanked them. "Gee. I never knew you carried so much fear and concern for my well-being. I appreciate the effort you've been going through to try to keep me safe, but, really, let's consider each of these fears and see how likely they all are."

I then went on to calmly and respectfully examine the claims of my inner critic, and integrated them into my conscious awareness. Once these fears had been heard, they no longer felt the need to shout, and they no longer generated intense sensations when they were ignored. That one blast of honesty went a very long way in helping me break my shame cycle.

There are several less intense ways to gain a deeper understanding of your emotional motivations. These include meditation techniques, such as the one described in *The Power of Focusing* by Ann Weiser Cornell, Ph.D. which I recommend very highly. Another tool is the kind of daily writing exercise that Julia Cameron, author of *The Artist's Way*, encourages. Journaling, twelve-step meetings, therapy sessions, or just shaking your fist at the moon and shouting your fears and frustrations out loud can all help loosen up some inner awareness. When you are done, a few moments of prayer can help calm you back down.

You can also simply take some time and calmly communicate with your emotional self through a process I call Internal Consultation.

Consulting with Your Emotions

Internal Consultation is a powerful tool for identifying the message of the sensations that your emotions are generating. It does not require money, tools or even a therapist, though they can often be helpful. If it sounds similar to other techniques you've used, it probably is. It isn't rocket science, but it can certainly take you places.

Here are the basics:

Sit quietly and comfortably.

Close your eyes if you like.

Become aware of your body.

Check for any sensations.

Be open to sensations that you can't put your finger on or give a name. Pay particular attention to the area around your throat, heart, chest and stomach. Check for sensations that might signal stress, like tightness, heaviness, heat, and pain. Also check for sensations that might signal positive reactions like lightness, warmth and calm.

When you become aware of a physical or emotional sensation, don't pounce on it. Approach it as you would a butterfly. Your goal is to give it a name or hear its message, not grab it and shake it.

The meaning of the sensation may not come to you in words, so be open to other forms of communication.

Become aware of your inner vision – your visual imagination.

Check for any images or pictures that might come to you.

Be open to images glimpsed out of the corner of your mind's eye.

Be aware of your inner voice – your inner community.

Check for any voices that would like to be heard.

Be open to random phrases, lines from songs or poems, quiet voices.

If anything comes to you, welcome it. If it has a name, say hello. If you're not sure of its name, ask open-ended questions to find out what it is and what it wants to communicate with you.

This is not an interrogation.

It is similar to what is often referred to as inner-child work, but what you hear won't necessarily be a child. You will want to maintain an attitude of welcome acceptance, curiosity, tenderness, empathy. Often, once you have a sense of what is present, all you will need to do is sit with it comfortably. Its presence is its own message – no more need be said. At other times, you will want to explore what is behind or accompanying a presence.

This process is called internal consultation rather than internal listening because you are trying to create a relationship with this part of you that has something to share. Whatever it has to share is always true – for that part of you – but not necessarily true for all of you. It is important to give it a voice without giving it power over you.

This feeling, sensation, belief, experience or observation deserves to be heard, but you are under no obligation to agree with it. In fact, the whole point of using this process is to uncover feelings and beliefs that have been misunderstood or have led you in unhelpful directions. The goal is not to accept them or reject them, but rather to gently guide them towards understandings that are more mature and consistent with your current vision. This is a process of guidance and education, not coercion.

Often is it enough to just acknowledge a feeling or thought without trying to change it or give it advice. This is because many times the message that a feeling is trying to send is simply, "I'm here!" Simply saying hello to it can release the energy that has been trying to get your attention.

If you've had any experience with working with a good therapist, then you may identify with this scenario. You can be in turmoil all week because of some event or personal interaction. You are sure it is going to take hours to work through with your therapist, but after hearing just a few minutes of your ranting, your therapist says, "It sounds to me like you might be feeling _____." ... And instantly the turmoil is gone. You've been heard. That's all you needed.

When we learn how to do this for ourselves, we can save ourselves a lot of turmoil (and therapy sessions).

I'm reminded of the scene in the movie *It's a Wonderful Life*, in which the child follows George Bailey around pulling on his coattails saying, "Excuse me" at successively higher volume until his father finally turns in exasperation and says, "Excuse you for what?" To which he replies, "I burped."

Like a burp that is not nearly as annoying as the bellowed request to be excused, the fears, transgressions and concerns that generate powerful internal sensations are often of much less significance than the irritation they generate when they are not acknowledged.

Even when the issues are of great importance, the resolution may not require any intervention because the "you" who is uncovering the issue has more internal resources than the "you" who generated the issue. In other words, issues that were buried when you were a child because you didn't have the emotional resources and experience to deal with them are now easy to handle – once they have a name.

Another reason why simply acknowledging a feeling can instantly resolve tension has to do with the nature of emotions themselves. Emotions tell us about the presence or absence of virtues in our lives. Simply naming the emotion can help us understand our situation more clearly and resolve all sorts of inner turmoil.

For example, sadness tells us that we perceive the loss of a source of goodness in our lives. It tells us, "You did have access to this source of virtue; now you don't." In order to hide sadness from ourselves, we must convince ourselves that either A) the thing we have lost isn't really gone, or B) the thing we lost didn't really have any value to us in the first place.

Any time we try to convince ourselves that something we love isn't really valuable, the part of us that loves goodness is going to start screaming at us. It will jump up and down, it will grab hold of our heart, our throat or our stomach and start squeezing.

If we want this tightness to go away, all we have to do is say, "I'm sad about ___." In doing so, we are admitting that we have lost something of value. Once we acknowledge that something has value to us, it is often much easier to accept the fact that it is gone and get on about the business of finding some other source of goodness to fill the void. So acknowledging sadness can make it go away. It's not magic. It's just dismissing the messenger after the message has been delivered!

If naming an emotion doesn't instantly clarify the nature of the message behind it, you might want to ask any strong emotional sensation what virtue or attribute it is responding to. There are, of course, some sensations that will require more than a name. They may be associated with traumatic experiences, major life events, long-term perspectives, or family systems. It is OK to call a feeling "something" and just sit with it to see what it has to share.

When you are done, say *thank you* and ask if it is all right to move on.

Then write down whatever of value you can put into words while the new awareness is still fresh. Creating an objective record of your internal experiences will help make them real and give you something to refer back to if your new-found understandings start to get cloudy.

Some additional tips and tricks:

The goal of internal consultation is to receive the message and honor the messenger, not become overwhelmed by either of them. The advantage of naming a sensation or an awareness is that it establishes a distinction between you and it. It creates a safe distance between you.

Don't eat or drink while practicing internal consultation. Physical sensations often serve double-duty. Physical hunger and spiritual emptiness, for example, can feel the same. Eating can interfere with an awareness of emotional cues.

I often visualize my mind as a rock tumbler. I toss an idea or word or feeling in and just let it roll around for a while until something tumbles forward and makes a connection.

Replacing Old Patterns

The third step in breaking shame spirals is to focus on *replacing* old patterns rather than resisting them. One of the great truisms of life is that nature abhors a vacuum. That is just as true of our spiritual lives as it is of the material universe. When we find ourselves caught up in a self-destructive spiral of inappropriate activity, our first impulse is to try to *stop* ourselves from engaging in that activity.

This approach is doomed to failure.

Every time.

Why?

Because negative behavior is caused by a need, a lack of some positive quality. One cannot remove a lack. One can only fill a need. We cannot remove darkness, we can only add light.

There is another reason. The soul hungers for sensation. Shame, fear and anger may be poor substitutes for love, peace and joy, but they are better than no sensations at all. To have no sensations feels like death.

We would rather be sad, angry, ashamed, embarrassed, dizzy, in pain, afraid, tense, irritated, needy or anxious than to feel nothing at all, because to feel nothing at all makes us question our very existence.

Think about it. The only way we know that we are alive is by our senses. If we could not see, hear, touch taste or feel, how would we know we were alive? People placed in sensory deprivation tanks for too long start to lose their sense of identity.

Just as the body needs *physical* sensations to feel alive, the soul needs *emotional* sensations to feel alive. If our unhealthy patterns are the only way we know to keep our emotions stimulated, then we sure as heck better keep those patterns going.

When we tell ourselves that we need to stop doing the things we are currently doing, what our soul hears is that we are going to stop doing the things that make it feel alive. To the subconscious, this sounds like a kind of spiritual death. It is frightening. Just as depressed people might cut themselves just to prove that they can still feel, the soul would rather continue experiencing painful emotional sensations than to feel nothing at all.

We *need* these sensations to feel alive, and will do almost anything to make them continue. That is one reason why we sabotage our own efforts at stopping our self-destructive behavior. It is better to self-destruct than to fade into oblivion.

This is why we can't just stop what we are doing. To change a behavior, we must replace it with a healthier behavior. To do that, we need to understand *why* we have chosen the behaviors we have, and find a new source of motivation that will urge us towards healthier behaviors.

Changing our Motivation

In order to be successful in adopting new, healthy behaviors, we need to look at what motivates those behaviors in the first place. So the fourth step in breaking our shame spiral is to change our source of motivation. To do that, it would help to understand exactly how shame, a negative emotion, manages to motivate so much of our behavior.

As I've explained, a little bit of healthy shame acts as a warning signal when we are about to make an unhealthy decision. It motivates us to stop and reconsider what we are about to do, or what we have just done. If a little bit of shame can stop us from making a small mistake, then wouldn't it make sense that a lot of shame would motivate us to avoid making a big mistake? No. Not after it becomes toxic.

Here is why.

If we only feel shame once in a while, then we know that we can make it go away by making a better decision. The ability to turn off the unpleasant sensation is an effective motivator. But if shame is with us all of the time, then we don't feel that we have the ability to turn it off. As our feelings of shame increase, we are motivated, instead, to *manage* our shame by doing one of several things:

Distract ourselves from it
Numb ourselves to its effect
Redefine it as something positive
Adopt it as part of our identity

When this happens, shame actually becomes the motivation for doing the very things that it was intended to discourage. That means that using shame to try to *stop* ourselves from the behaviors that are part of our shame spiral is counterproductive. Let me give you some examples:

Would you rather feel loved or shamed? Hmmm. So, if a person whispers in your ear that they love you and want to have sex with you, but your shame meter is going haywire telling you that this is a bad idea, which are you going to want to listen to? You are probably going to distract yourself from the shame by focusing on the promise of love. When given the choice, love (even imitation love) always wins. This is why shaming youth into abstinence doesn't work.

But it is not just sex that people can use as a distraction. There are lots of strong physical and emotional sensations that we can use to distract ourselves from shame's warning signals – lust, excitement, loud music, dangerous activities. These are sensations that overpower the sensation of shame and distract us from its warning signal. They don't necessarily have to be unhealthy activities, though many are, they just have to generate strong sensations. When we ask ourselves "why am I doing this?" we think it is because we are attracted to the strong sensations the activity generates. We don't realize that the *real* motivation is the need to distract ourselves from shame.

When shame becomes too strong to overpower, then the next step is to numb it. Some distracting activities can also numb shame, but usually numbing activities are more passive and serve to shut down our feelings or disconnect us from our bodies. Eating, watching TV, gambling, shopping, working, masturbation, loveless sex – these can all numb a little shame. As the shame increases, the need to numb also increases and so these behaviors can become obsessive.

As our cookie analogy illustrates, if one cookie numbs a little shame, it can take a whole box of cookies to numb a lot of shame. From the outside, the motivation appears to be a love of cookies, but beneath it all, the real motivation is the numbing of shame. Shaming ourselves for these behaviors just increases them, while a healthier motivation will lead us to healthier behaviors.

What happens if shame breaks through our efforts at distraction and numbing behavior? People can do what I did, and redefine the sensation of shame as feelings of love, or feelings of power, or feelings of excitement. By misidentifying shame as something good, it can lead us into all sorts of unhealthy behavior. It motivates us to do the exact opposite of what is best for us. For me, this happened when I faced an unexpected and strong source of shame that wasn't part of my usual shame spiral, but it can happen at any time.

The last stage in this progression is when we realize that we are *enjoying* the sensation of shame, and we give up trying to fool ourselves into believing that what we are doing is healthy. Shame becomes the central core of our identity. We behave in shameful ways because we see ourselves as shameful beings. We are "bad to the bone" or think of ourselves as outlaws or loners or wild ones, or simply broken. Doing shameful things is how we remain true to ourselves. The flashing red light of shame is no longer a warning signal, it is our destination.

If you have been told all of your life that you are sinful, evil, and deserving of punishment, and if you have given up hope of ever getting into heaven, then shame becomes a mark of honor, and self-destruction is a way of life. This does not have to be a conscious awareness. Many of us wear the mask of respectability while secretly believing that we are beyond redemption. Our subconscious is filled with the noise of inner demons and critics that only the numbing sensation of shame can drown out. Shame is our guiding light and motivating force.

These are just four of the ways in which we can allow our choices in life to be guided by shame. They also describe why shame is *not* the source of motivation we should choose for ourselves. But is there an *alternative* to shame that is strong enough to get us out of bed in the morning?

Yep. And it is a lot more fun.

Joy and Longing as Motivators

If shame makes a bad motivator, perhaps the opposite of shame would be a good motivator. At its essence, shame is the sensation of suddenly moving away from God, or away from your spiritual potential. It is the sensation of slipping backwards, or falling a short distance, as though you unexpectedly stepped off of a curb. The opposite of falling away is flying toward. This moving towards God and our highest potential is experienced as joy. As Teilhard de Chardin said, *"Joy is the infallible sign of the presence of God."* When we strengthen our virtues, accomplish something noble, and grow closer to God, our hearts take flight.

In the next few pages I will be explaining how we can replace shame with joy by changing our focus from pursuing positive physical sensations to experiencing positive spiritual sensations.

⊗

Physical Sensations Vs. Spiritual Sensations

Certainly, the concept of replacing unhealthy behavior with healthy behavior isn't new. People who are trying to diet don't just stop eating. They try to replace unhealthy food with the kind that will provide nourishment. They think of unhealthy food as bad and try to find the opposite of bad food to eat.

Likewise, people who are in unhealthy relationships will try to find the opposite of an unhealthy relationship in order to fill the holes in their lives. The problem is that people don't understand what it really means to do the opposite of what they are currently doing.

You see, the opposite of black, for example, isn't white. They are both visual sensations. They have more in common than almost any two random words in the dictionary. The opposite of black is God. Black is a physical sensory experience. God is a spiritual reality beyond sensation.

Likewise, the opposite of eating is not dieting—they are both ways of relating to food; they keep the mind focused on *food*.

The opposite of eating is *God*.

The opposite of *drinking* is God.

The opposite of *drugs* is God.

The opposite of *promiscuity* is God.

The opposite of *sickness* is God.

The opposite of *any* physical substance, experience or activity that draws our spirits away from God—is God.

So the cure for *all* of our ills… is *God*.

Focusing our attention on the names and attributes of God draws our hearts and minds away from the world of limitations into a world where perfections are infinite and our capacity for growth is unlimited. Turning towards God is not a process in which we beg God, over and over again, to change our behavior for us—concentrating our thoughts on what we don't want to do and hoping that God is strong enough to stop us. It is a way of turning our attention to a spiritual realm where our addictive behaviors simply do not exist—and therefore cannot take hold of us.

This is why, instead of trying to tell you how to *stop* getting into unhealthy relationships or how to *overcome* compulsive behaviors, the rest of this book - and its sequels - will try to direct your attention in a completely different direction, one focused on developing positive spiritual qualities rather than overcoming negative behaviors. We do this by focusing on *spiritual* sensations rather than physical ones.

Emotions as Spiritual Perception

I've mentioned several aspects of this idea since the beginning of this book, but now I want to explain it in detail because it really is one of the keys to achieving spiritual growth.

Emotions are spiritual sensations that tell us about the presence of virtues in our lives. These virtues are the attributes of God that are present in the world around and within us.

Emotions provide the spiritual eyes and ears with which to perceive the qualities of God in the world. When we perceive them, our hearts respond. When we experience their absence, our hearts are troubled.

Put another way, we could say that as physical beings, we need to be able to perceive and respond to our physical environment. Our physical senses allow us to do that.

As *spiritual* beings, we need to be able to perceive and respond to our *spiritual* environment. Our *emotions* allow us to do *that*.

Just as our physical senses communicate with our minds to tell us what is going on around us, our spiritual senses – our emotions – communicate with both our minds and our bodies to prepare us to respond to our spiritual surroundings. Our emotions generate a physical response. They *also* create spiritual feelings that are *more* than just physical.

Up to this point, I've focused on how these sensations can be misinterpreted and lead us astray. Now I would like to focus on how emotions, *when accurately identified as signals of the presence of virtues,* can generate a whole host of wonderful, ecstatic, and immensely satisfying physical and spiritual sensations.

I know, we don't usually think of emotions, let alone *virtues* as the source of wonderful sensations. We usually think of sensations in terms of *physical* pleasures. But our spiritual sensations are even more rich and varied than our physical ones.

When we think of *physical* sensations, for example, we start with our five senses, then combine them in an infinite variety of ways using an infinite number of sources of stimulation. We can't imagine ever feeling everything there is to feel, tasting everything there is to taste, seeing every kind of beauty there is to behold, or even experiencing every kind of sexual pleasure possible.

When we think of our emotions, however, we often limit our thinking to the six that most researchers acknowledge—happiness, sadness, anger, fear, lust and disgust. With only one pleasant, four unpleasant and one very confusing feeling in our emotional vocabulary, it is difficult to imagine our emotional lives ever being able to compete with the physical world as a source of pleasure.

But there are more than six emotions.
Emotions are sensations that tell us about the presence of
     the attributes of God.
Every attribute, every virtue, can generate a different sensation.
And the attributes of God are infinite.
Plus they can be *combined* in an infinite number of ways.
And the experience of each of those virtues *feels good.*

Misinterpreting, ignoring and denying the sensations that are associated with these virtues *feels bad*.

Trying to bend, push and squeeze the vast array of emotional sensations we experience into six cramped and rigid emotional boxes diminishes the good, exaggerates the bad, and impoverishes us spiritually.

It is very difficult to process an emotional sensation that we don't have a word for. As a result, we try to redefine our experiences to match the emotions that we have a name for. That is why we redefine shame as lust or love. That is why pity becomes love, or excitement becomes fear, or depression becomes sadness, or ecstasy is reduced to simple happiness.

I often wonder about how people who speak Spanish deal with loneliness, because in Spanish, they can only say, "solo y triste" which means "alone and sad." There is no word for that distinct feeling of being surrounded by people but still feeling lonely. This is the dilemma that all of us face every day when we experience sensations that simply don't fit the emotional labels we've been given. What do we do with them? How do we resolve them? If emotional sensations are messengers, how do we respond to messages that are written in bright red letters, but in a language we don't understand?

What's in a name?

Our ability to give a name to our emotional response to virtues is not just an exercise in semantics, it is an exercise in identification and knowledge. To name something gives us a kind of power over it. Being able to distinguish between related virtues and related emotions allows us to feel them both, understand them both, strive for them both.

It is important, for example, to understand the difference between the feelings of love, lust, need and pity. If we do not, then our relationships will never be honest.

Even more crucial, our ability to accurately name an emotional sensation gives us an invaluable clue as to the virtue that is involved.

In spite of the fact that most people do not think of emotions in terms of virtues, the vast majority of the virtues that humans strive to acquire *share the name* of the emotion or feeling that they generate.

For example, a kind person feels kindness. A patient person feels patience. A courageous person feels courage, and a compassionate person feels compassion. We feel grateful, happy, joyful, generous, pure, strong, noble, faithful, honest, and friendly.

Consider this:

Can you imagine someone saying "I woke up this morning feeling very...

Optimistic	Compassionate	Graceful
Patient	Confident	Grateful
Peaceful	Content	Happy
Radiant	Courageous	Hopeful
Resilient	Creative	Honest
Respectful	Determined	Humble
Reverent	Enthusiastic	Joyful
Serene	Forgiving	Kind
Strong	Friendly	Loving
Full of Wonder	Generous	Loyal

These are *feelings* that most of us have had at some point in our lives. If we think about them for a few moments, we can probably remember what they feel like.

Now consider whether you could also imagine the same person saying "for my New Year's resolution, I'm going to work on becoming more...

Graceful	Optimistic	Compassionate
Grateful	Patient	Confident
Happy	Peaceful	Content
Hopeful	Radiant	Courageous
Honest	Resilient	Creative
Humble	Respectful	Determined
Joyful	Reverent	Enthusiastic
Kind	Serene	Forgiving
Loving	Strong	Friendly
Loyal	Full of Wonder	Generous

These are *virtues* that many of us strive to attain. We recognize them as qualities worth having.

Look at these two lists. They are identical.

When displayed like this, the relationship between virtues and emotions is embarrassingly obvious, and yet few people have noticed. Perhaps it is because, though we have all felt these things, they don't show up on the standard list of six emotions. The feelings aren't overwhelming, and they don't set off physical alarms. They don't start wars, but they *do* inspire discoveries, build communities, connect hearts and add meaning to our lives.

So is it really fair to call these emotions? Do we really *feel* them in our hearts?

Well, consider the exceptions: Have you ever performed a generous act without feeling generous? Of course you have. We often leave a tip, provide a service or give a gift without *feeling* particularly good about it. We do it from a sense of obligation. In those cases, we are *not* feeling generous because we are not actually manifesting the *virtue* of generosity.

Other times, however, we *do* feel an internal desire to give freely of ourselves and our possessions. The fact that we can tell the difference between the two feelings even though the outward expressions are the same proves that the sensations are associated with the virtue rather than the material action.

Gratitude is another virtue that generates strong sensations when it is sincere, and none when it is forced. Here is a great description of this:

"Thankfulness is of various kinds. There is a verbal thanksgiving which is confined to a mere utterance of gratitude. This is of no importance because perchance the tongue may give thanks while the heart is unaware of it. Many who offer thanks to God are of this type, their spirits and hearts unconscious of thanksgiving. This is mere usage, just as when we meet, receive a gift and say thank you, speaking the words without significance. One may say thank you a thousand times while the heart remains thankless, ungrateful. Therefore, mere verbal thanksgiving is without effect. But real thankfulness is a cordial giving of thanks from the heart. When man in response to the favors of God manifests susceptibilities of conscience, the heart is happy, the spirit is exhilarated. These spiritual susceptibilities are ideal thanksgiving."

— 'Abdu'l-Bahá, *The Promulgation of Universal Peace, p. 236*

So expressing gratitude makes the heart happy. Remember that. I will mention it again in the section about happiness research.

Look at the list again. Pick any one virtue at random, then roll that word around in your heart. Try to *feel* what it is like to experience that virtue. Hold onto it for a few moments, then pick another word. Can you feel a shift in energy as you move from one word to another?

When you imagine yourself feeling forgiveness, for example, does it feel different from feeling wonder? Do some of these words resonate strongly with you? Do you resist others? Isn't it interesting that simply *reading* the name of a virtue can have an effect on you? Imagine how *receiving* one of these virtues might feel, or, better yet, *living* one of them.

What an amazing array of emotional sensations this list represents!

When you make an effort to replace old, unhealthy patterns with new, healthy ones, *this* is what you have to look forward to. Each of these virtues (and hundreds more) represent a change in behavior that will improve the quality of your life, generate positive spiritual sensations, and, because our spiritual and physical emotions are so closely linked, will make you feel better physically as well.

To understand why these virtues resonate so deeply in our hearts, please consider one more list—a list of qualities that you might turn to in prayer. If you were facing challenges in your life, might you not call upon God ...

the Creator,
the Compassionate,
the Forgiving,
the Most Generous,
the All Powerful,
the Lord of Joy?

God is loving, patient, wonderful, loyal, honest and determined. Every virtue that we possess is a reflection of God's glory, and every emotion is a signpost telling us which way we need to go in order to move closer to our highest potential.

⊗

The Down Side of Virtues

With all of these benefits going for them, why isn't everyone in the world rushing to experience the joys associated with experiencing virtues? Why isn't honesty and kindness as popular as beer and sex?

There are, of course, lots of reasons why virtues are not as popular as vices. Since you've read this far, however, I have to assume that you are at least open to the idea that virtues are good. Why, then, do you and I have such a difficult time focusing on virtues? If they really are as much fun as I say, it should be easy!

The problem is that in order to be open to the spiritual sensations associated with virtues, we must also be open to the sensations associated with their *absence*. Remember, emotions tell us about the presence or *absence* of a virtue.

Take another look at the lists on page 56. How often do you experience any of these virtues in your daily life?

You are a noble, radiant child of God. How often are you treated that way? As a child, you deserved to be cherished and celebrated. As a youth, you deserved to have your creativity unleashed and your enthusiasm appreciated. As an adult, you deserve respect and to be dealt with honestly. We live in an amazing world that should radiate reverence and joy.

In order to acknowledge that we long for these virtues; to even *begin* to look for them and try to identify them in our personal interactions, we have to admit that our lives are mostly devoid of them.

And that really *really* hurts.

A Story of Longing

One evening I went to hear a gospel choir concert at the Madame Walker Theater in downtown Indianapolis. I went because a Bahá'í choir had been asked to participate along with the choirs of half a dozen local black churches. I went expecting to hear good music. I didn't go expecting to be swept out to sea.

When the music started for the first piece, there were no choirs on stage, only a single director, but as he raised his arms towards the audience, almost a quarter of the room rose as one and lifted their voices up towards heaven in a wave of sound like nothing I had ever experienced in my life.

It was not just that I was surrounded by beautiful voices on all four sides. It was not just that the music was so full of life that you could almost feel the heart beat of the Holy Spirit. It was the ineffable blend of joy, praise, gratitude, reverence, and complete abandon that made me feel as though I had died and gone to heaven.

You see, I'm a white boy from a Lutheran background, and we just don't get that intimate with God. We praise God, all right, but with a slap on the back, not a full-body-contact embrace.

When my heart perceived the possibility of this level of spiritual expression, it experienced a brilliant flash of pure joy—and then immediately recognized its total absence in the rest of my daily life, and I began to weep uncontrollably.

Longing—deep, profound, personal, inconsolable. I believe that this is one of the main reasons why we are willing to limit ourselves to the five or six basic emotions. As soon as our hearts recognize something new, something transcendent, something beyond our normal daily experience, they leap for joy, then crash against the wall of longing.

To acknowledge that kindness exists is to face the overwhelming lack of it in our daily interactions. To experience generosity is to recognize the ubiquity of selfishness in our interactions. To receive grace is to become aware of how few things we have forgiven ourselves and others for. And so we almost instantaneously slide from the joyful sensation of the virtue to the painful awareness of its general absence and a deep longing for its return.

How many times have you been watching some silly movie, a sappy commercial on TV, or even listening to a country & western song, when a character says or does something kind, loving or generous *without a personal payoff* and suddenly you get a lump in your throat? I have to admit, I'm an easy touch. But what interests me is not that I am moved by sweetness, but how quickly my sensation flips from the joy of recognizing a virtue to the pain of that lump. That lump is longing, and it is the fear and embarrassment of experiencing that pain that prevents many of us from seeking out more encounters with divine virtues.

Usually, when I write books and booklets, I focus on the good stuff—how wonderful it is to develop our virtues, and how positive the sensations are when we learn how to be loving and kind and honest and forgiving.

But this isn't that kind of book.

It wouldn't be fair of me to ask things of someone who is struggling with personal issues and pretend that resolving them will be sweet and easy. It won't be.

As I said, we can't open ourselves up to the joys of Divine virtues without simultaneously opening ourselves up to their absence in our lives. And that absence isn't just today's absence. When we realize what we are missing now, we also realize what we've been missing for our entire lives.

There may be a hole in your heart that should have been filled with kindness. There may be a hole in your heart that should contain idealism. For every virtue that you come to fall in love with, there is likely to be a big empty space waiting for it. It hurts. It is supposed to hurt. That's how you know that something is missing. And it is good to take some time to grieve all that you deserved but didn't get. Acknowledge the loss. Understand that it may be appropriate to feel anger.

But it's very important to remember this: the sensation is just a messenger. The sensation tells you that there is something valuable that is missing in your life, but more importantly, it is telling you that you are longing for something that you don't have. That longing can either be pointed backwards into the past, or turned around and pointed towards the future.

This book is called *Love, Lust and the Longing for God*. Long-ing tells you that you really, really want something. That is a very good thing.

The stronger your longing, the more energy and motivation you have to go out and get all of the kindness and idealism and enthusi-asm you can grab. There is no limit. Your heart has infinite poten-tial for virtue, and God has an infinite supply.

The more you are motivated by longing, the less you will be motivated by shame, and the less attraction you will feel towards old behavior patterns.

Understand, though, that this is not a one-step process. Most people do not look at their life and say, "Gee, I didn't have much experience with positive virtues in my life, but that's OK. I'll fill up all my empty spaces with virtues and go have a happy life!"

Life is a process of uncovering and discovering. Sometimes a painful emotion or memory will point us towards a virtue that we need to develop, while other times our love for a virtue will shed light on our personal history. We grieve, we learn, we grow, we rejoice, then we grieve again.

Dealing with what is missing

Let's look again at the list of emotions that most scientists study: happiness, sadness, lust/love, anger, fear and disgust.

Happiness

We can now say that happiness is a catch-all name for the posi-tive sensations we experience when we become aware of any vir-tues in our lives. When we experience kindness, beauty, creativity, harmony, friendship, generosity, etc. it feels good, and we say that we are happy. You can, in fact, find entire books that claim that the secret of true happiness is one or another of these specific virtues. But the truth is, happiness comes from all of them, and hundreds more. Happiness comes from feeling close to God when we find signs of God around us. Since God is everywhere all the time, we should all be happy most of the time. It is our inability to *recognize* God's virtues in each moment of our lives that allows happiness to elude us.

Sadness

The nature of sadness, then, is equally obvious. It is a catch-all word to describe how we feel when we search for God's virtues and cannot find them—when something or someone who used to express those virtues is no longer available to us, or when the weight of the world's coarseness gets us down.

Lust/Love

Lust, as we've explored in detail, is the coarse physical side of the virtue of love. Love is the heart's attraction to the attributes of God in the world. Happiness tells us we are surrounded by virtues. Sadness tells us that they are absent, and love motivates us to go find more of them.

Love is attraction to virtue, while lust is simply the attraction of one body towards another body. It is, however, easier to measure, so it is the one that science can study and make pronouncements on. With both science and our culture focusing on the physical aspect of this virtue, the meaning of love has been debased.

So what about the other three—anger, fear and disgust? These sensations tell us that what is missing is one of the three most important virtues that we need to survive, both physically and spiritually: Justice, Security and Purity.

Anger

Anger tells us that we don't think we are being treated with fairness and justice. Some acts of injustice require an immediate physical response (fight or flight) which is why our bodies react so strongly to this perception. But many acts of injustice require a more measured, thoughtful response. This leaves our bodies all

fired up with no place to go. If we understand what we are responding to, we can walk our hearts and bodies back out of the
sensation of anger – by changing our perception of the event, resolving the cause of the injustice, or forgiving it and moving on.

If we *don't* understand anger's role as a messenger and cling,
instead, to the sensation, then we can carry this extra (negative)
energy around for hours, days, or a lifetime. If you find yourself
being angry much of the time, then chances are that you faced a
lot of injustice in your life that never got resolved. What is missing
in your life is a sense that the universe is fair and that God is just
and on your side. The virtues that will reduce anger are justice,
patience, faith, forgiveness, serenity and compassion, among others.

Fear

Fear tells us that we do not feel safe—either physically or spiritually. Now, we do not often think of safety as a virtue, let alone an
attribute of God, and yet scriptures such as these remind us that
safety, security and strength are, indeed, qualities of God that we
have a right to long for and attain:

"The Lord is my shepherd. I shall not want."

*"He only is my rock and my salvation: he is my defense; I shall not
be moved."*

*"My love is My stronghold; he that entereth therein is safe and se-
cure...."*

To feel physically safe means that we are confident that our
bodies are not going to be attacked or harmed and that our material needs will be met. To feel *spiritually* safe means that our *identi-
ties as children of God* are not subject to attack and that our spiritual
potential will be allowed to blossom. If we grew up with criticism,
nit-picking, ridicule, shame, abandonment, minimization of our
accomplishment or our feelings, and, of course, rage, then we lived
in a constant state of fear for our spiritual well-being.

The virtues that were missing—the ones that will eliminate
the fear—include self-acceptance, security, confidence, personal
boundaries, trust in God, detachment, courage and strength, along
with many others.

Disgust

Disgust tells us that something is impure or unhealthy. Physically, we are disgusted by rotten food, feces, dead animals and other things that our bodies tell us we should step away from. Spiritually, we are disgusted by actions and attitudes that we sense would degrade us, or sully us even by association. There are things that our minds and hearts do not need to see or experience. Some people lack positive virtues, while others actively pursue behaviors that harm themselves and others. We have pity on the first, but we are disgusted by the second.

Disgust is a legitimate and helpful response that protects us from exposure to harmful experiences, but it can be distorted in two ways. First, it is a sensation, and people who are numb to positive sensations will sometimes choose negative sensations rather than feel completely dead. That's why you will find plenty of television shows and movies that cash in on people's willingness to settle for fear, ridicule, injustice and disgust as a form of entertainment rather than seek out something spiritually uplifting.

Second, if people express disgust for *who we are as people*, as though our very existence makes the world a dirtier place, then we will internalize this attitude as shame.

This was a quick description of just the six emotions that science tends to study. There are obviously hundreds of different virtues, and therefore twice that many emotions – one for each virtue's presence, and one for its absence.

Just as each virtue feels different, the absence of each virtue feels different, as well. So, for example, as *freedom* and *independence* feel different, so do *control* and *manipulation*. When we name our feelings, we are better able to name the virtues that will heal them.

On the next page is a chart with just a few examples of virtues and the emotions they might generate when they are either present or absent.

The virtue	What we feel when it is present or expressed	What we feel when it is absent or removed
Security	serenity, peace	fear
Justice / fairness	satisfaction	anger
Purity	clean	disgust
Strength/competence	confident	helpless/incompetent
All virtues	joy/happiness	sorrow/loss
Connectedness	friendship/belonging	loneliness/isolation
Creativity	creative/alive	passive/apathetic
Integrity	noble/worthy	shame/unworthy
Patience	patient/calm	impatient/agitated
Trust	trustworthy	paranoid
Faith	assured	adrift/anxious
Generosity	generous/open	greedy/selfish

Each negative emotion gives us a hint of what is missing in our lives. By combining this awareness with the exercise of internal consultation, we can practice a kind of spiritual archeology. Just as fossils are made when hard rock fills in the spaces where soft tissue used to be, painful emotions fill in the spaces where we were most vulnerable. When we find ancient emotions set in stone in our hearts, we can use them to piece together a picture of what might have been missing in our lives. As we discover what is missing, we gain the ability to heal its absence. This is the essence of what it means to consciously engage in spiritual healing.

The Essence of the Healing Process is This:

To uncover a feeling or a memory that points to a
    virtue that was absent in our lives.
To acknowledge that absence.
To grieve that absence.
Then to foster the longing for that virtue,
even if it causes pain.
Then to create that virtue in our current lives.

This way of looking at what we are doing changes our whole way of thinking. By relating the healing process to virtues, we transform it from a shame-based escape from our failures to the noble enterprise of moving towards God. Our shame came from the belief that *we must not have deserved* what we didn't receive. The holes in our lives were seen as flaws in our character rather than virtues that we were never shown. As we heal our shame, we reclaim our right to strive to develop all of the strengths that we were denied as children.

Shifting our perception of what we are trying to accomplish from "healing an illness" to "developing our divine virtues" brings our efforts into the realm of the sacred. It sets our sights, not on our past, but on our future.

Developing Virtues in Our Lives

We heal ourselves—and grow spiritually—by filling the empty places in our lives with Divine virtues. There are two ways to do this. We can surround ourselves with people and experiences that reflect those virtues, or we can express those virtues *ourselves* in our relationship with ourselves and with others.

We would all like to fill our lives with kind, loving, supportive people, but if that were *easy*, I wouldn't be writing this book. Since the only person's virtues we have any control over at all is our own, the most reliable way to fill our lives with virtue is by practicing them ourselves.

It might seem unfair that after living so long without other people showing us the kindness, respect and patience we deserve, we should immediately be expected to try to practice these virtues ourselves instead of finding the "right" person to give us what we need. Yet it is absolutely fair.

Anyone who can show you kindness or understanding or support can also turn around and take it away. But if *you* develop your own capacity to express these virtues, then they will be with you always. You can show them to yourself, or you can offer them to other people, and no one will ever be able to take them away from you. The positive sensations you get from being a kind person, or a patient person, or a forgiving person, will never be conditioned on anyone else. They are yours forever.

This is not as difficult as it may seem. Remember, we are born with a longing for God, and that longing is expressed in our attraction to Divine virtues. The more we understand virtues—define them, visualize them in practice, understand their long-term benefits, experience the sensations they generate—the more we will long for them.

Understanding Virtues

*Virtues are the light of the Divine
reflected in the human heart.*

At first glance, this spiritual definition would not seem to have very much practical application. With deeper reflection, however, this metaphor offers a host of useful insights.

First of all, it reminds us that, like sunlight on a mirror, virtues come from a higher source that is both infinite and eternal. We don't need to be perfect in order to reflect these perfect qualities, all we have to do is point ourselves in the right direction and clean the dust off of our hearts.

Reflecting the light of the sun makes us brilliant, radiant, full of light and life, but that is not all it does. Sunlight is the originating source of virtually all energy – and therefore all physical life – on earth. Likewise, virtues are the source of our spiritual life.

While at first we notice the sun's light, we quickly begin to appreciate its heat as well. In time, we realize that white light is the source of all color in the world. When we really start to explore, we discover that sunlight contains infrared, ultraviolet, radio, x-ray, microwave, and an entire spectrum of energy that can be harnessed to accomplish amazing things.

Likewise, virtues start out as the idea of "being good," but as we explore all of their nuances, we realize that virtues are what allow us to do everything we do. They are the energy that powers our spiritual existence. Virtues are not one thing, nor are they a collection of many separate things, but like the rays of the sun, they express a full spectrum of capacities, behaviors, energies and attractions. Exploring all of their potential is, in the words of a Sufi poet, *"the science of the love of God."*

Other observations we can make from this metaphor are that:

A mirror allows us to reflect the light of the sun into dark places and illumine them. Reflecting virtues illumines the dark areas of our lives.

We are naturally drawn to heat and light, and enjoy diversity of color. Likewise, we are drawn to virtues and enjoy people who express a wide range of them.

We can reflect, experience and enjoy the bounties of the radiant Sun, even though we can never touch the sun itself and may never understand how or why it shines the way it does. Likewise, we don't have to *understand* or even *believe* in God in order to benefit from the qualities we were given. The sun will shine on us, even if we never look up in awe and wonder.

While I obviously love the metaphor of virtues as light reflected in our hearts, there are other analogies that also offer insights. For example:

We can think of virtues as spiritual food that gives us the energy we need to accomplish our goals. In fact, the Bible calls the virtues of love, joy, peace, longsuffering, gentleness, goodness, faith, meekness and temperance the "fruits of the spirit." The term "fruit" can be understood both as spiritual food and as the reward of a spiritual life.

We can think of virtues as our spiritual arms and legs, which allow us to work and serve. When we think of our physical qualities, we include our bodies, our organs and our senses – all of those things that allow us to function in the physical world. Our spiritual qualities are our virtues, combined with our minds and our will. Our virtues are all of the capacities that allow us to function in the world of the spirit.

We can think of virtues as tools in our personal toolbox. The more familiar we are with what tools we have access to, the more likely we are to choose the right one for the job and build the life we want.

Other Things It Is Helpful to Know about Virtues

Practicing virtues is a gift we give ourselves. It is not a sacrifice we make for others. Not only do virtues feel good, but they improve the quality of our lives. Having patience, for example, does not mean that we spend more time waiting for things to happen, it means that we enjoy the time we spend waiting, rather than being frustrated. (The wait will be just as long either way).

Virtues inform and guide our decision-making process. Our minds make decisions and our Will spurs us to action, but our virtues—and the emotions they evoke—set our priorities. The more we love what is good, the easier it is to do what is good.

Virtues need to be in balance with one another. Courage without prudence is recklessness. Honesty without tact becomes hurtful. Almost any virtue, without moderation, becomes a vice.

Our culture often values the wrong qualities. The ability to play guitar, shoot baskets or make money are not spiritual virtues, though the virtues of perseverance, focus and cooperation might make them more attainable.

Virtues are known by many names. When educators and psychologists talk about non-cognitive skills, good character and signature strengths, they are really talking about virtues, but they are ignoring where those virtues come from. By ignoring the spiritual nature of virtues, they loose access to much of their power, inspiration and meaning. That *doesn't* mean that the research is invalid, only that it is incomplete. You and I can use their research to validate the importance of virtues, then look for the deeper meaning behind it.

Virtues and Happiness Research

If the idea that practicing virtues can make us happy sounds more spiritual than scientific, you may be surprised to learn that the Positive Psychology Movement has some hard research to back up this claim.

The best-known research is described in the book *Authentic Happiness*, by Martin Seligman of the University of Pennsylvania. In his groundbreaking study, Seligman asked volunteers to do one of five different tasks. At the beginning of the study, and for six months after, they also took an online happiness/depression assessment to measure their state of mind.

Of the five tasks, one was supposed to be an "inert" or "placebo" activity. As expected, it had a small and short-lived effect on the participant's happiness. One of the other initial activities also had a small effect that lasted slightly longer.

Three activities, however, had a significant effect on the participant's happiness that lasted longer than expected.

In the one that had the strongest immediate effect, participants were given a week to write and then deliver a letter of gratitude—in person—to someone who had been especially kind to them but had never been properly thanked. These people's happiness went up dramatically right after the exercise, and then slowly returned to normal over a six month period.

Gratitude, of course, is a core virtue, so it should not surprise anyone that such an intense expression of it would have a positive effect on a person's feelings, but that this positive effect could last up to six months gives us reason for encouragement in our own lives.

The two other exercises had results that actually *increased* over time.

In the first, participants were asked to take an inventory of 24 "character strengths" that allowed them to identify five top "signature strengths." They were then asked to use one of these strengths in a new and different way every day for one week.

As I mentioned a moment ago, when psychologist use the term "signature character strengths" what they are *really* talking about are *virtues*. "Character strengths" sounds so much more scientific and less spiritual than the word "virtues", but look at their list:

Wisdom and knowledge: Creativity, Judgment, Curiosity, Love of Learning, Perspective
Courage: Bravery, Perseverance, Integrity, Enthusiasm
Love: Intimacy, Kindness, Sociability
Justice: Sense of responsibility, Fairness, Leadership
Temperance: Forgiveness, Humility, Caution, Self-control
Transcendence: Appreciation, Gratitude, Optimism, Humor, Spirituality

All of these "strengths" fit our earlier description of virtues. So in this exercise, participants were being told, "look, you have these five virtues that you are really good at. Now go out and be creative in finding new ways to practice them every day for a week."

The thing about practicing virtues is that, not only does it feel good, but it strengthens the virtues, making it even easier to practice them in the future. No wonder these people's happiness increased over time instead of drifting back down to its original level.

They were stepping beyond the bounds of happiness (the experience of virtue) into the realm of *joy* (the experience of *increasing* one's virtues).

So here is a case where science has measured a significant increase in a large number of people's happiness as a result of practicing a virtue. Who says science and religion can't agree?

The final exercise is a little more subtle in its mechanism. Participants were asked to write down three things that went well each day—and their causes—every night for a week.

We don't necessarily think of self-knowledge as a virtue, but of course it is. In order to fulfill the requirements for this exercise, the participants would have to go through a mini-version of the Internal Consultation exercise I described earlier in this book. They would have to ask themselves what made them feel good that day, which means they would have to explore their feelings and their causes. They would then also have to consider the degree to which they were or were not responsible for those feelings. This is a level of introspection that many people never take the time to experience. It sounds so simple, but after doing it for a week many of the participants would be more self-aware than ever before. No wonder they had the greatest long-term gains in overall happiness.

A completely different set of researchers, including Michael Norton of Harvard, and Elizabeth Dunn and Lara Aknin of the University of British Columbia, explored the relationship between generosity and happiness and discovered that people who were given a small amount of money ($5-$20) and asked to spend it on someone *else*, were happier at the end of the day than similar people given the same amount to spend on themselves.

A similar study gave money to individual members of sports teams or sales teams and, again, asked them to spend it on themselves or on other teammates. Not only were the teams that practiced generosity happier, but they performed better in their group activities. These experiments and several others led the researchers to conclude that money can buy happiness—but only when it is spent on someone else. Of course, it wasn't the money that created the happiness, it was the opportunity to successfully practice a virtue.

What this and other research can do is give us graphs and numbers to prove that practicing virtues can make us happier and more content. What mainstream science *can't* do, however, is explain that the reason why practicing virtues makes us happy is because it satisfies our longing for God; it is the path to becoming our true selves.

Right now, "Transcendence" which is the longing for the Divine, is just one more "strength" at the bottom of Positive Psychology's list of twenty-four character strengths. That's OK. Someday science will move the Transcendent from the bottom of the list to the top, and realize that our longing for God—*not* the search for pleasure—is the focal point of our lives.

In the mean time, we can take what science has to offer as proof that we are on the right track, and make a conscious choice as to which virtues *we* want to practice.

❇

Where to Start

So which positive sensations do you want to start feeling first? What virtues do you want to invite into your life?

I know, I know. We all want to invite love into our lives, but that is the wrong place to start.

Yes, love is a good thing, but if you put your energies into attracting love into your life—when that has already been your focus since the day you were born—then you are likely to just continue the same old patterns and get yourself into trouble.

Remember, true love is an attraction to a person's constellation of virtues. It is a *meta-virtue* if you will—the virtue of being attracted to virtues. What you want to do is develop your love for *specific* virtues within yourself. It is the virtue of love, but targeted at other virtues, not people.

If you say, "I want to become a more loving person," for example, what you are saying is that you want to recognize, identify and be attracted to every virtue that you see expressed in the world of creation.

In practice, however, you would likely use this goal as an excuse to become emotionally enmeshed with anyone and everyone who expressed even a glimmer of a virtue.

Becoming loving is the goal of a lifetime, not the first step in the process. There are *other* virtues that I recommend that you focus on first. These are core virtues that create the spiritual environment that will make it easier to practice any virtue, including love. I believe they are essential for spiritual healing and growth.

These are honesty, forgiveness, compassion and faith. Honesty and openness help us uncover the painful emotions that we are carrying inside.

Forgiveness allows us to free up the resentments that are keeping our negative emotions locked in place.

Compassion helps us feel connected with all of our fellow children of God, and faith heals our relationship with a God who truly is on our side.

Together they are the subject of part two of this book.

Summary of Part One

Though part one of this book is the shortest section, we've covered a lot of ground, so here is a brief summary of the main points.

God is love, and our longing for God is expressed through our search for love. Our emotional sensations tell us about the presence or absence of virtues such as love, but only if we know how to interpret them.

Our life history has caused us to misidentify love, and many of God's other virtues. Instead, we have mistaken the sensations associated with fear and shame for love. The close association between love, sex and shame has caused us to become trapped in shame spirals in which we try to numb our feelings of shame by engaging in behaviors that temporarily distract us from shame, but ultimately increase it.

We can break shame spirals and heal shame by using joy rather than shame to motivate our change in behavior, by facing and overcoming our unrealistic and crippling perfectionism, by being present and listening to the messages that our emotions are trying to send, and by focusing on developing our virtues instead of trying to find love by repeating our old patterns.

Our emotions tell us about the virtues we experience, and painful emotions tell us about the virtues that are missing from our lives.

By developing our virtues, we can fill the spiritual holes in our lives and gain access to a whole range of spiritual sensations that are more rewarding than the physical sensations we pursued before.

If these ideas have made sense to you, and you are ready to start focusing on what you can do to make your life better instead of how to stop doing the things that have gotten you into trouble in the past, then take a deep breath and move on to part two. Feel free to sit and meditate on all of this for a few minutes, hours, days or weeks before hand.

⚘

And Two Final Tips

Before you jump right into part two, the four tools of emotional healing, I would like to offer two tips.

First, take some time to process what you've read so far. Whether you take a deep breath and mediate for a few minutes, or you set this book aside for a few weeks, let the ideas sink in. Feeling comfortable with what you've learned is more important than barreling on to the next section.

My second tip is closely related.

Inner work *is* work, but that doesn't mean that it can't be fun as well. As we explore what it means to practice four specific virtues, I encourage you to *celebrate the process.*

No physical pleasure can compare with the joy of spiritual growth. But if we never acknowledge the progress we are making, we can't celebrate it. If we let perfectionism establish goals that are impossible to achieve, then we never let ourselves say "I did it!"

Before you begin the process of replacing shame with joy, and unhealthy behavior with spiritual activities, think a little about how you might celebrate the baby steps you will take on the way there.

Here are some ideas:
Set short-term goals that can be easily met
    (because success leads to more success).
Find someone you can celebrate with.
Give yourself appropriate rewards for success.
Keep a journal of the things you did right.
Say prayers of gratitude for every temptation avoided.

Part Two

Tools of **4Emotional HEALING**

Honesty, Forgiveness, Compassion & Faith

Introduction to Part Two

HEALING WHAT IS MISSING

The emotional pain caused by shame, anger, loneliness and fear is a message telling us that there is something missing in our lives.

Part of what is missing is honest self-knowledge, forgiveness, compassion and faith.

It is not our fault.

We can't be expected to have developed qualities that we were never shown as children, any more than we could be expected to know how to swim if we had never been taken to a lake or pool.

The question is, now that we are adults and can recognize the skills we lack, do we hide our heads in shame, or make a conscious effort to acquire them?

I will be blunt. Honesty, forgiveness, compassion and faith are what many people would call virtues, and virtues have been given a pretty bum rap lately. Even psychologists who study them for a living prefer to use the code words "character strengths" to refer to these positive qualities because no one wants to be asked to become "virtuous." People reviewing my books have even told me that they would sell much better if I could just find a better word to use.

Here's why:

Virtues have often been spoken of as though they were burdens. They were seen as effort you put forth on behalf of someone else—to make *their* lives better, not yours. To be honest, for example, was to lose the advantage of deceit. To forgive was to let go of revenge and become a victim. Compassion meant taking care of others at your own expense, and faith was something you had to feign in order to please an angry God.

But let me offer another perspective:

Honest people like themselves.

Forgiving people are at peace with themselves and the world.

Compassionate people feel connected rather than isolated and alone.

People with faith in the goodness of life are not afraid of the world.

These virtues are not obligations to anyone else. They are qualities that can fill the empty places in your life. They are the greatest gifts you can give yourself.

Perhaps you are unconvinced. That's OK. This is a short book. Just give me a few minutes of your time, and an open mind.

My prayer is that by the time you finish reading, you will be so enamored of the beauty and power of these virtues that you will hunger for them, and long for the day when you can experience even a glimmer of any one of them in your daily life. These four virtues save lives and restore souls. You need them, and if you read, think, meditate and pray about them, you will discover that you really, really want them too.

Honesty

I will talk about honesty first because it offers four great gifts in the process of emotional healing.

First, honesty allows us to overcome denial.

Second, it helps us to uncover and name the empty places in our lives that we long to fill.

Third, honesty shines a light on the dark corners of our past and chases away the shadows of shame.

Fourth, shared honesty is an important step in developing compassion and a feeling of connection to the people around you.

As I've explained, emotional pain is a messenger that tells us that there are things missing in our lives—some virtues that we all deserved to grow up with but didn't. These might be love, security, respect, encouragement, tolerance, or any number of other essential virtues. We may be consciously aware of some of these missing virtues, but many others are invisible to us. It is difficult to name something you've never experienced, and yet the emotional pain of its absence is still tangibly real.

Honesty is the virtue we use to help us uncover what was missing.

The kind of honesty I'm referring to is not about not stealing (though that is important) nor is it the tactless honesty that encourages you to say hurtful things to others. It is, instead, a tool for self-discovery. It is the kind of honesty that allows you to see yourself accurately, acknowledge the things that have happened to you, and take responsibility for your own future.

I use the word honesty to represent a constellation of virtues that includes openness, truthfulness, and an ability to discern what is real and speak about it without shame. Honesty requires courage—first the courage to *look* at oneself without flinching, and second the courage to risk *being* oneself without reservation.

The first gift of honesty that we will explore is the gift of escaping from denial.

In order to heal what is missing in our lives, we must first acknowledge that our lives were not perfect; that there were important virtues that were not practiced or expressed in our families, and that we need to make an extra effort to acquire them now. This first step is called overcoming denial, and it requires that most fundamental of acts of honesty: opening our eyes.

The Power of Denial

Denial is not just an attempt to ignore those parts of our lives that we don't wish to acknowledge. Denial is the ability to *block from our conscious awareness* anything that we do not want to be able to see.

Humans are amazingly good at this.

Our ability to block our awareness of our personal challenges is so universal that it is even referred to by Jesus in one of his more amusing admonitions:

Why do you see the speck that is in your brother's eye, but do not notice the log that is in your own eye? How can you say to your brother, 'Brother, let me take out the speck that is in your eye,' when you yourself **do not see** *the log that is in your own eye?*   Luke 6:41-42

Note that He does not say that we are *ignoring* the log in our own eye, but that we *do not see* it. The log represents our personal challenges and unhealthy patterns. Admitting that we *might* have them is the first step in being able to see them.

The classic metaphor for denial is that of an elephant in a living room. The elephant is a problem, but everyone in the family is committed to *not* seeing it, as it eventually destroys the home. Some people in the family ignore the elephant, but some are *so good* at ignoring it that it really and truly disappears from their mind's eye.

The elephant can represent an alcoholic parent, mental illness, divorce, financial problems, unwanted pregnancy, sexual infidelity, addictions, *anything* that is a source of unresolved stress. And it doesn't matter how big the problem is, there will be some who are able to ignore it, and others who will blind themselves to its existence completely.

In order to co-exist with the elephant, each member of the family will develop his or her own coping mechanism, and these coping mechanisms will *also* either be invisible or accepted as rational behaviors, even though they are anything but.

As long as we continue to deny that both the elephant and the coping mechanisms exist, then they will continue to sabotage our lives. Once we acknowledge that there are aspects of our lives that we cannot even see, and which are completely irrational, then we can begin to look for their footprints.

This awakening, which is critical to any real emotional healing, gives us permission to ask for help in seeing the things that we have blocked from our awareness.

What are examples of things we might be in denial about?

We can be in denial about stressful experiences that have caused us pain; about the coping mechanisms we have developed to numb, distract, or hide this pain; about the problems caused by these coping mechanisms; and about the emotional pain itself. Some of the things we deny might hide in plain sight, while others may be truly blocked from our conscious memory and awareness.

We hide things in plain sight by justifying stressful or abusive behavior as normal. If our parents beat us, we might tell ourselves that "spare the rod, spoil the child" was proof that they loved us. A sexual assault by a friend or relative might be rewritten in our memories as a short-lived romance. A parent's alcoholism might be remembered as "daddy was sick a lot." Our mother's perfectionism and constant criticism might be justified as "she could do no wrong." The pain of living in crushing poverty might be brushed off with "it was a hard time for everyone." The death of a sibling might be minimized as "I hardly remember them anyway." We allow ourselves to remember these experiences, but we do not allow ourselves to remember the emotional pain they caused. We use rationalization and justifications to create a barrier between the two.

Other stressful experiences really are hidden from our memory. Some may have happened at a very young age. Others were so painful or traumatic that even though they were experienced later in life, we have blocked them from our memory because we don't have the tools we need to process them. While consciously forgotten, the emotional memory is still with us and can still cause us pain and shame. The four tools of healing will make it safer for these memories to surface.

Whether we remember our sources of stress and shame or not, we live with our coping mechanisms every day. One would think that this would make it harder to deny them, but deny them we do.

I'm not an alcoholic, I just like to have fun. I'm not a sex addict, I just have a strong libido. I'm not addicted to porn, I am just bored at night. I'm not obese, I have a condition. I'm not addicted to gambling, I'm just sure my luck is about to change.

Addictions are the way many people cope with the pain of early trauma and shame. They numb and distract us. By denying the addiction, we deny the pain that causes it. But addictions are not the only coping mechanisms available to us, therefore denial is not just about addiction, nor is it even only about big things. Denial is about our blindness to *any* unhealthy or irrational activity we engage in as a response to some trauma or shame.

Here is a teeny tiny example of one of my personal blind spots.

Something I was unaware of in my own behavior was my inability to close a drawer all the way. I invariably left drawers open one or two inches. This seems like a small thing, but I was completely unaware of it until my wife commented on it (in some exasperation). What I came to realize was that I resisted *completing* the act of closing drawers because I resisted *finishing* projects because a finished project could be judged as a *failure*, whereas an incomplete project couldn't. Dealing with my fear of judgment and failure helped me finish projects and, yes, close drawers. The point is not so much about *why* I didn't close drawers, but rather that I was completely *unaware* of the fact that I didn't.

My wife, on the other hand, noticed one day that she was saving used tubes of toothpaste for no apparent reason. When she allowed herself to become aware of this habit, she realized that a part of her was still expecting a time to come when we would be so impoverished that she would need the last spot of toothpaste in each of these tubes. That unconscious fear of scarcity was filling up our bathroom drawers! (The same ones I was leaving open two inches).

Going straight from "I'm willing to admit that I am in emotional pain and may need help" to admitting that we have an addiction or that we were abused or traumatized may be too big of a leap for many people. That is why it is OK to start by acknowledging *any* blind spot or coping mechanism. As soon as we are able to see even *one* small irrational behavior pattern that we've been blind to in the past, we open ourselves up to the possibility that there might be more. Open eyes. That's all you need to start.

Whether it is leaving drawers open or drinking too much alcohol, it is sobering to realize that the behaviors that we are blind to or try to deny are *not* invisible to the people around us. Just as it is easy to look at our friends and know if they drink, eat, spend, and gamble too much, or have affairs, scream at their kids, or beat their wives, the chances are that they know what you are doing too. The only ones who think otherwise are you and your loved ones who have agreed to live in denial too.

Living in denial does not reduce shame, it just makes it harder to heal. Remember, the point is not to figure out who is to blame for your pain. The point is to figure out what virtues you grew up missing so that you can develop them yourself. Denying that something was missing makes it impossible to fill that unmet need. Becoming aware of these little blind spots opens the door to healing by revealing the empty spaces we are trying to hide from ourselves.

Becoming aware of *our* blind spots also lets us feel compassion towards all of the other people we know whose behavior seems completely irrational to us. We can be more forgiving when we understand that people are not being irrational *on purpose*. I was not leaving drawers open in order to irritate my wife. I was leaving drawers open because I didn't realize what I was doing.

Being aware that we have blind spots and unconscious coping mechanisms also gives us a small measure of defense against those who would use them to manipulate us. Advertisers, politicians and cult leaders know that if they disguise their lies as the right kind of elephants, we will be unable to look straight at them.

"Daddy is not an alcoholic," for example, is such a big lie, that in order to survive in a family a child must be able to believe very big lies and never challenge authority. This makes lies like, "The world is ending in September," or "I am channeling the spirit of an alien priest from the planet Beta-Max," relatively easy to believe.

Likewise, when you are trying to explain some clear and obvious truth to someone and they just refuse to see it, know that there is probably some large family secret standing between them and your truth, blocking their view. They are not stupid, they are coping. Either that, or there is some large family secret standing between you and *their* truth. That's the thing about blind spots. You never *ever* know for *certain* which side of it you are standing on. So be tolerant, compassionate, and forgiving of others, and pray for clarity for yourself.

What does all of this have to do with honesty? The fact is that, whether you *ignore* the elephant in the living room, or *blind* yourself to it, you are never actually blind. Some part of you knows the truth.

In order to be honest with yourself, you don't actually need to know what the family secrets or personal challenges are that you are hiding from yourself. It can take years to figure all of that out. All you need to do is acknowledge the fact that you are in emotional pain and that emotional pain is a clear sign that there is *something* missing. When you admit that something is missing, you can begin the process of creating it for yourself.

Once this first step is taken, there are places you can go to learn how to become even more honest with yourself so you can uncover more information. We learn how to be honest by exploring our own experience, but we also learn through witnessing the honest sharing of other people.

If you really want to experience the "mother load" of open, honest, profound sharing, then you really are ready for the first step—the first step of twelve.

⊗

A Model of Honest Sharing

I've been trying to figure out a way to talk about this deep level of honesty that *doesn't* involve introducing you to a twelve-step program, but I can't. The two aspects of honesty that are most important for your personal growth—self-honesty and letting go of secrets—are best addressed through the unique strengths of an Anonymous meeting. So even if there are no twelve-step meetings in your town, and even if you refuse to even think about attending one yourself, let me illustrate some of the healing properties of honesty by describing what happens at one.

First of all, twelve-step meetings are created to serve the needs of people who have recognized that they might be missing something in their lives. Just showing up for a meeting requires a level of honesty and openness that is outside of most people's experience. "Closed" AA meetings are only for people who absolutely know that they have a problem with alcohol, but "open" AA meetings and most other kinds of meetings, such as Alanon, CoDA and dozens of others are open to anyone willing to consider the possibility that they might not be in complete control of their lives. If you have read this far in this book, then you would probably benefit from the right meeting.

When you walk into your first meeting, you may be carrying with you an entire backpack full of shame, fear, distrust, and resentment. It doesn't matter if you are at a meeting for alcoholics, sex addicts, over-eaters, co-dependents, or drug addicts, you will see all sorts of people from all walks of life. You may look around the room and think, "These people are crazy and they have no idea what I am going through. That guy is too rich, that guy is too poor, that guy is too old, that one is too young. None of them is dealing with the problems I have."

When the meeting starts, they will explain that everything said in the meeting stays in the meeting and is not to be repeated or referred to. It is a safe place to share secrets. You may be thinking, "Right. Like I'm going to tell these guys anything anyway."

They also explain that there is no "cross-talk," which means that after a person shares, no one else is allowed to comment, give advice or express judgment. Each person is to share from his or her *own* experience, and not express opinions about others' experience.

"What?" you may be thinking. "What is the point of listening to other people's problems if I'm not allowed to give them any useful advice?"

When the first person shares, they say, "Hi, my name is ___, and I'm (an alcoholic, sex addict, or whatever) and you may think, "Why would anyone say something like that?"

But everyone in the room smiles and says, "Hi ___," and it seems to give him or her comfort.

Then they tell a story about something awful they did this week, or some problem they are dealing with, or some mistake they made that they are trying to learn from, and you may think, "I can't believe someone would actually admit to this in public."

In most settings, this kind of honest sharing would generate a wave of discomfort in the people around them. Listeners would feel embarrassed for the person for being so open and vulnerable. They would look for an excuse to change the subject or remove themselves from the conversation. They might decide that the person sharing is a little weird or strange and avoid them in the future.

But this is not most settings. As you look around the room expecting to see frowns of disapproval and judgment on everyone's faces, you discover instead expressions of acceptance and connection. You see people nodding in understanding, and even maybe a few tears.

You are expecting shame and tension and fear to settle on the group, but it never does. It is like someone has thrown a stink bomb in the middle of the room, but the love and understanding of the people listening have turned it into perfume.

It makes no sense. When families talk about their problems or reveal secrets, the tension usually increases, but here it does just the opposite. As your own tension decreases, you listen more closely. Strangely, you start hearing a little bit of yourself in his story— maybe just a hint—a shared fear or a similar sense of humor.

Then a second person shares her story and something different rings true ... and the next person's story, and the next. Pain is pain. Shame is shame. Longing is longing. The things that most people try to hold inside are even more universal than the things they are willing to share.

You may find yourself nodding in agreement along with others in the room. Those nods and that acceptance... maybe they could be for you too.

This sense of connection might not come with the first person who shares, or even in the first meeting. We have to experience a certain amount of honesty before we can develop an appreciation for it.

It may take time for our natural defenses to relax so that we can experience this kind of sharing as anything other than self-absorbed whining and complaint. It may take a while to calm our natural inclination to try to give advice and "fix" everyone else's problems. We may have to hear the stories and observe the progress before we begin to understand that the people sharing don't really need anyone's advice, let alone judgment. What they need is to take their secrets and their shame out of the dark corners of their isolation and lay them out where sunshine and fresh air can put them in perspective and blow the stink off of them.

Keeping our problems to ourselves makes us feel alone, which increases our desire to participate in inappropriate behaviors. Isolating ourselves allows us to believe that we are the only people in the world struggling with our problems. Keeping secrets allows us to believe that *our* problems, *our* mistakes, *our* patterns are so bad that they will never be accepted or forgiven.

When we listen to and share stories, we realize that we are *not* alone, we are *not* the only ones dealing with these issues, and, no matter what we have done, we can receive forgiveness and learn to forgive ourselves. Looking around the room, we see people who have made terrible mistakes, done destructive things and are struggling to deal with the consequences. Yet, when we look at them, what we learn to see is the nobility of the struggle.

Over time, the mistakes that people have made in the past become less important than the progress they are currently making. We are inspired by their growth. We are attracted to their perseverance. We begin to recognize virtues in them that we don't even have names for. In short, we begin to love them. We have no desire to condemn them, and we can't imagine a loving God condemning them either. If we can forgive them, and God can forgive them, then we can begin to imagine the possibility of being forgiven ourselves.

As I said, all of this sense of connection and acceptance will not magically descend upon you at your first meeting. It will take time, and, just as importantly, it will take an attitude of openness to the unknown. I hope you give it a try because I don't know of any other setting that even comes close to creating the healing atmosphere of the recovery community.

If you are unable or unwilling to try a twelve-step meeting, then keep in mind the essential requirements: safety, honesty, acceptance, mutual sharing, no advice. If you can find a group of friends or a support group to offer you these things, then go for it. It can work if everyone present understands what you are attempting and why.

Seeing a therapist is not the same. While there are some things a professional therapist can do better than a twelve-step group, therapists don't share their stories. Therapists are paid to be accepting. Therapists often like to give advice. Therapists charge by the hour.

Going to a meeting four to eight times a week for your first few months of personal work will give you the added advantage of hearing hundreds of stories and receiving thousands of nods of acceptance.

Now that I have described a meeting, and have, I hope, piqued your interest, let's take a look at what kinds of things it is valuable to share in this kind of safe setting. What are we being honest about, what are we disclosing, and what are we hoping to gain by the process?

Self-Disclosure

If we want to change our unhealthy, irrational behavior, then we will have to discover its roots. What is causing the shame that drives us to our unhealthy, numbing behaviors? What are we hiding from ourselves? What have we forgotten?

In the recovery community, there is a saying that goes

"The pain of remembering can't be any worse than the pain of *knowing* and yet not remembering."

Read that line again. It is important.

If we weren't in pain, we would not be engaging in numbing behavior.

If we had *truly* forgotten, if we did not carry an *inner knowing* of the source of our pain, then we would not be in pain. It would not have any power over us and our choices.

If some part of us knows why we are in pain, then, by removing one layer of numbing shame at a time, we can eventually figure it out.

We do that by shining a light on our feelings and behaviors, removing the shame, then looking beneath those behaviors to find the hidden motivation. We do this over and over again, one layer at a time by sharing our feelings and experiences with others. Sometimes, sharing will blow a little bit of dust off of our pasts. Other times it will dig deep enough to unearth skeletons.

The process of sharing is a way to call ourselves to account. So why does it need to be so public? Why can't we lie in bed and think about things that have happened to us and explore our feelings in the privacy of our homes using internal consultation?

There are several reasons.

Why We Self-Disclose

When we start to share with a group, things come out of our mouths that we didn't expect to say or know that we knew. Having witnesses solidifies the sharing and makes it real.

Self-disclosure is a way of shining a light on the shadows of our lives. When we remember painful things, we often take more responsibility for them than we should. Having witnesses who show empathy helps put what happened to us in perspective.

Honest self-disclosure that is followed by acceptance rather than judgment helps remove shame. When we remember shameful experiences, we often exaggerate their importance, making ourselves feel even more evil and shameful. Witnesses who are not shocked or appalled remind us that making mistakes does not make us evil.

Humans are social creatures. We discover ourselves through our interactions with others. We learn, not just from our own sharing, but by listening to the sharing of others.

Our understanding of our identity becomes clearer and more concrete when it is reflected in the responses of those who truly see us. Acknowledgment is a form of identity confirmation. Self-disclosure is a tool for integration of all parts of our personality and all past experiences into one coherent identity. When you share different aspects of your life with the same people over the course of months or years, they don't experience you as a collection of isolated stories. They don't see a parent, an employee, a religious person or a person who is struggling. They see a single, complex human. Their ability to accept that complexity makes it easier for you to integrate the different ways that you see yourself.

In addition to being a tool for self-discovery, honest self-disclosure is a form of profound sharing, which makes it an amazing creative process. Sharing is one of the ways that humans reflect the generative power of the Creator. It transfers knowledge or experience from one soul to another—effectively doubling its potential—at no material cost. By sharing experience, strength and hope, the amount of experience, strength and hope in the world is multiplied many fold.

As George Bernard Shaw said: "If you have an apple and I have an apple and we exchange these apples then you and I will still each have one apple. But if you have an idea and I have an idea and we exchange these ideas, then each of us will have two ideas."

The wisdom that is expressed in some of these meetings is staggering. The thought that that wisdom is now multiplying exponentially as it is internalized and then shared by others is one of the things that gives me hope for the human race. The belief that this wisdom can eventually heal the planet is why I'm writing this book.

What Self-Disclosure Isn't

It is important to make a distinction between therapeutic self-disclosure and confession—or such unhelpful, even potentially destructive behaviors as complaining, blaming, back-biting or self-flagellation.

First of all, we are not asking anyone to forgive us, give us penance, or tell us that what we did was acceptable. The people to whom we disclose are not stand-ins for God. They are simply witnesses. They help lock what comes out of our mouths into objective reality so that we can remember it and have it reflected back to us through other people's eyes.

The purpose is not to complain, blame or back-bite. The focus is not on what others may have done to us, but what we felt and internalized as a result of it. The experiences we relate are not *true* in the absolute sense. They are simply true for *us*. To the best of our ability, we do not reveal incriminating details about other people's behavior. We speak in "I" sentences.

The purpose is not to beat ourselves up for what we have done, but to shine a light on it so that we can understand our own hidden motivations and reactions. One of the paradoxical benefits of this type of honesty is that as we *increase* our sense of personal responsibility, we *reduce* toxic shame.

What We Self-Disclose

Whether it is in a meeting or in our daily lives, we should have a goal of being able to honestly share our feelings, our thoughts, opinions and observations, our experiences, and our positive regard for others. To the degree that these topics relate to our personal lives (rather than politics or gossip) they are also appropriate to share in a meeting.

Appropriate topics include:

Experiences that caused intense emotions that we might need assistance to identify and resolve. When we have strong sensations—good, bad or ugly—it means that *something* is going on with us. Talking them out can help us understand and identify what it is.

Experiences that we learned from. When we start paying attention to what goes on in the background of our lives, it seems as though every day brings a new flash of awareness. Journaling is a wonderful way to keep track of these insights, but there is a real joy and sense of empowerment that comes from being able to share these with people who care about your growth.

Experiences that we would like assistance in solving, resolving, interpreting or understanding. It might seem counterproductive to expect help from a group that is committed to not giving advice to one another, yet help does indeed come. First, the voicing of the dilemma often draws forth from our own well of wisdom the insight that we need. Second, while others won't tell you what *you* should do, they can share, using "I" statements, what *they* have experienced in vaguely similar situations. This might seem like a game of semantics, but the difference is very real. Advice invites either resistance or compliance. Parallel experiences invite exploration and contemplation.

Experiences that we simply need to have acknowledged as true, valuable or real. Sometimes all we need is to say "this happened to me" and have others sit in witness.

Sometimes the experience that we most need to share with others is the experience of sitting in silent, supportive witness to the other people in the room. Listening, in this situation, is not a passive activity. It is an active gift to the ones being heard—sometimes for the first time in their entire lives.

Phyllis Peterson, author of *Remaining Faithful*, writes about the value of external validation. She attended a twelve-step program for recovery from incest during which the pain of her inner child within was witnessed and validated over and over again by the compassionate listeners of the group. Through this process, the toxic shame and guilt she felt was finally transferred to her abuser. Without this external validation, she would have been unable to eventually develop the skill of internal consultation.

Letting Go of Secrets

Some of the most important self-disclosure involves letting go of secrets—personal secrets and family secrets. This is incredibly frightening. When I tell people this, they often protest—sometimes quite angrily—or even get up and leave the room.

Before you throw this book in the trash, let me clarify that secrets should only be shared in a safe setting. There are, however, several reasons why it is worth the effort to find or create such a setting for yourself—either in a twelve-step group or in private therapy.

It takes energy to keep a secret

Take a moment to consider the physical, emotional and mental cost of keeping secrets. The longer we keep one, the more energy it takes to keep it hidden—energy that is then not available for all of the other wonderful, creative things you could be doing with your life. The lifetime cost of just one big family secret might be enough for someone to have accomplished great things *if* they'd been able to use that energy constructively instead.

For example, I had three great secrets as a young child:

1) My father had left us,

2) The reason for his abandonment (in my mind) was that there was something profoundly wrong with me, and

3) The proof that I was defective (in my mind) was that I wet the bed.

These three secrets took enormous amounts of energy to keep hidden. Like all children, I still saw the world as a mysterious place. One of my beliefs was that adults—and especially women—could read my mind. After all, my mother knew when I had done something wrong, no matter how little evidence there was. Consequently, I was sure that every adult I met would be able to see right through my soul and know that I was flawed.

To prevent that, I tried to keep my thoughts from drifting towards the sources of my shame. That was about as effective as not thinking about pink elephants. It affected my ability to concentrate in school, my willingness to make friends, and my creativity, because part of my mental energy was always elsewhere, trying to block thoughts of how broken I was.

All of us have secrets. We have parts of our identity that we are ashamed of. Though most of us no longer believe that others can read our minds, we nevertheless devote an incredible amount of mental energy to trying to hide the subtle clues that might let someone else guess what we don't want them to know. Just think of the wasted energy!

Secrets hold us hostage.

Secrets can stop us from doing things we want to do for fear of exposure. For example, when I was in High School, I was so poor that I did not own a suit or a tie, and since I had no father or male family members, I didn't have anyone to borrow them from without revealing how poor I was. When my Graphic Arts Club took its annual field trip to a nearby city, dinner at a fancy restaurant was included as a treat. The only problem was that we were required to wear a jacket and tie. Rather than admit my situation to my fellow students, I simply didn't go. The teacher and students all thought that I was being a snob and didn't want to be seen with them, when the exact opposite was true.

How often do we subtly rearrange our lives so that we won't have to admit to our little family secrets?

Secrets blackmail us.

Shame can make you feel that you do not deserve success, but secrets can make you afraid to achieve success because you fear the scrutiny that comes with it. This subtle self-blackmail is more than just not doing something that might reveal a specific secret; it is avoiding doing *anything* that might draw attention to yourself. When we have big secrets, we are like families in protective custody. We are hiding who we really are, and trying to keep a low profile. This means we can't afford to excel in anything. We certainly can't go into politics, but even applying for jobs that do background checks or call references or check credit scores can send us into hiding. Acting, public speaking, making a lot of money, starting a business, traveling abroad, anything that would make someone—especially someone in authority—look at us closely provokes a fear that someone will figure out what our fatal flaw might. This background paranoia can keep us from giving life our best shot and reaching for our dreams.

Secrets disrupt honest interactions.

Many of us have more than passive secrets. We may be struggling with active addictions, fears, personality disorders, emotional pain and other issues that require conscious effort to keep under control when we're in social situations. I picture these personal issues as invisible monkeys that sit on our shoulders—poking, prodding, pulling our hair and screeching in our ears while we are trying to hold "normal" conversations with "normal" people. We can neither speak honestly nor listen objectively to what others are saying when our secrets are constantly threatening to highjack our conversations.

Secrets are not so secret.

If all of these reasons for letting go of secrets have not convinced you that should find a way to be more open with people, then you are really not going to like this last reason. The simple fact is, that many of our most closely held secrets are not really very secret to the people we work with or even meet on the street.

Those invisible monkeys that are screeching in our ears are often not so invisible—or silent—to others. To some degree or another, most of us are consciously aware of other people's blind spots as well as their supposed secrets. Like the abused spouse who tries to cover bruises with layers of makeup, we think that we are fooling people, but we aren't. To an even greater degree, we are often *subconsciously* aware of other people's issues because our hearts perceive what our minds try to hide. We notice the empty spaces in conversations, hear the tension in each other's voices, catch the nervous glances, read between the lines.

All of us subconsciously respond to each other's inner reality, secret or not. Usually our conscious and unconscious awareness of each other's secrets is papered over by small talk and polite redirection. Sometimes, however, people's secrets clash. Our "invisible monkeys" are not so invisible to each other. When angry secrets, guilty secrets and fearful secrets collide, all hell can break loose. One person's invisible "alcoholic monkey" for example may be secretly attacking someone else's "victim monkey," leading communication in completely unpredictable and unproductive directions. Workplace dynamics are often dominated by this kind of covert war of secrets, with the primary weapon being the threat of exposure. Sometimes I wonder how we ever get anything done at all.

The fewer secrets we keep, the less power they have over us. But secrets don't just disappear on their own. They must be transformed from *secret* to *known* and *accepted*. While I am certainly not advocating publicly sharing your secrets over the water cooler, it is important to know what your secrets are and to share them with *someone* so that these secrets can begin to lose their mystery and their power. By sharing them with *someone*, you can gain an objective appreciation for how few of them really need to stay secret after all.

❧

Becoming Whole

If keeping secrets from others robs us of a portion of our energy, then keeping secrets from ourselves robs us of a part of ourselves. It is amazing how much we can hide behind one secret and never let ourselves see.

My secret about wetting the bed, for example, was so shameful for me that I simply refused to think about it. Years later, in college, I would still mentally look away whenever the thought of it came up—until one day when I finally asked myself, "Why don't I like myself?"

What I discovered was a whole rat's nest of beliefs and attitudes hiding behind the skeleton in that closet. I believed that bed-wetting was a psychological and moral problem rather than simply the result of a slowly developing bladder. It was the proof that my sisters used in order to convince me that there was something wrong with me and that I should be shipped off to some institution for defective children. I seriously lived in fear that someday men in white coats would come and take me away (ha ha, hee hee, ho ho).

Such ideas are laughable to an adult, but the adult me had never given himself permission to look at the problem. It had been locked away in the secret closet since well before a rational perspective could take a look at it.

Shining a light on that secret allowed me to integrate my childhood fears with my adult understanding. Without that integration, my childhood fear of being defective would continue to subconsciously affect my decisions and influence my relationships.

Many people's deep, dark secrets turn out to be quite innocent and simple once they see the light of day. But they will never know this is true if they refuse to take a look.

As I've said, I am not advocating walking up to complete strangers and telling them all of your darkest secrets. The point is to find a safe time and place to let go of your secrets so that they no longer hold you hostage. This is a situation in which starting with a single, private therapist might be easier than sharing with a large group.

On the other hand, sharing with a group can shine a lot of light into your life all at once and air out a lot of fear and shame.

It is important to remember that self disclosure is not an end unto itself. It has a purpose, a goal. Some of the goals I've mentioned are: exposing your heart to the beauty of honesty, reducing shame, creating connections that can generate compassion, self-discovery and integration through self-disclosure, and reclaiming the wasted energy that it takes to hide secrets from yourself and others.

The result of all of these goals is an increased ability to be fully present; to be able to bring all of yourself—past and present, strengths and weaknesses—to every situation you enter. If we have secrets; if we are overwhelmed by shame, then we can't be fully present or feel fully accepted. The cumulative effect of being dishonest with ourselves—by constantly hiding who we really are and pretending that we are someone different—is that we end up living someone else's life.

We deserve better than that.

FORGIVENESS

Honesty helps us learn about ourselves and heal our shame. It also is an important part of forgiving ourselves, which, in turn, also helps us heal shame. Forgiving others helps us heal our anger and create more serenity in our lives. Reducing the level of anger in the world as a whole may do more than anything else to improve the quality of everyone's lives.

There is a well-known saying that holding onto resentment is like drinking poison and waiting for the other person to die. Resentment poisons our soul, but before we can let go of it, we need to understand the relationship between forgiveness, anger, resentment and injustice.

- ◆ **Forgiveness is a willingness to acknowledge anger, but let go of resentment.**
- ◆ **Anger is a healthy emotional response to a perceived injustice.**
- ◆ **Resentment is an unhealthy emotional investment in a *past* injustice.**

To invest in something is to store something of value in it for future use. When we invest our emotions in a past injustice, we have committed our energy to a particular outcome or response. Until we achieve that outcome, our emotional energy sits and festers instead of being used for something positive, productive, and in the *present*. When that outcome is unhealthy, inappropriate, unachievable or outside of our control, then we may cut ourselves off from that emotional energy forever.

Forgiveness releases this emotional energy so that it can be used positively. This frees us to experience *other* emotions and perceive the *presence* of virtues in our lives rather than focusing on the absence of justice.

Guilt, shame and anger stand between us and our ability to accept the virtues and positive emotions that are missing in our lives. Guilt and shame convince us that we still don't deserve them. Anger tells us that it is still someone else's responsibility to give them to us.

Many of us carry so much resentment that we *didn't* receive the positive treatment that we deserved, that we are oblivious to the fact that we can give *ourselves* the spiritual gifts that we need *today.* Forgiving ourselves and others opens up our capacity to receive these blessings.

◆ Forgiving others helps us heal our relationships.
◆ Forgiving others helps us let go of our victim mentality.
◆ Forgiving others helps free us from the past.
◆ Forgiving ourselves helps us heal our shame.
◆ Forgiving ourselves involves letting go of our feelings of guilt— for who we are and for what we've done.
◆ Forgiving ourselves makes it safe to admit our mistakes.
◆ Admitting our mistakes makes it easier to make amends ...which makes it easier to forgive ourselves.

Forgiving both ourselves and others for the mistakes we've all made makes it easier to let go of old beliefs and explore new ones.

Why Not *Forgive?*

With all of these wonderful reasons to practice forgiveness, why do so many people resist? I believe that most of the reasons why people are afraid to forgive are based on mistaken ideas of what forgiveness really is. Forgiving is not forgetting. It does not give people permission to commit additional injustices. It is not being a patsy, wimp or coward.

Forgiveness does not let people off the hook. It only lets them off of *your* hook. People will still suffer the natural consequences of their own actions, it is just that you won't be keeping score. Will they "get away with it?" No. Their unjust action will follow them around for the rest of their lives and beyond. Don't let it do the same for you.

Some people believe that holding onto anger is a way to punish the person who hurt them, so they hold onto it as a form of revenge. Of course, anger hurts the person feeling the anger more than the one they are angry at, so it kind of backfires. Buddha is claimed to have said that holding onto anger is like picking up a hot coal with the intention of throwing it at someone else. You are the one who gets burned.

Holding onto anger until someone apologizes is equally counterproductive. The anger creates tension; the tension creates distance; the distance makes it harder for the other person to apologize and increases the likelihood that they will find a way to feel as though *they* are the injured party.

Forgiveness is not reconciliation, which involves reestablishing a harmonious relationship with the person who hurt you. Sometimes reconciliation is appropriate, but it takes two people and a safe situation. Sometimes we have to forgive from a distance, and even forgive people who still hate us and want to hurt us. That's their Karma. Ours is to let it go and move on to something better and brighter.

If we *fear* reconciliation, we have a right to listen to that fear, but we shouldn't let that get in the way of forgiveness.

If we *long for* reconciliation, we have a right to feel that longing, but we would be wise to direct it towards a relationship that is worthy of our longing.

For example, our parents represented God to us when we were infants, and no matter how badly they treated us, we still long to reconcile with them because we spiritually want to reconcile with God. Fortunately, we don't need our parents' cooperation to do that. We can bypass the human symbols of God and express our longing towards the virtues that a loving God has blessed us with. Forgiveness is a good one to start with.

Apologies, punishment, forgetting, reconciliation—these are all specific outcomes that we may cling to through our resentment. Since they are all outside of our control, clinging to them may leave us swimming in resentment for decades. Letting go of these expectations will free our energies for more productive pursuits.

❀

The Stages of Anger

There is a school of thought that says that the secret of forgiveness is to never judge other people's actions as inappropriate so that you never get angry in the first place.

If you will forgive my French, I think that is bull shit.

Emotions are messengers. Ignoring them or slamming the door in their face will not make them go away.

Anger is an emotional response to the absence of justice. Justice is *very* important, and there is very little of it in the world today. That makes anger very important. Ignoring injustice will not make it go away, and will not give us the opportunity to correct it.

Being able to **feel** anger, **recognize** its source, **confirm** its validity, **identify** the injustice that is being perpetrated, make wise choices as to how to **respond** effectively, and then take positive **action** are among the most important things we can do as humans.

Let me put that in a bulleted list so you can find it later:

- ◆ Feel the Anger
- ◆ Recognize its Source
    (this is an emotional process)
- ◆ Confirm its Validity
    (your right to have emotions)
- ◆ Identify the specific Injustice
    (this is a rational process)
- ◆ Choose an appropriate Response
- ◆ Take positive Action

When anger is allowed to follow its natural course, it only lasts a few minutes and results in positive corrective action, even if that corrective action is nothing more than a smile and a friendly, "That's OK. I don't mind."

When your perception of an injustice is *not* allowed to take its natural course, then it gets blocked and the energy of anger builds instead of being released through action. When anger lingers, it can turn into resentment or rage. That is when it stops being healthy and starts being dangerous.

Anger's natural progression can be blocked at any point along the way. Perhaps you are trying not to **feel** anger; you are having a difficult time **recognizing** its source; the **validity** of your feeling is being denied, you can't identify the specific **injustice** you are responding to; you are either having a difficult time finding an appropriate **response**, or you are emotionally attached to an inappropriate response; and/or you are unable to **act** on the response you have chosen.

Practicing forgiveness, then, is not simply about ignoring injustice or letting go of anger, it is removing the internal blocks to anger's natural progression—one step at a time—so that the anger can serve its purpose and walk away, leaving you feeling informed, respected and empowered.

Feeling Anger

The first step in forgiving is allowing yourself to get angry.

Anger, remember, is a messenger. It tells us when we have experienced an injustice.

If we try to forgive before we listen to the message, the messenger will not go away. It will just go into hiding.

If we try to forgive before we listen to the messenger, we are ignoring the injustice—we are saying that the injustice was not real, it did not matter, or that it was not really an injustice at all.

This is really the same as saying that *we deserved it.*

You see, anger is an automatic sensation, like wrinkling your nose when you smell something bad. You can't choose to *not* sense it, you can only choose to acknowledge it or ignore it. If you ignore the sensation—if you pretend not to smell anything foul—then what you are telling yourself is that nothing unfair happened; that stinky is really sweet.

In order to perceive the unjust as just, and for the foul to seem fair, you must convince yourself that you deserved whatever unfair treatment you received. You are, in essence, saying, "The way I've been treated isn't so bad after all; this is normal; I deserve it; I can live with this stench for the rest of my life."

Believing that you deserved whatever bad things were said to you—or done to you—makes you feel unlovable, unworthy, dirty, or sinful. This is not healthy. We can't hold these beliefs about ourselves and still feel full of life, love and energy. Negative self-talk, even if it is completely unconscious, drains us of hope and enthusiasm. It makes us small. It weakens us.

In other words, when we deny that we have been treated unfairly so that we can avoid acknowledging anger, we are telling ourselves that we deserve to be treated poorly. If we believe that we deserved to be treated badly in the past, then we will also believe that we deserve to be treated badly in the future.

Because of this belief, we will do things that are self-destructive, like start relationships with unhealthy or abusive people, or engage in compulsive behaviors.

This is why processing anger and learning forgiveness is one of the four tools of healing. It is not just about letting go of resentment, it is about releasing the depression and self-loathing that is sitting on top of the resentment, trying to keep the anger in check.

❦

Why Not Feel Angry?

If anger is a natural and healthy response to injustice, why are so many people afraid to acknowledge their anger?

Here are just a few reasons:

♦ They fear that anger will spill over into rage or violence.
♦ They fear anger will fester into resentments that will keep them focused on the bad that has happened in their lives.
♦ They fear that anger and resentment will cut them off from the people they love, who may have unintentionally treated them unjustly.
♦ They fear that if they show their anger, the people who hurt them will respond with anger and hurt them even more.
♦ They have been told that "good" people don't get angry.
♦ They fear getting angry at the people in authority in their lives— especially those who represented God—for fear it will cut them off from salvation.
♦ They fear "rocking the boat" and attracting disapproval.
♦ They fear damaging their family's reputation.

All of these fears are perfectly reasonable if you haven't learned how to work through your anger to find forgiveness and serenity. It is prudent to not start a process that you don't know how to finish. Allowing yourself to feel anger with no end in sight can have dire physical, emotional and social consequences. Fortunately, that is not what I am asking you to do. Go ahead; hold your anger in for just a little while longer. Let me walk you through the steps that will get you all the way to the other side. Knowing all of the steps that are in front of you makes it less likely that you will get stuck when the emotion of anger tries to overwhelm you. When you can see where you are going, you will know in your heart that you can control the anger rather than letting it control you.

The next steps, after giving yourself permission to feel anger, are to recognize the source, validate the anger and identify the specific injustice. Since recognizing the source and identifying the specifics are closely related, I will discuss both of them after explaining the importance of validating our emotional perceptions.

Validating Anger

When we hear voices, we instinctively look around to see who is speaking. If we can't find anyone, then we begin to doubt our sanity.

When we feel angry, we instinctively review our situation to see if we are being treated unfairly or unjustly. If we can't find a source for our feelings, then we, again, begin to doubt our sanity. That is why most of us will do whatever it takes to identify some source of irritation to justify our anger.

After identifying a possible source of our emotion, our next step is to mentally *confirm or validate* the spiritual perception. Our mind asks "do I see evidence of an injustice?"

Anger, by its nature, is a kind of accusation. When we feel anger, we are saying "someone or something here is not fair." This attitude of accusation sets us up for resistance—both internal and external. If we are angry at a person, they are likely to say, "Hey, wait a minute! I didn't do anything wrong." If we are angry at a person we love or fear, we don't even need *them* to argue with us, we argue with ourselves. Part of us wants to defend or justify their actions so that our anger does not hurt or anger *them*, while another part of us needs to acknowledge *our* hurt and anger.

Even if all we are angry at is a *situation*, one part of us will be thinking "This is not fair!" while a contrary voice inside our head says, "It is not the world's fault. If something bad has happened to you, you must have deserved it!"

This sets up a tug-of-war between our emotional perceptions and our mental need to validate what we feel. We try to pull the world, the other person, or even ourselves towards one perception of reality, while they try to pull us back towards another.

Until these dueling realities are resolved; until we can mentally validate our perceptions, it is impossible for us to formulate a reasonable and rational response to the situation. And until we do, we are stuck feeling angry, and rational action is almost impossible.

How long can we stay in this emotional limbo—angry, but not quite sure if we have a right to be? An entire lifetime.

Just listen to people.

Anyone who feels the need to explain *why* they are angry is in the process of trying to convince themselves that they have a right to be. Once our head and our heart are in agreement, there is no longer any need to talk about it. It is time to move on to action.

So how do we escape this tug of war?

By letting go.

If we keep pulling, our anger will keep us emotionally bound to this situation forever. We can't convince them they are guilty and they can't convince us they are innocent.

If we stop pulling but don't let go, we get dragged into the opposing perception. We are accepting their innocence. In doing so, are pretending that the situation was not really unjust at all; that we had no valid reason to be angry. We are denying our reality and saying that we deserve to be treated badly. This will just lead to depression.

When we let go, we stop trying to convince the other person (or our inner voice) that we are right. We look for a *different* kind of validation that our feelings are legitimate.

When our conflict is with another person, this can be as simple as saying to ourselves, "I do not need them to agree with me on this. I can allow myself to feel slighted by this situation even if they don't think I have a reason to. They don't have to understand my perspective." Since we ultimately have absolutely no control over other people's thoughts or feelings, letting go of the need to convince them that *our* feelings are valid is the only rational path to serenity. It allows us to validate our own feelings, and prepare to respond.

When our conflict is bigger than one person or is left over from childhood trauma, then self-validation may not be enough. When we are having a tug-of-war with God, the Universe, or our own inner demons, then telling ourselves that we are right won't end the argument. These internal conflicts often involve deep, painful injustices that have never moved from anger to response because the anger was never acknowledged as legitimate. Our fingers are gripping the rope so tightly that we are afraid to let go.

In these cases, we need someone to hold onto the rope for us while we let go—someone standing on our side in the tug-of-war to let us know that if we let go, we won't be alone in our perceptions. We need someone to stand witness to the injustices we have experienced.

What does that look like?

It looks like open, honest sharing. Find a trusted friend or therapist to whom you can describe the situation in private. Tell them that you don't want advice, just confirmation that what you are perceiving is valid. Before you can *let go* of anger, you first need to hear someone say, "that sounds awful. That was really unfair. You have a *right* to be angry."

Once you are reassured that your feelings can be trusted, only then is it safe to let them go and begin to formulate an appropriate response to their message.

Note: you need to hear that your anger is valid *even if it isn't true*. You can't see a situation clearly until the fog of anger clears, and the fog of anger will not clear as long as it is being argued with, dismissed or minimized. While this might seem dishonest, what we are really doing at this stage is validating our *right* to have our emotional response. We will address the validity of our *reason* for feeling angry later.

Arguing over the *reason* for our anger before establishing our *right* to feel angry is why small fights can escalate so easily. When both people are wrong, neither is able to see their part in the problem until the other person's wrongs are acknowledged first. It is not so much about making the other person wrong as it is about legitimizing our own experience of reality.

The most terrifying thing in the world is to fear that you can't trust your own perception of reality. It is like hearing voices without being able to find the speaker. Feeling anger and being told that you have no reason to makes you feel crazy. The fear that you might be both wrong and crazy makes you work even harder to prove that you do have a reason. Once someone else validates that you do have a *right* to be upset, then the fear dissipates and you can consider your reason more dispassionately. Then your desire for connection, understanding, compassion and forgiveness can take over.

Once fear and anger are not clouding our judgment, we can find a rational and appropriate response to whatever situation it was that we felt was unjust.

Often, once fear and anger, guilt and depression are not clouding our judgment, we immediately realize that the most rational and appropriate response... is to forgive.

What We Are Angry About

With so much injustice in the world, we have a lot to be angry about. However, it helps to make a distinction between the deeper sources of our anger and the specific injustices that trigger our day-to-day flashes of irritation. In a way, our life-long feelings of having been mistreated, abandoned, misunderstood, abused and all the rest are like red-hot coals just under the surface of our awareness, while the individual events that trigger our awareness of that anger are like drops of gasoline that make a bright light, but are not the real source of the heat.

When you read those words, "mistreated, abandoned, misunderstood and abused," some of you thought, "Yeah, that's right," while others thought, "Come now, aren't you being a bit melodramatic?"

Not at all.

We live in a culture whose underlying beliefs—religious, scientific and psychological—are that humans are fundamentally sinful, violent, competitive and in need of fixing, when in reality, humans are glorious, noble reflections of God in need of education and guidance. That disconnect between our reality and the way the world sees us is so unjust and unfair that it is enough to make anyone who feels it very, very angry, or very, very sad.

Both the deep-seated injustices and the day-to-day slights need to be validated so they can be resolved, but the nature of the resolution is somewhat different. Deep-seated injustices are often very old, and the range of appropriate healthy responses may be very narrow. If resentment is an emotional investment in a specific outcome, then it is important that we choose an outcome that is within our control. Deep-seated injustices changed our beliefs about ourselves, so a healthy response must be more about transforming those beliefs than changing someone else.

Specific injustices can be approached on a more pragmatic level, with a much wider range of appropriate choices and actions. We will work through what some of those might be shortly, but let's start by looking at some of the deeper reasons why we are angry—starting with why we are angry with ourselves. Exploring why we are angry with ourselves and the things we think we might need to be forgiven for will give us a pretty good idea of what our core sources of anger are. When we move on to forgiving others, we will have a better idea of what it is they might need forgiveness for.

Once we appreciate our core sources of anger, it will be easier to separate them from our day-to-day sources of irritation. That way we don't end up fighting life-long battles every time something upsets us, and it will be easier to choose an appropriate response.

From Anger to Forgiveness

Forgiving Ourselves

Feeling angry with ourselves, feeling guilt and feeling shame are not the same, but they are close siblings. Healing one will help heal the others.

John Bradshaw, the author of **Healing the Shame That Binds You**, says that the difference between healthy shame and toxic shame is that with healthy shame, you know you've *made* a mistake. With toxic shame, you believe that you *are* the mistake.

We could say something similar about *feeling* guilty and *being* guilty. We feel guilty when we commit a sin—that is we do something that we know in advance is hurtful to ourselves or others. We *are* guilty when we feel that we *are* the sin—that our very existence is a stain on the world, and there is nothing we can do to change that.

Shame tells us that we are a mistake and must change who we are to be acceptable. Guilt tells us that we are sinful—that we have committed an unforgivable injustice—and we must be punished before we will be acceptable.

The way we punish ourselves is to refuse to forgive ourselves. We commit to remaining angry with ourselves—even when we have no idea of what it is we have done wrong, or why it is we *are* wrong.

As children, many of us felt this sense of "wrongness" and tried to make sense of it. We created elaborate explanations as to what our sins might be. Just because we can't remember what those explanations were doesn't mean that we don't still believe them. Until we forgive them, we will continue to live in anticipation of an unspecified punishment every single day.

So the big question is, what do we believe that we are guilty of? What kinds of things must we be telling ourselves in order to justify carrying around this burden of unforgiven guilt?

For those of us who live with guilt and anger, we have a conscious awareness of many little sins that we are guilty of, but these often just serve to hide a bigger sin from our awareness. For example, we use all of the people we've hurt in relationships as an explanation of why we are so evil, rather than asking ourselves why we are afraid to commit to a relationship in the first place. If we can find a way to name these big sins, then we shine a light on them. When we do that, we usually discover that they are either something that we have made up, they are misunderstandings, or they are exaggerated. Naming the "sins" that we have been hiding from ourselves for years often exposes them as laughable.

As children, we believe ourselves to be the center of the universe, so in our attempts to make sense of the confusing events of our lives, we take responsibility for everything that goes wrong.

I don't know what you feel guilt for, but I felt guilty for: being born (original sin and all of that stuff), being born a male, wetting the bed, causing my parent's divorce, letting my sister be sent away to a children's home when I was obviously the one who was defective, allowing women to fall in love with me knowing I would break their hearts because I was defective and unable to meet their needs, and for taking up space on the planet when there were so many more worthy souls who deserved my place.

On top of these major sins, I added a daily list of every failure to anticipate the needs and expectations of the women around me—because they were proof positive of my biggest sin of all: I didn't love and care for other people enough to earn my place in the world. Life was not a gift, it was a debt, and I was failing to make my daily payments. I was guilty, and I couldn't forgive myself.

All of these "sins" seem funny to me, now that I have given them a name. They are absurd. No sane person would believe them. Yet I can assure you that these, and many more just like them, rattle around in the heads of most people. If they *didn't*, then most people would behave much differently than they do. Consider, for example, the popularity of such songs as *Highway to Hell*, and

Bad to the Bone, or video games such as *Grand Theft Auto.* These were created for people who have given up on believing that they are forgivable.

If people liked themselves; if people forgave themselves for their imperfections, then people would treat themselves (and each other) with more kindness and respect.

Forgiving a Belief

In *The Secret of Emotions,* I described an exercise called "internal consultation" in which you try to get in touch with inner emotions and sensations. This same technique can help you get in touch with the beliefs behind your feelings of guilt and anger, and create an opportunity for forgiveness.

In my original description of internal consultation, we started with physical sensations and tried to get in touch with emotional sensations that were hiding in the background. In this brief review of the exercise, you will start with sensations relating to guilt or anger at yourself and try to walk it backwards to find the underlying beliefs or events that triggered them. While this exercise can be done alone, it may bring up some deep emotions, memories and questions. Having a professional therapist to help you sort out your feelings and mirror your experience can be very helpful.

Emotions have sensations associated with them. Guilt, shame and anger all have a slightly different "flavor." Sit quietly for a few moments and try to sense these emotions in your heart and body. Which is dominant for you? What do these sensations tell you about your internal belief system? What "truth" about yourself are you avoiding looking at? Don't go in with a search light. Go in with a candle and see what beliefs are willing to introduce themselves to you from the shadows.

As memories, fears and stories return to you, make friends with them. Get their names, and if possible figure out the years they were "born." When you think you know what you have been telling yourself, take the time to write it down, and then get ready to have a conversation.

In Part 1, I said that you couldn't *get rid* of old habits and patterns, you had to *replace* them, instead. Well, the same principle applies to old beliefs.

These beliefs, no matter how absurd, childish or painful, are not your enemy. They developed over time for a reason. They helped you make sense of your world and your place within it.

Once you recognize them, you need to honor them, thank them, and only then gently explain to them why they no longer apply to your life today. You want to take that old belief by the hand, and walk it towards a more mature and functional perspective, not shame it out of existence.

For example, I felt responsible for my parent's divorce. It would be easy to tell myself, "Don't be stupid. It isn't your fault, so just get over it." But then my sense of responsibility would just go into hiding.

Instead, I can tell myself that every child of a divorce feels responsible; that children see themselves as the center of the universe and interpret parental behavior accordingly. I can remind myself that children need to feel that the universe makes sense and that things don't happen without a cause. It was safer to believe that I was the cause than to believe in a chaotic world.

I can find all of the reasons why I was sure that I was to blame, and then—only then—go back and assure myself that I can know better now. As an adult I can understand adult motivations, I can see the bigger picture, I can put my childhood fears in perspective. "Thank you for helping me make sense of the world, but look at how much more sense the world can make if we look at it this way."

If you are having a difficult time finding replacement beliefs for these old sources of guilt, a professional therapist can help you find alternative perspectives with which to comfort and educate your inner child.

Recognizing and then letting go of the guilt will likely be accompanied by copious amounts of tears. Many of us have been holding in a lot of guilt for a long time. We were afraid that if we ever actually admitted *what* we felt guilty for, we would be proven guilty and punished accordingly. After all, what *is* the punishment for not being worthy to live? Why would we ever want to risk finding out?

The process of forgiving ourselves follows the pattern of feeling our anger and guilt, *recognizing* the source, *validating* our inner child's right to feel these feelings, but then *identifying* the specific injustices that we blamed ourselves for and *changing our beliefs* about them so that we no longer feel the need to punish ourselves. The choice we made was to validate the emotion but redefine the injustice. Our action was to educate ourselves and let go of our need for punishment.

So what do we do when we *can't* redefine our sins or change our beliefs about them? How do we forgive ourselves when we really have done bad things?

The first step is to look at your behavior in the context of the pain, anger, hurt and guilt that informed all of your decisions from early childhood on. When you make choices as to how to act, you are doing it based on who you believe you are. If you are given faulty information about who you are, then that will influence your choices. Forgiveness of anyone, including ourselves, requires a bit of compassion and understanding. But perhaps, before you forgive yourself completely, you do need to consider additional appropriate responses. Your response to your own acts of injustice may need to be similar to your response to other's acts of injustice. We will explore those in a few pages.

But there is a well-established system in place that is designed to help people forgive themselves for their defects of character and the harm that they have caused. It is called *Making Amends*.

If you know anything about twelve-step programs, you probably know that they encourage people to *"make direct amends to all people we have harmed wherever possible, except when to do so would injure them or others."* What you may not know is that it takes the first nine of the twelve steps to prepare for this process.

You may be under the impression that making amends to people is designed to make people feel ashamed and guilty. Actually, the result is just the opposite. It releases shame and guilt, and breaks the emotional bonds that keep us tied to our mistakes.

When we prepare to make amends, we are asked to acknowledge the pain we have caused others. This process invites us to feel compassion for them; to put ourselves in their shoes and imagine what our actions might have felt like from their perspective.

This is a powerful exercise that gives us the opportunity to see ourselves through their eyes.

Their view of us mirrors our perception of those who hurt us. That is, we can imagine them feeling about us the same way as we feel about those who hurt us.

Seeing ourselves as both the abuser and the abused breaks down barriers. We begin to realize that abusers are often just victims who are doing the only thing they know how to do. Understanding that abuse is a cycle does not excuse our behavior or theirs, but it does make it easier to forgive. The question of blame and the need to hate lose their power over us.

This is a profound and complex process. I don't expect or even advise that you set out to make amends to those you have harmed until you have done a lot of preparatory work. I just wanted you to know that the step is out there, and it does help.

The last bit of advice I have for healing guilt is to encourage you to use affirmations. Once we have introduced ourselves to our deepest, darkest sources of guilt, made friends with them and offered them a new perspective, we can solidify this new perspective in our subconscious by developing phrases that reinforce our new beliefs about ourselves and saying them several times a day. While giving yourself a daily pep-talk may sound silly, it is much less silly than continuing to listen to all of the negative self-talk that is currently bouncing around inside your head. I will talk about affirmations in book three, or you can go online to find more information, or ask your therapist about how to use affirmations to shift your internal beliefs.

❀

Forgiving Others

Exploring the core issues that made us angry and feel guilty about who we are has probably given you a clearer feel for the source of your anger towards other people.

When we look inside to figure out what we feel guilty for, we can see that much of what has worried us for years is truly absurd. We are not evil, worthless, or guilty of any major transgressions against humanity.

When we realize that we are not really evil, we start to wonder how we came to believe these bad things about ourselves in the first place. Some of these absurd beliefs are the result of childish thought processes, but some of them were taught to us by the people we grew up with. In many cases, we were *encouraged*, either directly or indirectly, to believe that there was something wrong with us.

If we think about this for very long, it just might make us angry. After all, who *told* us that we were sinful creatures who deserved to go to hell for eternal punishment? Who made us feel as though *nothing* we did was good enough? Who failed to rescue us from the bullies and abusers that made us feel dirty or ugly or helpless, or guilty?

You see, while a part of us believed that we had a reason to feel guilty and needed to be forgiven, another part of us—sometimes stronger, sometimes beaten down—knew that we were innocent. *That* part of us is angry. *That* part recognizes the fact that we were treated unjustly and accused of wrongs we did not commit or could not control. *That* part knows that we were lied to about our nobility and our humanity and our essential goodness.

That part needs to learn how to forgive others.

Just as a quick reminder:
Forgiveness is a willingness to acknowledge anger, but let go of resentment.

Resentment is an emotional investment in a specific outcome that is never achieved. Holding onto resentment is the result of feeling anger but not following through to positive action.

Working through our anger towards others follows the same progression we've been talking about. First, you allow yourself to feel the feeling. Second, you recognize the source. As with your anger at yourself, the source of your anger may include very old injustices that are difficult to name, as well as current or ongoing injustices in your daily life. In either case, you need to validate your right to be angry before you can begin to sort out the details of the specific injustice. Whether you are angry at your mother for not supporting you when you were young, or your spouse for not supporting you today, you need to accept that anger as valid in order to give yourself permission to explore just *how* valid the anger may or may not be.

Once we identify the specific injustice that has sparked our anger, we then choose an appropriate response and take positive action.

Identifying the Specific Injustice

Up until now, I have been defining anger as an emotional response to the absence of justice. If we want to overcome the mental fog of resistance, fear and anger, it is important to *start* by validating our *feeling* as legitimate. Once we have done that, however, it is time to take the next step. We must turn our *rational minds* back on and confess the obvious:

Anger is *really* an emotional response to the <u>perceived</u> absence of justice.

In order to continue the process of resolving our anger we need to identify the specific injustice and choose an appropriate response. When we reach the stage of identifying the specific injustice that we want to resolve, we may discover that, with the fog of resistance, fear and anger gone, it really *is* an injustice. We may also come to realize that it is *not*.

So the next step is to assess our perception of the experience that has generated our feelings of anger.

As I've said, anger is a sensation. It is *only* a sensation. It tells you that you have perceived an injustice in your life. Since justice is an important spiritual principle, anger is a very valuable tool for understanding your social environment.

BUT... anger doesn't tell you how big the injustice is. It doesn't tell you how accurate your perception is. It doesn't tell you what the other person's motivations were. It doesn't tell you what you should do about it. All it does is let you know that something doesn't feel fair.

Think of it like the smell of smoke. When you smell smoke, you don't throw your arms in the air and go running in circles screaming, "FIRE!" You use the information to guide you while you investigate your surroundings. The purpose of anger is not to get you all riled up and agitated. It is to give you useful information and the energy you need to act on it. When you feel angry, use this information to guide your rational exploration of your current situation. Why are you angry? What triggered your emotional sensation?

In order to get an accurate picture of the source of a current feeling of anger, you need to be able to distinguish it from two related kinds of anger: Displaced Anger and Rage.

Displaced anger is when we are angry at one person or situation, but we project that anger onto someone or something else. There is a classic cartoon in four panels: In the first, a boss yells at a man. In the second, the man yells at his wife. The wife yells at her child, and the child kicks the dog. When I described this cartoon to a class of fifth-graders, they immediately understood the message. "So when my dad yells at me, he might not really be angry at me?" one kid asked. It broke my heart to hear the question, but the realization that he understood the idea gave me hope for his future.

We displace our anger most frequently when the cause of the injustice is more powerful than we are. To protest the injustices we receive from parents, teachers, clergy, bosses, bullies, police, or city hall would just invite additional punishment, and so we either express it towards someone even less powerful than we are, or we store it up as depression or rage.

The sensation of *healthy* anger is in proportion to the size of the injustice you are facing at this moment in time. The chemicals that shoot through your brain when you experience anger only last about 90 seconds. If your anger is overwhelming or builds over a long period of time, then it is probably rage.

Rage takes the injustice of the moment and throws it on the pile of every other injustice you have ever experienced, producing a literally raging fire of emotion. It is important to deal with the many injustices of your life, but it is impossible to deal with all of them at the same time. If you want to deal with one specific injustice, you will have to set the intense energy of rage aside to be dealt with later. Just knowing that it is *possible* to separate anger from rage can be a source of serenity and strength. It means that you can acknowledge the injustices of your past without wrestling with them every time something goes wrong. By dealing with one source of anger at a time, even deep and debilitating rage can be resolved and healed.

When you have identified a single issue or source of injustice that you want to resolve—and you are sure it isn't the victim of displaced anger—then you are ready to take the next two steps: choosing a response, and taking positive action. Choosing an appropriate response is dependent on the answers to the following questions:

1) Are my perceptions accurate—would it still seem unjust from a different perspective?

2) Is there anything reasonable and non-inflammatory I can do to correct the injustice?

3) Can I let go of my need to respond to this injustice?

4) Can I find a way to look past the injustice and love the person behind it?

5) Can I see something positive that came out of it?

❅

Mentally Assessing Your Emotional Perceptions

Anger is the result of a *perceived* injustice. Sometimes what we perceive is inaccurate. Sometimes what we perceive is colored by our beliefs, by immaturity, by lack of information, or lack of experience. There are many situations, for example, that would seem unfair to a child that, to an adult, would seem perfectly reasonable. As a child, you had a right to be angry, but when you remember this source of anger as an adult, you can understand it and therefore let go of the emotional charge.

There are also situations that adults experience that seem completely unfair from one perspective, but are understandable when seen from a different perspective or when more information is available. For example, if you think someone has hung up the phone on you, this belief will color your perception. What a mean thing to do! If you later find out that their cell phone battery died, then anger can evaporate in an instant.

It is not what *happens* to us that makes us angry, it is our perception that someone has treated us unjustly. As we mature, we become better at distinguishing between intentional harm and accidents; between malicious intent and distracted thoughtlessness.

Acquiring the virtues of patience, compassion, flexibility and objectivity can assist in this process and help to mitigate or eliminate anger through understanding. We may decide that what our parents did to us really wasn't so bad. That doesn't change the pain we felt at the time, but it does help us let go of the anger now. We may realize that our expectations in life were naturally immature as children, and may currently be unreasonable as adults. We don't always get what we want, but that doesn't mean life is unfair.

Many of us live our lives feeling defensive for good reason. We have not been treated well. But this attitude can be counter-productive. If we already feel victimized or unworthy, then we live in a constant state of needing positive feedback from others. *Anything* less than that can feel like an attack, and it can keep us feeling resentful and angry. In this condition, even "have a nice day" can be perceived as an unjust imposition, and really tick us off.

When *we know* that we are good, noble souls, it becomes easier to forgive the thousands of little slights we can encounter or perceive in a confused and distracted world. We don't take things so personally. It becomes easier to forgive.

Separating the Injustice from the Blame

I have said that anger is a natural response to injustice, but what *is* injustice, really?

Each of us is a noble child of God. We all deserve to receive kindness, respect and encouragement. We deserve safety, security, education, food and shelter. We feel sad when the virtues of God are absent from our lives. We feel angry when those virtues are denied to us through the actions of another person.

In other words, we are *sad* when we feel that there is an absence of virtues in our lives, but we feel *angry* when we convince ourselves that it is someone else's fault. So anger is a two-step process: first the recognition that we aren't receiving the virtues that we deserve, and second, the blaming of someone else.

As children, we are relatively powerless, so if there is a lack of kindness, encouragement, security or food, it probably *is* someone else's fault. The ability to recognize that you deserve these things is very important for your spiritual growth. The need to blame is *not* so important. When we understand that what we are feeling is the absence of the virtues we needed, we can begin to consider the fact that no one can give us something that they, themselves, do not already have. How does one blame one's parents for not passing on a set of qualities that they never received from their parents?

We are absolutely right to be angry. But what is the point of holding on to resentment? What positive outcome can we possibly imagine might be the result?

As adults, we have a great deal of control over the virtues in our lives. Anger tells us that someone may be trying to threaten our security, self-esteem, or other virtues, but in most situations, *we* are the ones who control whether or not they succeed. Someone may insult us, but *we* choose whether to let it affect our self-esteem. Someone may cut us off in traffic, but unless they actually cause an accident, it is *we* who decide whether to be distracted the rest of the drive home. Someone may leave the toilet seat up, but *we* can interpret that as a sign of forgetfulness, or a sign of disrespect. The ability to recognize rudeness, recklessness and forgetfulness is a valuable skill which anger helps us develop. The desire to blame, retaliate or fume over these lapses is not so helpful.

From Judgment to Discernment

In Part 1 of this book, I explained how perfectionism and black-and-white thinking kept us in a constant state of failure, and therefore kept us ashamed. A similar dynamic happens in our relationship with others. We are taught to judge people and actions as either good or bad, and then allow ourselves to get angry or offended based on that judgment.

Our tendency to get angry is affected by three dynamics. First is our sensitivity to unjust behavior, second is the starkness of our division between acceptable and unacceptable behavior, and third is our tendency to globalize.

People who have been hurt a lot as children tend to swing in one of two opposite directions. Either they numb themselves to the pain of injustice and become doormats, or they become hypersensitive to injustice and become prickly complainers or rageaholics. Neither extreme is helpful.

The ability to recognize rudeness goes hand-in-hand with the ability to recognize kindness. Being able to discern *exactly* how kind a person is on a scale from one to a hundred would be very useful. It would help you choose who to spend your time with, and even more important, it would help you identify what behaviors you should practice.

Here is where we get into trouble: if, on that scale from one to a hundred, we say, "I prefer to be around people between ninety-five and one hundred," then we are being way too sensitive to imperfections and will constantly be disappointed by the normal humans who populate our lives.

Or, if we say, "Anyone who falls below fifty is rude and deserves to be punished," then we are being judgmental, and will carry resentments towards all sorts of people.

We are also globalizing based on one virtue. We could, for example, say instead, "That person has horrible manners, but he tells funny jokes and is a great dancer."

When we do all three—have high expectations, have strong judgments against anyone who falls below them, and judge a person's entire character based on one failure to practice a particular virtue, then we doom ourselves to being constantly angry at everyone. We have also placed our own serenity firmly in the hands of every stranger we meet.

The way we perceive injustice affects our ability to forgive in the same way that the way we perceive right and wrong affects our ability to heal shame.

To counteract this common tendency, some forgiveness counselors recommend instantly forgiving everyone all the time for everything. They say that, since every experience is a learning experience, all injustice is an illusion.

I disagree.

The only way to learn from an experience is to identify it accurately and then respond appropriately. Anger tells us that we are not receiving something that we deserve. If we ignore the anger, we will never know what it is we've lost. Instead I recommend using discernment. Discernment allows us to identify what is missing, protect what is threatened, strengthen all needed virtues, and only *then* let go of any need to pursue additional outcomes. In other words, discernment allows us to both change our perception and *change the situation.*

Looking at the experiences that have hurt us from another perspective, separating injustice from blame and using discernment rather than judgment are all ways of reassessing our perceptions. In many cases, the injustice will now seem so small that it no longer calls for a response. Our positive action will be to let go of any need for vindication, restitution, revenge or apology. The messenger was wrong; it was a misunderstanding; or it wasn't worth worrying about. Anger has been dismissed—with gratitude—but dismissed all the same.

But sometimes the messenger is right.

❀

Choosing a Response

Not all injustices are the result of misunderstandings or minor irritations. Sometimes situations really are significantly and painfully unjust. There is a lot of injustice in the world, so chances are good that you've experienced your share. What do you do then?

You've probably heard of the Serenity Prayer:

"God grant me the serenity to accept the things I cannot change, the courage to change the things I can and the wisdom to know the difference."

Once we have determined that the specific injustice that caused our anger is real and significant, then it is time to choose an *appropriate* response. Is there something you can do that would actually make the situation better for everyone? Often the answer is *No*, in which case, you need to take a deep breath and move on to letting go and finding a way to forgive the person involved. But sometimes the answer is *Yes*.

Often these are times when the injustice is ongoing. Taking action can protect us or someone else from physical, emotional or spiritual harm.

Children don't have the resources to correct most unjust situations, but as adults we have an obligation to at least consider trying. Even if we can't fix an entire problem, we can make an effort. Helping even a little bit can give us a sense of power and accomplishment that tempers our anger. Shame and depression are often linked to feelings of powerlessness. It is amazing how even little efforts in the cause of justice can lift our spirits and discharge our anger.

We must be careful, though, that our efforts at correcting an injustice are not excuses for exacting revenge instead.

Revenge is not about correcting a situation, it is about punishing a person by causing them harm. The desire for revenge is unhealthy for several reasons.

First, revenge does not resolve anger, it simply perpetuates the cycle of abuse. Healing an injustice is not about punishing the perpetrator, but simply protecting the victim, whether it is yourself or another. If the injustice is severe enough, then it is the job of the courts to punish.

Second, the desire for revenge actually increases our feelings of powerlessness. Protecting ourselves is something we have a fair amount of control over, so in taking steps toward this, we can satisfy our need to respond and let go of resentment. However, if our goal is punishment, we are emotionally invested in a type of response that we have little legitimate control over. While we wait for the slow wheels of justice to turn, our resentment will fester and grow, making us more angry, feeling less in control of our lives.

Third, it is impossible to feel both compassion and revenge at the same time. Looking forward to someone else's suffering—even if they absolutely deserve it—is a form of spiritual poison.

Putting Your Energy to Better Use

Perhaps you aren't quite ready to let go of your resentments. After all, anger is what gives many people the energy to get up in the morning. But resentment is an emotional investment in an outcome. What if you took all of that investment, all of that emotional energy, and directed it towards a *different* outcome—one that was still directly related to the injustice you suffered, but was not about revenge, punishment, or even reconciliation?

If we find that there is nothing we can do for the specific situation that we faced or are facing, perhaps there are things we can do in a related area that can make us feel that we are helping to address a larger injustice than our own. Volunteering at shelters, doing educational work with children, becoming a mentor in a youth program or sponsor in a twelve-step program can all be manifestations of the "courage to change the things I can."

The outcome we dedicate ourselves to can also be more personal. Injustice robs us of the opportunity to experience important virtues. An appropriate response would be to learn everything you can about the virtues that were denied you in the past, and commit yourself to developing them to the fullest in the years ahead. Every challenge we face in life is an opportunity to learn and grow. Anger is like a flashing red arrow pointing to the challenges in your life that you are being invited to learn from. Not everyone is blessed with such clear road signs on the path of spiritual growth. Use them.

Perhaps more clearly than anything else, anger tells us that our lives have been devoid of compassion. The best response to injustice is an effort to develop compassion—if not compassion for the people who hurt you, then perhaps for the many like them that you meet at twelve-step meetings, in your daily life, or when looking in the mirror. You are not the same as the people who hurt you, and for that you can be grateful. But you carry a part of them around with you. Developing compassion for others will help you feel it for yourself.

I will be discussing compassion in great detail in the next section, but I wanted to mention it a couple of times in this section on forgiveness, because it takes on a different character when combined with forgiveness. Feeling compassion for those who have hurt us is like putting a blowtorch to a candle. It melts the resistance and rearranges everything.

When the Appropriate Response Is No Response

Many situations are so far in the past or are so large that we have no appropriate way to respond to them. What do we do then?

When the injustice is real and there is nothing you can do about it, then you *could* stew in your anger forever and let it eat away at your faith and joy. But that wouldn't be very helpful. Instead, you could turn your need to respond over to God.

That doesn't mean that you pray to God that the guilty party be hit with a lightning bolt or sent to hell. It means that you allow your faith in a higher justice—in the Karmic Principle of *you reap what you sow*—to melt the chains of resentment that keep you attached to the one who wronged you.

The recovery community of twelve-step programs encourages people to, "Let go and let God." That one phrase has helped keep millions of people sane and sober. It is the *surest* way to let go of resentments and allow the peace and serenity of forgiveness to seep into our souls. Yet, for many people, it is also the hardest.

At first, the act of letting go might just be a grudging, "OK, I'll stop obsessing about this and let God handle it. God will make sure they reap what they sow."

But the deeper meaning of *you reap what you sow* is that if you sow true forgiveness and compassion and positive thoughts towards those who have hurt you, that is what your life will be filled with. That is why the highest form of forgiveness is more than simply letting go of resentment, it is a stepping past the injustice and looking for the lost child of God who perpetrated it.

This is where experience in a twelve-step community can once again be helpful. It can give you the experience of loving and forgiving people who have made terrible mistakes in their lives, including ones that may have hurt others. It is easier to forgive strangers because what makes forgiveness difficult is not the size of the injustice, but the size of our emotional investment in responding to it. When we don't have personal resentments to get in the way, we can see the good person behind the unjust act or the hurtful mistake. That experience makes it easier for us to see the good in the people who have hurt us and been unjust.

One of the side benefits of developing this capacity for forgiveness is that we can then apply it to our other tools for resolving anger. An attitude of compassionate forgiveness provides us with a new perspective on our old hurts. It is easier to see things from another person's point of view if we have already forgiven them and are giving them the benefit of the doubt.

Likewise, compassionate forgiveness makes it easier to rectify unjust situations because we approach them in a more loving, non-confrontational manner. We look for win-win solutions to problems rather than exacting revenge on those who may have hurt us in the past.

❀

Permission to Forgive

Why is it that many people resist this most basic kind of forgiveness? What are we afraid might happen if we just "let it go?"

I think our deepest fear is that if we forgive someone, what we are really doing is ignoring the injustice, and that by doing that we are saying that the injustice was not real, it did not matter, or that it was not really an injustice at all.

Our fear is that to forgive is to accept that we deserved what happened to us.

We began the process of dealing with our anger by validating the legitimacy of our feelings. Now that we have looked at our experiences from different perspectives and explored different possible responses—including understanding and compassion— we can remove our final barriers to forgiveness by validating our *understanding* of our experience at the end of the process. This validation encompasses our feelings, our interpretation of the injustice, the response we have chosen and the actions we are taking.

Once again I encourage you to talk to a therapist or share with a twelve-step group, or at least have a gripe session with a close friend *before* your final effort to let go of anger and resentment. You need to hear someone say—in words or with their silent encouragement, *"I'm so sorry that happened to you. You did not deserve to be treated that way."*

This *external validation* can go a long way in helping you get rid of anger and resentment.

This is where I believe a good therapist is better suited to help than friends or recovery groups because a therapist can both be objective, and say *the words you need to hear.*

A therapist can help you through the steps of processing anger. They can help you determine if what you experienced was an injustice or if you need to change your perspective. They can help you find a safe and reasonable course of action to take. They can listen to you describe the injustice and help you can name it so that you can let it go.

Friends are not objective, and may try to take sides or give advice on how to get revenge. In twelve-step groups, as I've said, people don't generally speak directly to one another after sharing—though you can often see compassion and empathy in their eyes.

Serious injustices, though—especially ones that you dig up from your past—really require an objective witness who can verbalize the legitimacy of your pain. That's why a good therapist can remove one of the biggest obstacles to forgiveness. You can let go of the anger because it has been made real. It exists outside of your inner world because someone else has perceived the injustice and named it as such.

In fact, a therapist can often give the injustice an actual name. You might be surprised how healing this can be. Yes, that is *emotional abuse*. Yes, that is *spiritual abuse*. Yes, that is *sexual abuse*. Yes, that was *controlling* and *manipulative*. Yes, that was *abandonment*. Yes, the threat of violence is still *violence*. Yes, you were right to be frightened and angry for being treated that way. Yes, you can forgive this, even though it was an injustice. That is what forgiveness means.

Can it really be this easy? Sometimes, yes.

Resentment is an emotional investment in an outcome. Sometimes, sincere validation is the only outcome that you really need. Wrestling with your fears and anger, betraying family secrets, asking for help, these are the hard parts. Once your pain is validated, forgiveness and letting go often come easily. Validation gives you permission to forgive.

This kind of letting go is exactly the opposite of the kind of letting go you did when you changed your perceptions. In the *first* case, you looked at what happened to you and realized that what you had perceived as an injustice when you were a child was not unjust after all. In *this* case, however, you look at what happened and receive external confirmation that it really *was* unjust. It is the *validation* of your perceptions that allows you to say *"I was right. They were wrong. Now I can give myself permission to stop clinging to the proof that I was wronged and move on."*

How do we know
when we have succeeded in forgiving?

As I said when describing people's misunderstandings about forgiveness, forgiving does not mean that you like, trust, or want to spend time with the person who hurt you. It doesn't mean that you have forgotten what has happened or will make yourself vulnerable to future injustices. All it means is that you are no longer emotionally invested in the injustice. Thinking about the person or the event does not give you a twinge of anxiety, a rush of adrenaline, or an elevated heart rate. You no longer dwell on the event, or relive it in your mind. You do not feel the need to respond to the person or event in word or deed, nor do you feel the need to *avoid* thinking about them. Your emotional serenity no longer has anything to do with that particular situation.

It is a great feeling.

*The first section of this book, **The Secret of Emotions**, focused on the relationship between emotions and virtues, and looked particularly at the role of shame in pushing us toward unhealthy behaviors. This section has expanded the focus from just shame to shame and three other emotions that tell us that there is something wrong: anger, loneliness and fear. The first two sections have looked at the benefits of honesty in healing shame and forgiveness in healing anger and shame. Let's move on, now, to exploring the role of compassion in healing anger, shame and loneliness. I've already mentioned how compassion and forgiveness can work together to help us understand ourselves and those who have hurt us. Now let's look more deeply at what compassion is and how it can serve us.*

COMPASSION

Compassion is sometimes the fatal capacity for feeling what it is like to live inside somebody else's skin. It is the knowledge that there can never really be any peace and joy for me until there is peace and joy finally for you too. — Frederick Buechner

My dictionary defines compassion as a "sympathetic concern for another person's pain or suffering." It defines "sympathetic" as the ability to feel what another person is feeling. So compassion is concern for another person's pain and suffering that is motivated not only by an *intellectual* appreciation of his difficulty, but by a shared *emotional* response to it. This is a much more profound and meaningful definition than many are comfortable with. Some would prefer to place compassion alongside pity, concern or kindness, as an activity that can be done at arm's length. But the mingling of emotions is what distinguishes compassion from these other virtues, and is also what makes it such a fascinating subject of exploration.

By defining compassion in terms that include shared emotions, we change the dynamics of our response. We behave differently when we feel another person's pain than if we simply pity him or her.

There is another reason for making a distinction between compassion and pity, concern or kindness. The word itself can be broken down into the prefix *"com,"* meaning "with or together"—as in com*munication, com*munity, and com*mune* (as in prayer)—and *"passion,"* which means strong feelings or emotions. So *compassion* literally means to have a strong emotion together with another person.

Pity, on the other hand, means to feel sorry for someone. We can feel *pity* for someone who is blissfully unaware that he or she is the recipient of our sorrowful attention. Pity can be self-righteous and even cruel. Compassion can't be. Compassion requires an act of transcendence—a temporary and perhaps even miniscule setting aside of oneself in order to perceive life for a moment through another person's heart.

The Five Steps of Compassion

There are five steps in the process of practicing compassion. For some they may take a lifetime to learn, while for others they can be traveled in the twinkling of an eye.

First, you see another person from your own perspective. We all start here.

Second, you recognize some point of unity or commonality between you. This will be easier with some people than others, but we all share our common humanity.

Third, you use this point of commonality to shift your perspective and begin to see them and their situation from *their* perspective.

Fourth, when you begin to *see* the world from their perspective, you will begin to *feel* the world from their perspective because our feelings are shaped by the virtues we perceive in our environment.

Fifth, your feelings will motivate you to act. Perhaps all you will be able to do is express sincere concern, but it is also possible that you have knowledge or resources that the person whose feelings you share does not have. Being able to perceive a situation from *two* perspectives creates an increased capacity for wisdom and understanding.

Why Practice Compassion?

If you want others to be happy, practice compassion. If you want to be happy, practice compassion. — The Dalai Lama

When we think of practicing compassion, we tend to think of it as an obligation. We are compassionate for the sake of someone else. But that is only half the equation.

One of the themes of this book is that the practice of virtues serves us in two ways. First, virtues heal our emotional pain by filling our lives with the qualities that have been missing. So honesty helps heal the shame that came from carrying secrets and forgiveness heals the pain of anger and resentment. Likewise, compassion is a wonderful tool for helping us feel connected and easing our loneliness.

But virtues also serve another function: they offer us positive activities and enjoyable sensations to replace the activities and sensations that generated and reinforced our shame. In this regard, honesty and forgiveness make us feel good, but compassion? Compassion makes us feel amazing.

Compassion helps us tear down the walls of isolation that keep us separated from the people around us and make us feel lonely. The first thing we notice is that we no longer feel lonely, but feeling connected is *more* than just not feeling bad.

Compassion allows us to experience the sensation of *transcendence*—that is, the feeling of being connected to something *bigger* than ourselves. This is not a metaphysical connection, but a heart connection that expands our perspective of our place in the universe. This, according to happiness research, is one of the keys to deep life satisfaction.

By connecting to people and experiences that are bigger than we are, we also gain access to a source of wisdom that can guide our choices and protect us from foolish mistakes.

Combined, these gifts of compassion go beyond healing old hurts. They bring us true joy.

The Science of Compassion

"By compassion we make others' misery our own, and so, by reliev-
ing them, we relieve ourselves also."   — *Thomas Browne, Sr.*

One of ways in which shame keeps a grip on us is through our sense of isolation. When we believe that no one else has done what we have done or felt what we have felt, then we feel even more broken and ashamed. This shame, in turn, acts as a wall around us to keep us from even *trying* to connect with others. Shame and isolation work together to build a wall of loneliness between us and everyone else. Compassion breaks down that wall.

Practicing honesty by sharing your story and listening to others' stories allows you to *see* that you are not alone; that other people have had experiences similar to yours, but practicing compassion allows you to *feel* that you are not alone by recognizing that even when experiences are different, the feelings are the same.

How can we do that? How can we possibly *know* what someone else is feeling if we have not had the exact same experience? How can we *feel* what they are feeling if we are not them? If I have not lost my friend, or my job or my health or my home, how is it that I can *feel* your loss?

We know how to *think* what another person is thinking. We simply ask them to explain their thoughts, and in the process of listening, we end up thinking the same thing (though we may think that they are wrong, we are, nevertheless, thinking the same thoughts.) But how do we get our hearts to respond with the same feeling that another person is feeling? Even if they tell us what they think their emotion is, "knowing" and "feeling" are not the same thing.

I would like to offer three different theories as to how emotions can be shared, based on different understandings of how humans are connected to one another. The first is for people who believe we are connected in an abstract, conceptual way; the second is for people who feel we are emotionally connected; and the third is for the more metaphysically minded who believe we are all spiritually united.

The theories on how one person's emotional state can create a parallel response in another person's heart include:

1. The use of cues
   a. Physical cues
   b. Psychological cues
   c. Spiritual cues
2. Emotional resonance
3. Psychic connection

Physical Cues and Mirror Neurons

On one level, we can explain our capacity for compassion in terms of neurology. It would appear that we are biologically hard-wired for compassion. That's right. It is in our DNA to identify with the feelings of others. This may not be obvious from your personal experience, but it *is* the lesson of recent scientific studies. These studies aren't from the schools of psychology or sociology. They are studies of the way our brains respond to the actions of the people around us.

The lessons of these studies are both astonishing, and so obvious that we all understand them intuitively.

If someone near us stubs their toe, we wince.

If they smile at us, we instinctively smile back.

If they laugh enthusiastically, we start to laugh.

If they cry, we fight back tears.

If we watch them do a running long-jump, our muscles tense as they run and relax when we see them land.

From gross physical movement to subtle emotional cues, humans are hard-wired to mirror the actions of the people around them. Neurologists theorize that, not just humans, but other animals as well, have "mirror neurons" that fire in the brain in areas that correspond to the actions that we observe.

In humans, this mirroring process is not just about physical actions, but responds to perceived intentions as well. For example, the brain reacts differently if it sees a person pick up a cup, pick up a cup in order to take a drink, or pick up a cup in order to clear a table of dirty dishes. The parts of the brain that react correspond to the parts of the brain that would activate if the observer were to do the behavior him or herself—*for the same reason.*

What this means is that when you watch another person's actions, *you identify with him or her whether you want to or not.* If a person is hurt, your body *will* respond. If a person is feeling strong emotions, your body *will* mirror those emotions to some degree.

We all know this. We've known it for centuries. But until now it has been an intuitive knowledge that we could dismiss and ignore. Now we have hard scientific proof that we are all strongly influenced by the actions and emotions of the people around us.*

In fact, we are not just *influenced.* It is as though a shadow part of ourselves steps into the other person and goes through the same motions and *emotions* as they do. In doing so, do we learn, experience, perceive or feel what they do? If watching a golfer swing his club makes neurons fire in our brains, does that make us a better golfer too? Scientists seem to think it might. And if watching a mother care for her child makes our neurons fire in ways that are different from watching her bake a cake, then how does that change us?

The grand implications are somewhat staggering. Knowing about this innate capacity for connecting with others gives us a powerful tool for developing our compassion—especially when we understand that this capacity to identify with others is not limited to those we see in person, or even those we see in videos, but also those we experience in our imaginations.

If we want to develop our capacity for compassion, then one way is to surround ourselves with compassionate people to emulate, but another way is to choose uplifting sources of entertainment. There are many wonderful movies, documentaries and books that provide opportunities for us to reflect upon positive behavior, be moved by expression of virtue, and feel compassion for people who can expand our sense of connection with the world. The trick is to make the effort to surround ourselves with *positive* images, *positive* emotions, and *positive* people. Then when our mirror neurons kick in and we are drawn into a compassionate connection with the world around us, it will be a rewarding and enlightening experience.

The alternative is to allow the world to subject us its barrage of negative images, stories and people.

When we understand the power of watching, we grasp the importance of making conscious choices about what we put in front of our eyes. When we understand our innate tendency to step into the shoes of the people we spend time with, we grasp the importance of choosing our friends and activities wisely.

This book is not the place to explore all of the ways in which we are influenced by the TV shows, movies and videos we watch, or the books we read and the games we play, but we would be foolish to try to improve our behavior and spiritualize our lives without considering the power of that influence.

I think that the prevalence of sex and violence and simple *meanness* in the visual images we are bombarded with every day has two contradictory effects on us.

First of all, we are forced to desensitize ourselves against the violence and cruelty we see everywhere—both in the name of humor and in the name of excitement. If we are hard-wired to wince when we see someone stub their toe or hit their head, then how can we possibly sit through The Three Stooges, Tom and Jerry, America's Funniest Home Videos, Home Alone, or any of the thousands of other videos that use violence as a form of humor, without working mightily to resist our urge to feel compassion?

The fact is, none of these forms of entertainment are funny. They are incredibly stressful, and one of the tools our bodies use to release stress is to exhale explosively in something resembling laughter. Okay, it *is* laughter, but there is happy laughter and *laugh so you don't cry* laughter.*

When we surround ourselves with slapstick humor, it trains us to distance ourselves from other people's pain. This is just as true in the case of emotional violence. Most situation comedies rely on a constant stream of insults and put-downs. Our natural response to this kind of personal attack is an emotional wince. Then we feel the relief of realizing that the insult was not directed at us, but at some poor schmuck on the screen, and we release the tension with a laugh. We are grateful that we *don't* identify with him or her (too much, anyway), and remind ourselves to *not* feel too much compassion. That the poor schmuck doesn't dissolve in a puddle of tears tells us that insults aren't that bad after all, as long as you don't care about the person being insulted (and it isn't you).

Likewise, violent images in adventure, mystery and horror movies use our natural "wince response" to get our bodies all worked up, and then convince us that we are excited and having fun.

We aren't excited. We are expending energy to try to *not* identify with all of the pain we are seeing so that we are not overwhelmed. We are actively working to *not* allow our natural compassion to send us running from the theater.

All that this does is make it easier to ignore *real* pain and suffering when we see them on the news, or on the street in front of us. And we call it entertainment because, as I said earlier, *any* sensation is better than no sensation at all.

We are so afraid of *real* compassion, and so ignorant of how to generate positive *spiritual* sensations that we allow ourselves to be manipulated to accept these base and ugly sensations as the best entertainment we have.

So, on one hand, video images desensitize us to feeling other people's pain. On the *other* hand, they manipulate us to try to *make* us feel other people's sexual impulses. If watching a person put a cup of water up to his lips causes our mirror neurons to fire in a way that resembles *our* taking a drink, *what* in heaven's name happens in our brains when we watch two people kiss on a 40-foot screen—or four people have meaningless intercourse on a computer screen?

If, as studies have shown, our brains react not just to the movement of limbs, but to the perceived *intention* behind those movements, then watching a well-acted drama in which two people express their sincere love and commitment to one another with a kiss might actually be *good* for our ability to identify with healthy relationships.

On the other hand, watching people have meaningless sex for the purpose of getting paid to make a video might leave one feeling both aroused and empty. What effect would *this* have on one's ability to feel compassion? How do these base and ugly sensations compare to the feelings our hearts truly long for? We deserve better.

The Art of Compassion

Mirror neurons cause us to identify with the physical actions of others whether we want to or not, whether we choose to or not, whether we are conscious of it or not. But true compassion is literally not a knee-jerk reaction. It is a choice to create a bond with another person. We can choose to numb, distract or ignore our biological reaction to another person's experience, or we can embrace it. Most people prefer to avoid pain and sadness, so a willing desire to experience the same emotion as someone who is grieving or suffering is an act of great courage and generosity. It requires more than the science of neurons, it requires the art of watching, listening, feeling and *connecting*.

Physical Cues

Having chosen to express compassion, I can choose to augment my mirror neurons' natural response by looking for a wide range of cues to tell me what you are feeling. The most obvious cue is your physical state. Tears, crying, sobbing, trembling, flushed skin, weakness, are all clear signs of an emotional crisis. These are the cues that our mirror neurons are most likely to reflect. But stress, depression, pain, anxiety, hopelessness, and fear *also* have clear physical signs for those who are attentive enough to notice them. People who grew up in dysfunctional or abusive families may have particularly well-developed "emotional radar" because their very survival was dependent upon accurately reading the non-verbal signals that forecast their parents' emotional state. The twitch of a lip, the speed of a movement, or the texture of a voice can all provide innumerable clues as to what a person is feeling.

There may even be much more subtle physical cues to help people in close proximity to loved ones pick up on the emotional state of those they care for. They say that animals can smell fear and it is true. Humans release unique scents and odorless pheromones in accordance with our emotional states. Though we may be consciously oblivious to these subtle cues, millions of years of biology may provide unexplored subconscious chemical hints as to the emotions of our companions.

Psychological Cues

In addition to purely physical cues, we can use our minds to tease out psychological cues as to what another person is feeling. Most obviously, we can either observe their situation, or ask them point-blank what they are feeling. If someone's dog is missing and they say they are worried sick about it, then you have a pretty good starting place for figuring out what they are feeling. Clarifying questions can help fine-tune the exact emotional state. "How long has it been missing? How long have you owned it? Is it an inside pet or an outside guard dog? Have you ever lost a pet before? Do you have other pets? Have you always had dogs?" etc. Now if you love dogs too, then this information may make it easier to create an emotional connection. If you don't like dogs, then an emotional twenty-questions may create more distance than compassion. Psychologists are experts at drawing people out so that not only does the therapist have a clear understanding of the emotion involved, but the patient himself also has a more precise label for his emotional state.

Spiritual Cues

The final cues that we can use to figure out what another person is feeling are spiritual. Though the word spiritual often implies some kind of metaphysical connection, in this context, spiritual cues can be used even if we assume that there is absolutely no direct spiritual connection between the people involved.

Compassion invites us to see ourselves in another person, and in so doing, see the world through their eyes and feel the world through their heart. In the process, hearts become one. They feel the same feelings because they perceive the same spiritual need, and are pulled by the same longings.

In other words, since feelings are a response to the presence or absence of a *virtue*, it is the *virtue*, not the specific experience, that generates the feeling. That means that we can feel what someone else is feeling even when we have not had the same experience because we have longed for the same virtues that they long for, and rejoice in the same virtues that they rejoice in. When we listen to their stories, a part of us is saying, "Yes, that is the virtue I would recognize; that is the loss I would identify; that is the injus-

tice I would perceive in that situation." And in recognizing, identifying and perceiving the presence or absence of these qualities,
our own hearts are moved to generate appropriate sensations. We
feel along *with* them, and even when it hurts, it feels good.

Through this compassion, we know that our shared longing
for virtues connects us to other people, even though our material
circumstances may be very different.

From this understanding of emotions, we can see that in order
to feel the same thing as someone else, we don't necessarily even
need to know what they are feeling. What we need to know is
what virtues are present, and what virtues have been lost to them.
Faced with injustice, we, too, will feel angry. Faced with the loss of
something good and true, we, too, will feel great sadness and loss.

To illustrate this concept, I must again turn to my experience
with a twelve-step program. I was sitting in a meeting for cocaine
addicts. I was not a cocaine addict, but when you are in recovery,
you take the meeting that is there when you need one. As a non-
addict, I was trying to hold myself at arm's-length from "those
people" while still participating in the process.

Then a young woman shared. She talked about living on the
street, and her family and her shame, and her efforts at recovery,
and the things she was learning... and somewhere in the middle
of the story, I realized that there was no "arm's-length" between
us. There was not a hair's-breadth difference between her pain and
mine; between her shame and mine; between her longing for God
and mine.

Paradoxically, sharing this woman's pain was one of the most
joyful experiences of my life. It broke down barriers and helped
me see myself as part of an interconnected web of life. It helped
me transcend my limited vision of myself.

Compassion as Emotional Resonance

Okay, now that I have established the fact that compassion is possible even if there is no underlying spiritual connection between human hearts and minds, allow me to take a step into the more esoteric field of emotional resonance.

Resonance is an amazing phenomenon. Here is how it works in the material world. Suppose you have two guitars that are in perfect tune with each other. If you hold them three feet apart and pluck the bottom string on one guitar, the bottom string on the other guitar will start to vibrate. In fact, the top string, which is an octave higher than the bottom string will also start to vibrate—but the ones in between won't. When you see it happen, it seems like magic, but of course it isn't. Sound waves may be invisible, but they are not magic, and their movement of a corresponding string is physics, not psychic. The question is whether the principle of resonance—that objects in tune with each other can influence each other over a distance more easily than objects that are not in tune with each other—can be applied to spiritual realities. If it can, then it provides one more potential means by which one person's emotions can influence another's.

People have talked about "heart strings" and emotional vibrations for thousands of years. In fact, resonance is often referred to as "sympathetic vibrations." I personally believe that our spirits may carry emotional vibrations the way the air carries sound waves, and that people who are emotionally in tune with each other may instinctively vibrate in response to each other's strong emotional states. This is an intermediate level of connection between hearts. It allows for a view of human nature that is essentially independent, but recognizes that there may be a spiritual atmosphere in which we all operate.

Applying the phenomenon of resonance to our emotions allows the possibility of feeling what another person is feeling without being in their physical presence and without understanding the exact nature of their situation. It allows for compassion in silence, and even in ignorance. Certainly this kind of emotional intimacy is rare, but I don't think it is impossible. I do believe that when it operates, it is most often used to fine-tune an emotional understanding gained through more direct contact. Resonance allows us to go from the gross awareness that someone is in pain to the more subtle understanding of exactly how they feel and what they need with a minimum of invasive questions and prying.

Resonance is also a cooperative effort. A person who is in pain is not going to fine-tune his emotions. We are the ones who have to open our hearts to him and adjust our emotional understanding of what he is experiencing until our understanding and his experience harmonize and reinforce one another. A "G" string can't get an out-of-tune "C" string to vibrate, no matter how loud it is played. A man who is suffering cannot move the heart of a selfish person no matter how loud he cries. But if you have ever played an instrument, then you know that special satisfaction that comes from getting your instrument to blend exactly with the one beside you. There is a special purity, a "rightness" that says "Yes! We are on the same wavelength." I think that "magical" sensation is one of the added benefits of experiencing compassion as an act of resonance, not just one of understanding. It is not a requirement, but it is a nice bonus.

Compassion as Spiritual Connection

The third theory of shared emotions is direct psychic connection. Well, perhaps not *conscious* psychic connection, but there is a belief that since we are all connected on a spiritual level, we can gain direct access to another person's strong emotions. Though I don't have much personal experience with this level of connections, I'm not ready to dismiss it as a possibility. After all, when I hit my thumb with a hammer, my whole body jumps—even though my feet had nothing to do with the accident.

According to this view, the reason we can feel compassion for other people is because we are intimately connected to them on a spiritual, psychic level. Their pain is our pain and our pain is their pain. There is certainly plenty of evidence for this view in many spiritual traditions—most obviously in Buddhism, Hinduism and the Baháʼí Faith, but also to a lesser degree in every western religion.

Perhaps all of these views are equally correct. Perhaps people who are apathetic towards one another are like islands, responding only to the strongest mirror neurons, people who respect each other breathe the same spiritual atmosphere and resonate with each other's emotions, and people who love each other deeply are like fingers on one hand or even one soul in many bodies. Perhaps our capacity for compassion increases exponentially with our practice of compassion because it brings us into closer relations and deeper connections with other human hearts.

Whether we are spiritually connected to others, or just emotionally connected, the result is the same: compassion makes us feel part of something bigger than ourselves. It helps us transcend our own limited reality and care deeply about something or someone outside of ourselves. It breaks down the walls of isolation and removes the pain of loneliness.

And through all of that, it makes us wise.

Gaining Wisdom through Compassion

The heaven of divine wisdom is illumined with the two luminaries of consultation and compassion. — *Bahá'u'lláh*

This is a book about emotional healing, but it is also a book about changing our behavior, and gaining a little wisdom can go a long way in avoiding a lot of mistakes.

Wisdom is the virtue that allows us to recognize what virtue is needed in any given situation. Put concisely, wisdom allows us to squeeze maximum spiritual gain out of minimum spiritual pain. It allows us develop our virtues efficiently and effectively. Common wisdom is that wisdom only comes through experience—lots and lots of experience. We need to be able to try many different responses to the same type of tests to see what works and what doesn't. Wisdom, it seems, comes from trial and error.

But does it have to?

We all learn through experience. The more experiences we have, the more mistakes we make. The more mistakes we make, the more we learn and the wiser we become. But life is only so long, and many mistakes are fatal. If I want to learn a lot *and grow old*, then I would be wise to learn as much as I can from *other* people's experiences. Through consultation—sharing thoughts, ideas and experiences with people *verbally*—I can experience the world through other people's minds. Through compassion, however, I can experience the world through other people's *hearts*. I can learn how to identify the presence or absence of virtues in different situations. I can come to feel passion for the virtues that other people love, and grieve the absence of virtues that other people value.

The mind may be able to guess what virtues are present, but it is the heart that is specifically designed to be able to *sense* the presence and absence of virtues. Your mind might be able to guess that a brown liquid in a cup is coffee, but without the sense of taste or smell, it would be difficult to prove. Likewise, there are the virtues that *should* be present in a situation, and then there are the virtues that actually *are*. Our hearts, through our emotional response to a situation, tell us what virtues *we* perceive. But it is only through compassion that we are able to experience the emotional response to the virtues that *someone else* may perceive.

We have all had the experience of expecting a person to react emotionally to a situation in one way, only to discover that they responded completely differently. People's emotional perspective is just as unique, just as personal, and just as *filtered* as their intellectual perspectives. It is *not* that these people are being "illogical." It is that their experience and filters are causing them to sense the presence or absence of a different set of virtues. The only way to understand them—and increase your level of wisdom in the process—is to develop compassion.

Compassion, then, is the virtue that allows us to identify and appreciate a wide range of virtues through our *emotional* connection with other people. When we feel compassion for people who suffer from poverty, sickness, drug addiction, abuse, and other personal loss, then we acquire a great longing for the virtues that would help ease their pain—without ourselves having to suffer from their difficulties. This is a kind of wisdom that no amount of talk will provide.

The capacity for compassion does not only apply to sadness. To feel what another person feels and be compelled to take action can also apply to hope, love and wonder; to courage and conviction; to faith and joy.

When we see a mother cry at the loss of her son, do we not cry? When we see a child laugh in delight and wonder, do we not laugh? Compassion allows us to benefit from *everyone's* experience and be uplifted by *anyone's* joy. It connects us to the entire human race.

"A human being is part of a whole, called by us the Universe, a part limited in time and space. He experiences himself, his thoughts and feelings, as something separated from the rest — a kind of optical delusion of his consciousness.

This delusion is a kind of prison for us, restricting us to our personal desires and to affection for a few persons nearest us. Our task must be to free ourselves from this prison by widening our circles of compassion to embrace all living creatures and the whole of nature in its beauty.

Nobody is able to achieve this completely, but the striving for such achievement is in itself a part of the liberation and a foundation for inner security."   *— Albert Einstein*

Compassion versus Passion

When we see ourselves in other people, we are focusing on the signs of our common humanity. This encourages us to find the things in other people that make them easy to love, which in turn makes it easier for us to love them. In learning to love the people we see ourselves in, we learn to love ourselves a little more. In loving ourselves and others, we become more loveable. Love attracts love. So compassion helps bring love into our lives.

But there is a twist.

In learning to see ourselves in other people, we are actually doing the *opposite* of what we normally do when we go out searching for passionate love.

In Part One, I explained that in spite of our professed interest in finding people that we have common interests with, what most people find themselves attracted to is the *exotic and mysterious stranger.* We shun the boy or girl next door, and dive into relationships with people who make our pulse race.

Focusing on our common humanity, however, *short-circuits* our creation of this fantasy mystery lover. When we see ourselves in others, they are no longer mysterious or frightening. Our common humanity makes them *interesting* rather than exotic. Because of this, the passionate part of compassion does not lead to lust, it leads to understanding and connection and concern and respect.

Feeling what another person feels through compassion puts you both on the same side of a window looking out and emotionally perceiving reality. Because our emotions are designed to respond to the presence of virtues, and virtues are expressions of the attributes of God, at its most pure, compassion allows you to have a shared experience of the Divine. This shared experience has nothing to do with how old or young, cute or ugly, male or female, rich or poor the other person might be. Compassion is not about romance. It is a spiritual connection.

Fear-based romantic feelings, on the other hand, are very different. They are not about a shared experience of reality, but rather sharing the experience of alternating between being predator and prey. *Having* the same feeling is not the same as *sharing* the same feeling. If I'm afraid of you and you are afraid of me, then we are both *having* the same emotion, but we are not standing together looking out at the world. Instead, we are like wolves facing each other and wondering who will be eating whom.

When we see ourselves in others, however, we no longer want to conquer or be conquered. We want to be in harmony. What a pleasant idea!

Compassion versus Codependency

So is feeling compassion really a good idea? Won't it just mean that you will get sucked into other people's lives so they can use you to fix their problems? No. That isn't compassion. That is codependency.

Codependency causes us to lose ourselves in another person. Compassion invites us to expand ourselves to include another person. The difference is significant.

In the five steps of compassion I outlined, the third step was to be able to see another person and their situation from *their* perspective. Seeing things from their perspective as well as your own gives you *two* ways of understanding a situation. When we are codependent, we come to see ourselves through another person's eyes, and we are only able to hold onto one perspective— *theirs.*

Codependents define themselves by the way other people see them. To be compassionate, you must first see *yourself* clearly before seeing yourself in others. You are not finding yourself in the way others see you, but rather, you identify with the common virtues that you share with them.

Not everyone who is struggling with emotional healing is codependent, but many are. Fortunately, there are many skills that codependents have developed that can be used in developing compassion—sensitivity to other's needs, listening skills, an interest in helping people in need, etc.

The other good news is that practicing seeing ourselves in others and expressing compassion will strengthen our sense of identity and make us less codependent. By being more aware of the subtle difference between codependency and compassion, we strengthen the one and reduce the other. It is win-win.

Seeing Ourselves in Others

Of the five steps of compassion, we have mostly been exploring the fourth step, the art and science of how to feel what others feel, but in practice, before we can get to the feeling part, we must first take the second step, which is to find a point of unity or commonality between you and another person.

I encourage you, then, to start your practice of compassion by focusing your efforts on *seeing yourself in other people.*

We are all children of the same God, and we all reflect the same Divine virtues, yet we spend most of our time looking at the things that set us apart from everyone else. When we look for differences, we find differences. But if we look for similarities, we quickly discover that we are all more alike than we are different.

See ye no strangers; rather see all men as friends, for love and unity come hard when ye fix your gaze on otherness.   —'Abdu'l-Bahá

Trying to see yourself in the people around you is the first *conscious* step in the practice of compassion. Finding points of commonality will help you see things from their perspective. Seeing things from their perspective will help you understand their feelings about things. Understanding their feelings will provide opportunities for you to feel the same way that they feel, at least once in a while, and will move you to service. In the long run, it will make you more compassionate.

But you don't have to worry about the long run. Focus on finding positive similarities with every single person you meet—even if at first they are ridiculously shallow. *Ah,* that person has the same color of hair as I do, and that one buys the same brand of milk. That person laughs at the same jokes, and that one also has a child they love. Someone here is a writer, or at least speaks English. Is anyone here worried about global warming?

Start with the obvious, and keep going. Make it a game, or be completely serious. Just thinking about finding something in common with the people around you will change your entire perspective on life. On some deep level, it will connect you to the world.

Compassionate Service

What separates compassion from sympathy or empathy is that it is expressed through acts of kindness. When you begin to see yourself in others and feel what they feel, then *you are moved* to act in an appropriate way. This kindness rises from an inner knowing of what the other person needs, and an inner desire to *do unto others as you would have them do unto you.*

By putting compassion into action, you achieve the third goal of this book. The first is to heal emotional wounds. The second is to enjoy life more by experiencing positive emotional sensations. The third is to discover alternatives to unhealthy behaviors, because it is always easier to replace bad habits than to hide from them.

What can you *do* to find opportunities to practice compassionate service? How do you go from the abstract appreciation of the value of compassion to the actual face-to-face experience of it?

Note: Before you look at my list of suggestions, remember that you should not choose a population or activity that might trigger inappropriate or obsessive behavior. Whoever it is you are attracted to, *go serve someone else.*

At the risk of repeating myself, the first place to go might be to an appropriate twelve-step meeting. There you can practice honesty, forgiveness and compassion all at the same time. But there are many other fields of service you might want to consider as well.

You can start with your own family. Are there family members—adult or child—that you are taking for granted or even avoiding? Call them up or take them out and listen, listen, listen.

Are there members of your religious or social group who are alone, sick, or going through difficulties? Offer to help. Often the greatest service you can provide another person is to simply be there as a caring witness to the other person's experience, whether it is one of joy or grief.

Neighbors, hospitals, nursing homes, Big Brother, Big Sister, Scouts, soup kitchens, homeless shelters, Habitat for Humanity— the list of people and organizations that need your help is endless. Many cities have a non-profit volunteer coordinator or office that can direct you to an appropriate agency. Even if you are homebound yourself, you can make phone calls to shut-ins, send sympathy cards to the grieving, write letters to prisoners or soldiers, or say prayers for any and all of the above. I have a friend who stands in parking lots handing out stickers to children just to see them smile. She lives in a beautiful world.

Even the smallest act of service can change your focus from yourself and your problems to the needs of others. It may sound trite but it is true: the best way to help yourself is to help someone else.

*We have come to the last of our four tools of healing. This is the shortest section, not because faith is the least important, or because I have less to say about faith than the others, but because I have already written an entire book about the value of trusting in a loving God who allows us to suffer trials and tests in order to help us grow spiritually. That book is called **Why Me? A Spiritual Guide to Growing Through Tests**. If you believe in a God who is active in your life, then that book will be a great source of comfort and encouragement.*

FAITH

The kind of faith you need for emotional healing does not involve a specific religion or doctrine. It isn't about holding on to dogma, or pledging love to one Messenger of God versus another. It is an attitude of trust in the general goodness of the universe, and a confidence that you have an important part to play. It is the kind of faith that speaks of purpose and meaning and belonging.

We all have faith in something. The question is whether we have faith that we will succeed, or faith that we will fail; faith that the world is a safe place, or faith that it is out to get us; faith that there is meaning to our lives or faith that the universe is a great cosmic accident in which we are just a tiny blip.

We also all believe in a Transcendent Higher Power, no matter how vehemently we try to deny it. This belief began before we were even born and was reinforced every day of our lives for the duration of our emotional development.

We are born helpless and dependent upon adults who had much more power than we did. We believe, to the very core of our subconscious beings, that there is a power outside of us that is greater than we are because we *experienced* such a power every day of our early lives. Our feelings of helplessness and powerlessness were therefore embedded in our emotional reality at birth. They are the foundational scaffolding upon which our early emotional and intellectual world-views were built.

Our pre-verbal awareness that as infants we were subject to the whims of forces more powerful than ourselves was reinforced by at least 10-15 years of additional experiences during our childhood and youth. It would be unrealistic to think we could erase these feelings from our psyches. No matter what our head tells us, our hearts tell us that there is something bigger than us out there.

It would do no good to engage in an intellectual argument with our hearts over whether or not there is a God.

If we resign ourselves to the idea that a part of us will always believe in a Higher Power, we can still do three things. First, we can accept that our hearts will always long for a source of power, strength and protection. This is not a sign of weakness; it is simply a universal aspect of the human condition.

Second, we can work to uncover what our subconscious and emotional beliefs *about* that Higher Power might be. We will always believe in a force bigger than ourselves, but we can wrestle some power back from it by being able to name it and describe how it has influenced us.

Finally, we can use this use this understanding to slowly redefine our Higher Power, both mentally and emotionally, to be more supportive and loving. Instead of denying or doing battle with the Higher Power we grew up with, we can transform it; educate it; turn it into the loving Force that we need it to be in our hearts.

The God We Know

In Part One of this book, I explained that when we were children, our parents were our gods. If our parents were angry, we internalized an angry god. If they were unpredictable, being loving one minute and cruel the next, then our god was erratic. If they were judgmental, always finding fault with us, then our internal god was judging us and looking for a reason to punish us.

If we did not feel that our parents were on our side, looking out for our best interest and doing whatever they could to help us succeed, then we internalized more than just the belief that life was unfair—we believed that God Himself was working against us.

To a lesser degree, this belief was reinforced by our relationships with other sources of authority in our lives, such as teachers, clergy, police, and bureaucrats of all sorts.

Because of these negative associations with God, some of us rejected the idea of God entirely, while others continued to believe in God. Some of those who continued to believe worked doubly hard to please him, while others gave up and identified themselves with those damned to go to Hell.

For those who consciously believe in God, the association with power and authority works both ways. If the authorities in your life were untrustworthy, then you will tend to believe in a capricious God, and if you believe in a vengeful God, then you will tend to not trust people in authority.

This means that how we see God, and how we perceive our relationship to God both have a huge impact on our emotional and psychological health.

While this statement seems self-evident, it is only recently that science has dared to study the effects of belief and faith on mental health.

Belief in God and Depression

Two small studies, one at Harvard and one at Rush University both suggest that belief in God can be a factor in the effectiveness of treatment for depression. One found that belief in God—even if the patient had no specific religious affiliation—doubled the effectiveness of a treatment program compared to patients who said that they had "no" or "slight" belief in God. A second found that patients with a strong belief in a personal and *concerned* God were 75% more likely to respond to treatment with antidepressants than people who didn't.

A third study that analyzed a large-scale survey found that people who believed in an angry or judgmental God were more likely to suffer from general anxiety, social anxiety, paranoia, obsession, and compulsion than those who believed in a loving God.

This study, done at Marymount Manhattan College, had a large sample size, but both the beliefs about God and the diagnosis of psychiatric symptoms were based on self-reporting, so the results are far from conclusive, and yet, based on what we know about how beliefs shape feelings and behaviors, the findings make sense.

The researchers write, *"We propose that belief in a benevolent God inhibits threat assessments about the dangerousness of the world, thereby decreasing psychiatric symptoms."* They also write, *"Belief in a punitive God... facilitates threat assessments that the world is dangerous and even that God poses a threat of harm, thereby increasing psychiatric symptomology."*

Since this study was based on self-reporting, what it can't show is the degree to which *subconscious* beliefs about God affect all of us and increase the overall level of anxiety, paranoia, obsession, compulsion, and yes, depression, in society.

The question *you* have to answer is whether your subconscious beliefs are undermining *your* mental health. If you are dealing with depression, anxiety or fear then you might find it helpful to use Internal Consultation, therapy, and the support of a good twelve-step program to uncover exactly what it is you believe about your relationship to your Higher Power.

One of the first times I used the technique of Internal Consultation was to help me uncover my subconscious feelings about God.

Many years ago, when I was going through my divorce, I started attending twelve-step CoDA meetings. Affirmations were a popular tool for developing self-esteem and I used them regularly, saying nice things about myself repetitively in a meditative state. One day I decided to use what I thought would be the most powerful, positive affirmation I could imagine: "God loves me!" I said it over and over as I tried to relax. But a strange thing happened. I noticed that my chest started to feel heavy, as though my heart were sinking. "That's odd," I thought, and tried switching to a different affirmation about being precious. Sure enough, the weight in my chest began to lift. I switched back, and my heart became heavy again.

This is the point at which I could have told myself that I was imagining things—that I was crazy, stupid, or simply wrong to have a negative reaction to the words "God loves me," but instead I adopted an attitude of curiosity towards the sensation my body was generating. While continuing to say the affirmation with one part of my mind, I opened myself up to whatever information my heart, mind or body was willing to share with me about the message behind the sensations I was experiencing.

Since I'm a visually-oriented person, what came to me was an image—an image of God holding me by the heel over a tub of soapy water, and dunking me repeatedly into it while holding his nose! The message was clear: Yes, God loves me, but as an unpleasant obligation because I stink! I am a dirty diaper in God's eyes—or at least I thought I was. Being able to acknowledge how I really perceived myself was the first step in being able to redefine myself.

Turning inward with openness and curiosity allowed me to realize that I had conflicting feelings about my relationship with God. Acknowledging this conflict was the first step in beginning to resolve it. If I hadn't been willing to listen to what seemed to be a random and illogical sensation, I would have missed out on an important piece of self-knowledge. Now when I say "God loves me," I know that I really mean it.

Faith and the Marshmallow Test

The fourth scientific study I want to tell you about puts the issue of faith into very practical terms. Here, faith is not just affecting those hard-to-pin-down aspects of life like depression or anxiety. Here, faith in the general goodness, trustworthiness and predictability of life can impact the hard-core and infinitely measurable qualities of success, income, graduation rates, unintended pregnancies and drug abuse.

This kind of faith helps us overcome fear. Fear tells us that the world is unsafe, unstable and unfriendly. Faith tells us that the world is full of wonder, possibility and goodness. Without this kind of faith, we are predisposed to making a never-ending spiral of self-destructive choices that will hold us back for our entire lives. This is because having faith that everything will work out in the end—that there is enough good to go around and the world is on our side—does more than simply make us feel better or give us a sense of peace and hope, it also has a direct impact on our ability to control our impulses, resist temptation and delay gratification. This is what this last study is about.

Researchers have known for decades that people who have trouble with controlling their impulses, or delaying gratification have a much harder time succeeding in life. They are more likely to do drugs, drop out of school, experience an unintended pregnancy, etc. Researchers know this because of a long-term follow-up study of children who participated in what is known as "The Marshmallow Test" at Stanford University in the 1960s. In it, researchers leave a four-year-old alone in a room with a single marshmallow or other treat and tell them that if they can wait until the researcher comes back in ten minutes to eat it, they can have TWO treats instead of one. Children who were good at this—who waited the longest without eating the treat—were found to be more successful in many areas of their life as they grew into adulthood.

The fact that this one test correlated with a long-term pattern of behavior seemed to indicate that it was exposing an innate character quality in these children. A child was either good at delaying gratification or he wasn't, and if he wasn't when the test was given, he would probably never be. This consistency suggested that an ability to wait for a greater good was somehow written into a child's DNA.

The fact that poor kids tended to do less well on this test was explained, not by their poverty, but by an inherited predisposition for irresponsible behavior and short-term thinking.

So where does faith come in? Well, about 50 years later, as it turns out.

In a 2012 study of 56 three-to-five-year-olds, researchers at University of Rochester found that children who experienced *reliable interactions* with a researcher immediately before the marshmallow experiment waited on average *four times longer* to eat the marshmallow than children who had an unreliable interaction.

For this new version of the study, children were given *two* activities. In the first activity, they were promised a reward if they did an art project as requested. After doing the project, half of the children were given the promised reward, and half were not. Later, this same researcher told them that if they waited to eat their marshmallow, they would get a second one.

The children who had faith that the researcher would do as he promised waited a mean time of twelve minutes, while those who expected the researcher to let them down waited a mean time of three minutes—only one quarter as long.

The ones waiting three minutes were not poorer, less bright, or less able to control their impulses. They had less *faith* that waiting would gain them any advantage.

They had *learned* from experience that promises are broken, people are unreliable, and pleasure should be grabbed while it is sitting in front of you. As one of the researchers said, "If you are used to getting things taken away from you, not waiting is the rational choice."

This new study provides strong evidence that the kids who lacked self-control in the '60s were probably living in unstable households *before* they ever walked through the door to take the test. Is it any wonder, then, that the follow-up studies found them to be less successful?

Many of us also grew up in unstable homes. Even if we had religious faith, we did not necessarily have faith that God and the universe were looking out for our best interests. The idea that there was plenty to go around never occurred to us. We expected to run out; we expected to be disappointed; we expected to be lied to; we sometimes even expected to be hurt and abused. These expectations were developed as a result of our interaction with those whom we should have been able to trust. As a corollary to these expectations, we also expected to fail, to have the rug pulled out from under us, and to be caught in an endless Catch 22 of bureaucratic gotchas.

The expectation that life will kick you when you are down creates a self-sabotaging attitude. Why study if you will never graduate? Why wait to have sex if you will never have a career? Why *not* take drugs, if they make you feel good now?

When we combine this expectation of failure with feelings of guilt and shame, it is not surprising that many of us go through our days subconsciously looking for proof that the world is out to get us. When that is what we expect to see, that is exactly what we find.

Today, for example, my proof that the world is out to get me is the fact that both my favorite coffee flavoring and my favorite style of facial tissues have been discontinued by the manufacturers. Could life get any worse? Well, yes, of course it could. And if I keep looking, I am perfectly capable of *making* it worse. But I have the option to use my free will and my conscious choice to start looking for the good instead.

If faith in the general goodness of the world is what it takes to keep from spiraling down into self-destruction, then we all need to work on developing a little faith, no matter what our childhood experiences taught us.

Choosing to Believe

As the four studies I have described indicate, it is good for your mental health to have faith in something. As I have already explained, we are all shaped and guided by our subconscious beliefs, whether we like it or not, so doesn't it make sense to consciously choose what we want to believe so that as we uncover unhealthy beliefs we will have something better to replace them with? We can't create a vacuum in our belief system, so we might as well be ready with something really great to fill the void created by fear and mistrust.

What might that kind of faith look like?

The kind of faith I suggest breaks down into four different aspects, none of which involve a specific religion or doctrine. They aren't about holding on to a theological belief, or pledging love to one Messenger of God versus another. They are about reflecting an attitude.

These aspects of faith invite us to accept the possibility of a power in the universe greater than ourselves; maintain an attitude of openness to the unknown; anticipate the good; and trust that everything will work to the good in the long run.

Contemplating a Higher Power

If we subconsciously believe in a force in the universe greater than ourselves, then we might as well make friends with it. You can call it God if you like, but if that seems too anthropomorphic, you can call it Higher Power, Creative Spirit, the Unknowable Essence, Gaia, or any other cosmic name that appeals to you.

The twelve-step community has understood our need for a Higher Power from the beginning. Step number two is *we came to believe that a power greater than ourselves could restore us to sanity.* Its members also understand how hard it is for people who have been abused by religious authority to accept a traditional God figure. The term "Higher Power" originated with the recovery community. Many there have chosen less god-like names for whatever it is that watches out for them. Some call their Higher Power "HP" for short. You can call it god with a small "g", Friend, your Guardian Angel, or Harvey the 6′ tall invisible rabbit. The die-hard agnostics sometimes use their recovery community as a whole for their higher power. It doesn't have to be mystical, it just has to be bigger than you.

The point is that, whether you want to believe in it or not, whether it really exists or not, your mental health will improve if you have faith that there is a force in the universe that is looking out for your best interests; that cares whether you live or die; that you can lean on when life feels out of control.

For some of you, this will require a bit of humility—an acknowledgement that there just might be something more to the universe than what you already know. That's a good thing, because the second aspect of faith that I encourage you to try is to simply maintain an attitude of openness to the unknown.

Remaining Open and Anticipating the Good

Fear of the unknown keeps us returning to *the Devil we know* rather than opening ourselves up to the Angels that we never dreamed existed. When we think we know how the universe really works, we project our past pain, abuse and failures into our future and then live up to our low expectations.

Faith means believing that things can be *different*—not *only* different, but different in ways we can't even begin to predict.

This attitude of openness to the unknown also helps counteract perfectionism. Perfectionism leaves us terrified of the unknown because it is outside of our control, and because to be perfect is to know everything that needs to be known. To be able to say, "I don't know, and that's OK," can open new paths of personal exploration.

Most of us live our lives on auto-pilot, putting one foot in front of the other in a predictable pattern, day in and day out. Faith invites us to look up, look around, and maybe, just *maybe,* veer off in a new direction. It also reminds us that it is OK to do this, and that the unknown can even be a safer, friendlier option than the step we normally take.

To be open to an unknown good allows us to take the next step of faith, which is to *anticipate* the good.

This phrase reminds me of the old bumper sticker, "Expect a Miracle!" I always felt that that was pretty damn demanding on my part. To expect something, to me, implies that someone else is going to provide it for you.

I decided I preferred the phrase, "anticipate blessings." Anticipation is a state of readiness. It implies an openness to what is possible, rather than a demand for what is impossible.

If I am open to seeing and receiving blessings, then I am more likely to recognize them when they arrive, yet there is no time limit on anticipation. Good things could come today, tomorrow or next year. But the feeling of anticipation is a positive one, full of hope and enthusiasm.

Trust That Everything Will Work to the Good

In a world filled with pain and suffering, having faith that everything will be all right in the end may be the most difficult thing that I've asked you to do in this book. So let me offer you some perspectives to help you set aside fear and distrust and look forward to the future with faith and hope.

If we define "everything will be all right" as "I will live a long and prosperous life," then I cannot guarantee that you will get your heart's desire.

If, however, we define "all right" as "I will continue to grow and experience the joy of fulfilling my spiritual potential," then I can, with absolute confidence, assure you that you will find the good you seek.

The purpose of each individual's life is to become the best, most fully developed expression of that individual's potential that is possible. Or, to be more specific, the purpose of *your* life is to be the best *you* possible. This is achieved by developing your inner character qualities—*your* virtues—which in turn will heal your pain and bring you joy. No matter what life throws at you, you still have the choice to follow this path and live your potential. You don't need to have faith that the external world will be pleasant. You only need to have faith that whatever unpleasantness you experience will help you to grow.

Summary of Part Two:
The Power of Synergy

Honesty gives us the capacity to see what was missing.
Forgiveness gives us permission to speak it.
Compassion gives us the ability to understand it, and
Faith gives us the opportunity to turn it over to God.

I started this section by saying that I would tell you about four different tools of emotional healing. By now, however, you have probably figured out that these are not separate tools. They all work together with each other, and with every other virtue that your heart is anxiously waiting for the opportunity to develop.

Faith gives us the courage to be honest. Honest self-discovery helps us discover what we need to forgive, but it also shows us why we have so little faith. An attitude of forgiveness makes it easier to be honest with ourselves about what we have done and what those we love have done to us. Compassion helps us see situations through the eyes of those who hurt us, which makes them easier to forgive.

As we expand our capacity for each of these qualities, we enter an expanding spiral of growth. Each step forward in any area opens up new possibilities in all areas.

And it is not just these four qualities that will be strengthened. Faith builds courage and courage releases creativity. Creativity generates enthusiasm. Enthusiasm replaces anger as the energizing force behind our actions.

Honesty builds trustworthiness, which reinforces nobility, which creates confidence which releases joy.

The connections never end.

No matter where you start; no matter what qualities you decide to develop, you will begin to fill, one by one, all of the empty spaces in your heart, and heal the wounds you thought could never be healed. You were created to be whole. It is what you are destined to be. Whether it takes a year or a lifetime, you will achieve it.

Have faith.

PART THREE

Longing for Love

RETRAINING YOUR HEART

The problem with most relationship guides is that they assume that we are rational people and then give us rational advice as to how to attract another rational person.

But we aren't rational. If we were, life would be much easier, but our behavior doesn't often proceed from our logical minds—no matter how much we may want to believe that it does.

The way that most people find their life partner is to find someone they are attracted to, enter into a relationship, and THEN, if the relationship gets serious, go through a checklist of qualities that they would like their spouse to have, in order to see if the relationship has potential.

If you want to have a healthy relationship, you must do the exact opposite of this.

By exact opposite, I don't mean that you should start by finding someone you are NOT attracted to. I mean that you should do these things in the reverse order.

Start by figuring out what qualities a person needs to have in order to be a healthy life-partner. Honesty, Forgiveness, Compassion and Faith, from Part Two are just a few of the many you should consider.

The next step is to teach your heart to *recognize* these qualities when you encounter them.

Finally, through exposure, you can inspire your heart to be *attracted* to these qualities when you see them expressed in the people you meet.

Please note that I am not suggesting that you force your head to override your heart. I am, instead, saying that your head can *guide* your heart so that your heart and head can work together to create wonderful, nurturing, and long-lasting relationships.

The reason why it doesn't work to try to build relationships in the usual order is that if your heart is attracted to emotionally unhealthy people, then your heart will blind you to the absence of the qualities that you are looking for. Love is not blind, but the naïve heart sees what it wants to see, whether it is there or not. Teach the heart first, and it will see accurately, and love truly.

A Quick Refresher in
Why We Need to Retrain Our Hearts

If our hearts keep leading us astray, we have three options:

1. We can stop listening to our hearts and live our lives in our heads.

2. We can resign ourselves to a life of chaos and heartbreak, or

3. We can retrain our hearts to give us accurate guidance.

In Part One of this book, I explained that our hearts, the center of our emotions, respond to the presence and absence of virtues. Since this is such a central point in understanding how romantic relationships work, it might be helpful to quickly review the issues involved. The next few pages will revisit what emotions are; how they respond to the presence of virtues; how this ability to perceive virtue is similar to physical perception in some ways and different in others; and how, like our physical senses, we can learn to identify and appreciate sensations that we were previously unaware of. Instead of just *understanding* our emotions better, now we need to *train* them to respond to healthy people and situations.

The reason why so many of us have difficulties in finding and building healthy relationships is not that our hearts are faulty, but that we have not taught them to look for the right things, and we have misunderstood the sensations they have generated.

Retraining, then, involves both learning and unlearning—*teaching* our hearts how to recognize and become attracted to the sensations created in the presence of virtues and noble character traits, and *unlearning* our attraction to unhealthy sensations. This unlearning involves being able to correctly identify the sensations we are feeling, and overcoming our culture's fascination with the sensations of lust and intensity at the expense of love and intimacy.

In Part One, I explained that we were taught how to identify emotions by our parents and early childhood experiences. Now I would like to revisit this idea from the perspective of the need to train our perception. Unless we understand how our hearts have been taught to recognize and respond to virtues up until now, we can't appreciate the need to retrain them so that we can recognize and respond in a healthier manner.

Hearts are Trained to Perceive Virtues

We spend the first five or six years of our lives calibrating our physical senses to accurately identify a wide variety of sensations. First we learn what hunger and pain feel like. Then heat and cold. Eventually we are given names for these sensations, and we learn to make ever-finer distinctions. Cold, cool, normal, warm, and hot each take on subjective meanings. Oval, circle, square; sweet, sour, salty; blue, green, purple. Children take delight in demonstrating to adults their mastery of these ever more subtle sensory distinctions.

Eventually we can be trained to distinguish between musical notes, the letters "b" and "p", and even the smell of roses versus lilacs. While some of the sensory training we go through is simply a labeling process, much of it actually allows us to sense distinctions that would have been invisible to us without the training. Musicians train themselves to hear subtle variations in pitch, cooks can determine what spices are in similar foods, and artists can pick from maroon, burgundy, wine, plum, purple and violet. Publishers can tell you what typestyle this book is printed in.

The ability to make these subtle distinctions in sensations requires time, training and practice.

In a very real sense, our physical survival depends upon our ability to distinguish between the sensations that signal health and safety and those that signal dangerous, disgusting or diseased input. Our instincts supply us with some of this knowledge, but much of it is only available as a result of conscious training. Our physical senses and the sensations they produce are a gift from God that allows us to function in the physical world.

Physical sensations are also a source of pleasure—the sweetness of an apple, the touch of a cool breeze on a cheek, the smell of cinnamon rolls in the oven. Sensations are much more delicate than is absolutely required for survival. They do more than keep us alive; they help us to discover the reflection of spiritual qualities in the material world.

The reason I am rambling on so long about the beauty, subtlety and value of physical sensations is to reintroduce the idea that emotions are *spiritual sensations*. I explored the broad implications of this idea in *The Secret of Emotions*. Now I want to look at it more deeply within the context of *relationships* and our ability to *train our hearts*.

While we train our children to identify *physical* sensations, we fail to train children in the identification of *spiritual* sensations, which leaves our hearts unable to accurately identify our emotions or the spiritual qualities present in the people we meet.

If God has been so kind and loving as to give us the physical senses we need in order to both survive in and enjoy the material world, would it not be logical to think that God would give us a set of spiritual senses that would enable us to survive in and enjoy the spiritual world as well? We are both physical and spiritual beings. Our physical reality consists of our bodies and our senses, while our spiritual reality consists of our souls and our virtues. Just as our physical senses tell us about the condition of our body and its physical surroundings, our spiritual senses tell us about the condition of our soul and the spiritual virtues that surround us.

This understanding of the heart as a perceptive tool that responds to virtues provides several useful perspectives in our quest for healthy relationships.

First, it gives us some useful questions to ask when we find ourselves in an emotional situation.

- What is this sensation?
- Where am I feeling it—in my heart or in my body, or both?
- In what other situations have I experienced this sensation?
- Can I identify an emotion associated with it?
- What virtues might be associated with this sensation/emotion?
- Are these reasonable virtues to associate with this situation?
- Could this sensation be caused by a misreading of the situation?
- What virtues could I apply in this situation to change my response to it?
- What virtues could I apply in order to increase my enjoyment of it?

Asking these kinds of questions allows us to train our hearts to recognize and respond to virtues more effectively. This is not an instantaneous process. We do not go from being blindly buffeted by our emotions to self-control and development overnight. Awareness of the process is helpful, but it does not replace time and effort. Making a conscious effort to ask questions about our emotional responses might seem too difficult, too contrived, too analytical for real life. Yet we ask similar questions when we try to improve our understanding of other parts of our lives.

You might gain an appreciation for the process and the questions outlined above by relating them to the process of becoming a master chef. Think of emotions as being flavors and virtues as being spices. Most of us eat dozens of different foods every day and have a general idea of what flavors we enjoy, but very few of us understand or appreciate the complex interplay between base ingredients, spices, leavening, temperature, texture, and so forth that makes the difference between edible food and aesthetic cuisine. Wave a spice bottle under my nose and I can identify garlic, pepper, cinnamon, clove, mint and half a dozen other favorite spices.

But with training and a love for the art of food, a person can learn to taste one bite of a dish and tell you exactly what ingredients are used and in what proportion—as well as making suggestions as to what spices might be added to make it even better. While most of us have a flavor palate of a dozen tastes, an expert can choose from hundreds of unique spices and ingredients so that every meal of every day is a new and wonderful experience.

Just for fun, let me rewrite the questions about spiritual sensations as though they were about food:

- What is this sensation?
- How am I feeling it—taste, texture, on my tongue, through the smell?
- In what other foods have I experienced this sensation?
- Can I identify a flavor associated with it?
- What spices might be associated with this flavor?
- Are these reasonable spices to associate with this type of food?
- Could this flavor be caused by an unusual combination of ingredients?
- What spices could I apply to this food to change my response to it?
- What spices could I apply in order to increase my enjoyment of it?

Our culture's move towards fast food and prepackaged meals has impoverished our ability to identify and appreciate excellence in the art of food preparation. Our culture's shaming of emotions and obsession with physical rather than spiritual pleasure has impoverished our ability to identify and appreciate the breathtaking beauty of our spiritual reality.

We can think of our spiritual sensations the same way as we think about our physical sensations, and train our heart the way a chef trains his palate. But train it to do what?

We train it to identify and respond more positively to virtues.

In other words, we *teach it how to love God.*

For some of us, the phrase "teaching our heart how to love"

sounds blasphemous. Shouldn't we just listen to our hearts, and not try to tell them what to feel? Well, in a way we are. The heart, like your tongue, will taste whatever is there. It is our job to learn how to identify and appreciate the right things.

For example, most people don't like the taste of beer, whisky or cigarettes the first time they taste them. Our culture tells us, however, that these are tastes that "mature" people acquire, so, given time, many of us override our initial response and cultivate a taste for things that our bodies have correctly identified as unhealthy. Similarly, as children we often have very clear and strong emotional reactions to certain situations. Observing cruelty, for example, often makes children cry. Given time, however, we can shame, ridicule and retrain children to enjoy the abuse of other children and become numb to the abuse of themselves. By the time we are adults, we have already had our hearts trained. But do we want to follow the guidance of our current social conditioning, or do we want to retrain ourselves to respond in more loving, healthy ways?

It is not too late

❈

Is It **Possible** *to Retrain Our Hearts?*

Just as an adult palate can be trained to truly *enjoy* healthy foods, we can train our hearts to recognize and truly *love* healthy character traits. While it is true that some people will never like brussels sprouts, *everyone* can develop a taste for a wide range of properly prepared healthy foods. How could it be otherwise? If humans couldn't recognize and enjoy the taste of healthy food, our ancestors would have died out eons ago.

Likewise, if our souls could not recognize and become attracted to the attributes of God when reflected in the character and actions of the people around us, the human race would not be able to fulfill its role in creation.

We were *created* with an innate longing for God, and that longing can best be fulfilled when we allow ourselves to become attracted to the Divine Virtues reflected in the people around us.

There are those who will say that it is impossible to change
our attractions, but if that were true, then not only are we all
doomed to unhealthy relationships, but the very foundation of
religion is a sham.

The purpose of religion is to teach us how to love God—that
is, to recognize and be attracted to God's qualities. If that is what
we were created for, then it is irrational to think that we cannot
teach ourselves how to do it. If we can't learn how to be attracted
to the attributes of God in our primary relationships—the people
we will spend our daily lives with—then when, where and how
else will we do it? What good does it do to love God in the abstract
if we are unable or unwilling to do it in the concrete here and
now?

How I Discovered My Attractions Could Change

When I was in college to study art, I liked to think that I was
attracted to beauty and repelled by ugliness. Why would I want to
retrain myself? Shouldn't I just go by intuition? My teachers, I
thought, should just teach me how to get my vision down on can-
vas, not try to expand my vision.

Early in my freshman year, I was working in the pottery studio,
throwing a cup, when I saw a poster on the wall. It pictured a
Japanese bowl that was brown, lopsided and cracked. I thought,
"Why on earth would someone spend good money to produce a
full-color poster of such an ugly bowl?" I was taking a class in
Japanese art and culture that semester, but it was out of curiosity
rather than a desire to emulate their style.

Three months later, I was back in the pottery studio when I
happened to glance up at the wall. "My God, what a beautiful
bowl!" I thought to myself—and then realized that it was the exact same poster that I had found so disgusting just a few months
earlier.

Please note, *and this is important*, when I glanced up at that bowl, my automatic response was a heart-response, not an intellectual appreciation. I was not *thinking* about how pretty the bowl was, I was *feeling* an attraction to its innate beauty. Also, I had not *set out* to fall in love with a brown, lopsided, cracked bowl. I had not convinced myself that I *should* find it pretty, nor had the bowl changed in any way.

I was the one who had been changed by the simple fact that I had opened myself up to another culture. I had not consciously chosen to find beauty in Japanese pottery, but I *had* consciously chosen to expose myself to a new way of looking at the world. In doing so, I had increased the range of "visual virtues" that I was capable of responding to.

The point of this story is not that you should learn to appreciate cracked Japanese bowls. The point is that *through exposure*, we can train our hearts to be attracted to those things that we *want* them to be attracted to—the virtues that will make us and our relationships nurturing and healthy.

Once we accept the idea that *what we love* is not determined by *fate* or set in *stone*, we can take control of and responsibility for the promptings of our heart. We can choose what we expose our hearts to. We can open ourselves up to healthy people and behaviors. Because these virtues are expressions of our true nature, with enough time and enough exposure, we *will* become attracted to them, and we *will* find that they bring great joy into our lives.

This brings us to three critical questions:
- *What* virtues or character traits do we want to develop an attraction to?
- *How* do we recognize them when we see them, and
- *Where* do we go to experience them in a safe environment so that we can open ourselves up to them and learn about them?

Let Me Start With Some Basics

I'm going to assume that you are reading this book not so that you can go out and have a string of one-night-stands, but because you would like to enter into a long-term committed relationship.

With that goal in mind, there are a number of virtues or character traits that it will be important for you to learn how to recognize and be attracted to that otherwise might not be high on your list of priorities. Likewise, some qualities that are very important in a fling or trophy relationship may not be important at all. Good looks, hot body, expensive car, fashion sense, a biting sense of humor and even a captivating public persona all become irrelevant when it comes time to change a diaper in the middle of the night.

So what qualities *are* important? The four I described at length in *4 Tools of Emotional Healing* are critical: honesty, forgiveness, compassion and faith (in *something*), along with responsibility, attentiveness, patience, listening skills, humility, confidence, optimism, courage, joy and many more. Picture yourself ten, twenty and thirty years in the future, possibly with children, probably with rent or mortgage payments and health issues, dealing with all of the challenges that life throws at you. What kind of person do you want to spend your days with? What kind of person do you want to *be* in the future?

Thinking about these virtues, it is fairly obvious that jumping from romance to romance is *not* the best way to learn about them. These qualities are best observed in intimate friendships—especially with people who are *not* romantically available to you. Hanging out with people who are already married, are older or younger, or are otherwise unavailable gives you the opportunity to observe people objectively.

You might be surprised at how much you can see when you aren't jockeying into a romantic position.

Watching a group, even from across a room, you can see who talks and who listens. Is the speaker engaging or boasting? Are the listeners attentive or waiting for a chance to jump in? When they laugh, are they laughing at others or with others? Do they radiate confidence or vanity, humility or shame? Do they encourage others or put them down? Do they look nervous? Do they smile, and is it real?

Study people.

Some virtues are amazingly easy to identify once you step back and watch rather than trying to impress or seduce the people you meet. Other times, vices masquerade as virtues and it takes time, attention and insight to tell the difference.

Open your heart, but don't assume that you understand what your heart is telling you. Pay attention. Your heart will respond to both the presence and the *absence* of virtues, so just because your heart is moved by someone does *not* mean that he or she is expressing a virtue that you want to spend your life with. If your heart responds to that nervous person, that does *not* mean that insecurity is a virtue, but rather that you are accustomed to associating love with rescuing people. If your heart beats faster when you hear a snarky laugh from across a crowded room, that does *not* mean you are enchanted, it means that you recognize cruel laughter and it scares you.

Hanging out with friends gives us the opportunity to study virtues, but we really *don't* want to develop intimate friendships with dishonest, judgmental or cruel people. Unfortunately, most of us don't know how to recognize these qualities in a person until after it is too late.

In the physical world, we are carefully taught the difference between dolphins and sharks, even though our chance of encountering either is fairly slim. But spiritually, we are introduced to sharks every day and are expected to ignore any spiritual sensations that might indicate danger. Indeed, we are often told that these people are exciting, suave or hard workers, thus associating positive virtues with the spiritual sensation of fear. But when we open our hearts to them, we find cruelty, deceit and selfishness.

Stock brokers, for example, are often considered smart, hardworking, good providers, with an admirable desire to get ahead. They would be considered a "great catch" and a good choice for a friend. A Swiss university, however, discovered that the stock brokers *they* studied (there are exceptions, of course) took more risks, were more manipulative and more focused on damaging their competitors than a control group of convicted psychopaths. In this case, the quality we identified as "smart" was really arrogant, "hard-working" was really workaholic, "good providers" meant materialistic and a "desire to get ahead" was actually cutthroat competitiveness.

If our hearts told us to be frightened of such a person, our minds (and our friends) would tell us we were wrong.

Because our hearts have been fooled so many times, we have programmed ourselves not to respond too quickly or feel too deeply when meeting a new person. Our fear of being hurt or overwhelmed by unpleasant sensations has caused us to shut down our spiritual sensors almost entirely. We are, spiritually speaking, holding our breath in order to avoid the stench of the moral swamp we are living in. This response is perfectly reasonable, but it is emotionally stifling.

What we need is a way to know when it is safe to let our guard down and respond to a person. In other words, we need to know how to identify a person's virtues with our minds *before* we open our hearts too wide.

There are two steps to this, one emotional and one intellectual. Emotionally, we need to learn that it is OK to experience emotional sensations without naming them or acting on them. Intellectually, we need to increase our vocabulary so that we can eventually identify virtues when we see them and find the right name for them when we feel them.

Our culture has called many vices virtues and taught us to name many things "love" and "attraction" that really aren't. When we are too quick to try to identify a strong feeling, we can fall into the trap of believing we are attracted to a person or quality when we are not. I will describe some of the many sensations that we mistake for love later on in this book, but for now what I encourage you to say to yourself as you explore the relationship between virtues and emotional sensations is this:

"When I am in this situation, have this experience or am with this person, I experience a strong sensation that I feel compelled to integrate into my emotional vocabulary."

This lets you be "open to the unknown" without pushing you to respond in any particular direction or take any specific action. *Not* taking action gives us time to observe and study.

We observe what is going on with our minds and then we compare what we see with what we feel in our hearts. Over time, we will be able to correlate our emotional sensations with our intellectual understanding of virtues and name our feelings accurately.

Or, put another way, if we pay close attention, we can get our knowledge of virtues and our experience of virtues to line up and make sense. Then we will be able to use our emotions to tell us about the virtues we see in the people around us. We will also be able to use our minds to tell our hearts what our emotional sensations really mean.

When our hearts and our minds agree on what they see, and what they see is *good*, then we can feel safe and confident opening ourselves up to true intimate friendship. When we are sure that what we are perceiving is happy laughter, not cruel laughter, is compassionate sharing, not codependent complaining, is kindness, not manipulation, then we are on our way to developing the skills and the virtues that will attract intimate friends and lifetime companions into our lives.

Four Tools for Identifying Virtues

If we want our hearts to be able to trust our minds, we must start by actually making an effort to learn about virtues. How do we do that? Where do we go to learn the names and descriptions of virtues so that our minds know what it is we should be looking for? Here are four options.

A Religious Approach to Identifying Virtues

The first thing we need is a new vocabulary. One of the best places to learn the names and descriptions of virtues is in religious scripture. Though the world's religions rarely agree on theology or dogma, they all extol the value of virtues, and they do it in a language that is poetic and inspiring.

The stories, lessons, prayers and examples that can be found in the Holy Scriptures of the world's religions provide helpful tools in identifying, naming, appreciating and practicing the virtues that God wants us to develop.

When Jesus said, *"Blessed are the peace makers,"* He was naming a virtue. When King David sang, *"Justice and judgment are the habitation of Thy throne: mercy and truth shall go before Thy face,"* he was exalting virtues.

Religions help us define virtues by providing us with the names and descriptions of the virtues that God wants us to develop. You will not find these virtues in your economics classes, sports commentaries or studies of animal behavior. They do not include good looks, material wealth or power over others. Some—like meekness and selflessness—are completely counter-intuitive and at cross-purposes with our cultural expectations. There is a reason why God's Messengers were rejected by the people of Their time. They were calling us to adopt virtues and behaviors that people really didn't want to practice—things like *turning the other cheek.* But the virtues of God's Messengers are the virtues that our hearts were created to reflect. They are expressions of our true spiritual nature and are, therefore, the ones that will ultimately lead to our happiness.

Scripture does something else with its description of virtue: it inspires us. Reading the definitions of virtues from a dictionary might give you a more precise description, but reading the stories, proverbs, songs and poems of the world's great religions helps us integrate our intellectual and spiritual understanding of virtues. Our hearts are moved while our minds are expanded. We do more than *learn* about virtues, we *long* for them. Verses like *"Surely goodness and mercy shall follow me all the days of my life,"* make us hope for lifelong friends who would be good and merciful. Scripture may even help us imagine becoming good and merciful ourselves.

As we learn to identify virtues by studying the Holy Writings of the world's religions, we then have to look around us and try to recognize what they might look like in real life. It's like seeing a picture of a rose in a book, then finding one growing in a garden. The Holy Books describe virtues so that we will be better able to recognize them when we see them.

When you read scripture with an open heart and an open mind, your heart trains your mind to identify the virtues that move it emotionally. With practice, your mind can then help your heart identify when it is safe to open up in your personal relationships.

The Twelve-Step Approach to Identifying Virtues

When people think of twelve-step groups, they think that they are about quitting some behavior, but much of the sharing that goes on is not about the addiction, but about the virtues needed to kick the addiction—virtues like humility, strength, hope, forgiveness, compassion, service, detachment and faith. At meetings you will hear stories about these virtues, and witness people putting them into practice. Virtues take on a concrete quality as we watch them transform people's lives right before our eyes.

In church, virtues are a way to get you into heaven *when you die*. In recovery, virtues *keep you alive*. It is that simple and that stark. It is not about sweetness and light. Virtues are the weapons we use to fight our personal demons.

The other benefit of studying virtues in a twelve-step setting is that it gives us opportunities to practice making friends that are emotionally intimate without being sexually intimate. We see virtues being practiced by people of all ages and both genders. It helps us fine-tune our emotional compass.

The recovery community also uses affirmations to counteract the negative self-talk that many of us engage in. Many of these affirmations incorporate the names and descriptions of virtues that the recovery community has found to be useful in building healthy lives and relationships.

Using Our Life Experience to Identify Virtues

Now that you have a larger vocabulary of virtues from scripture, and have heard them talked about and seen them practiced in the recovery community, you can take what you've learned and go digging into your own life experience to uncover more examples of virtues and the emotional sensations they have generated.

Every relationship we can remember is an opportunity to learn something about what virtues look like. Instead of labeling relationships as good or bad, we can use our powers of discernment, combined with 20/20 hindsight to identify the virtues that each person did or did not have.

Were they kind? Honest? Generous? Supportive? Gentle? Creative? What is our evidence? What virtues did we *think* they had when we began the relationship? Why did we think that? What virtues did we see at the *end* of the relationship? If they weren't the same, how did we get fooled? What sensations did we experience when we first met? What did we *think* those sensations were telling us, and were we right? Can we now identify those sensations more accurately?

Are there patterns to what we are attracted to, and the ways we are fooled or confused? Do we often mistake pretty for sweet? Do we mistake wealthy for generous or arrogant for confident?

Now turn those questions around. How did we treat the people we were with? Were *we* kind, supportive, confident and loving? Do we mistake bossy for helpful, or needy for loving? What virtues could we have practiced to make the relationship more successful?

The goal of these questions is not to beat ourselves up for our relationship errors, but to mine gems of understanding from the most detailed and complete source of information we have access to—our own lives. If we are willing to look and ready to learn, then we can make our current and future relationships richer, more intimate, and more enjoyable.

Using Great Literature to Explore Virtues

While many characters in pulp fiction are two-dimensional, there are also some profoundly memorable characters, both good and bad, who exemplify the presence or absence of virtues. If we are moved by a story, we can be sure that there are virtues being explored. We can be passive readers (or viewers), or we can think deeply about why characters make the choices they do, what they might be feeling, and what this says about their character. As long as you remember that these are *imaginary* characters and don't go looking for your own princess or hero, you can learn a lot from literature.

That Was Easy... or Was It?

In order to have happy, healthy relationships, you simply stop looking for a relationship, then go out and learn how to recognize and become attracted to the virtues that make long-term healthy relationships possible. Once your heart is trained to love *these* virtues instead of being moved by shallow characteristics or imitation love, then you will only fall in love with mature, healthy people.

Now that you know how to do it right, you will never be tempted to fall for the wrong type of person again.

Right.

It is not enough to know how to create healthy relationships. You need to see the *whole* picture. That means that you need to recognize the sensations and behaviors that have led you into *unhealthy* relationships. These are the things you need to *unlearn*. Unless we discuss some of your old habits and why they don't work, and how to avoid temptations, and how they came to be accepted as normal behavior, you are likely to fall right back into old patterns.

LETTING GO OF OLD PATTERNS

Recovery groups don't just talk about how great it is to be sober; they talk about all the things that might cause people to slide back into addiction.

This section, then, will explore some of the many emotional sensations that we mistake for love, and why the things that masquerade as love will lead us astray in the end.

Our Love Affair with Lust

In Part One, I explained that the sensations that are most often mistaken for love are a combination of fear, shame and lust. This mix of sensations creates the sweaty palms, racing heart, weak knees and tingling groin that many people interpret as a sign from God that they have finally met their soul mate.

The belief that these intense sensations are signs of love is almost universal in our culture. If we want to have any hope of having a healthy relationship based on love instead of shame, fear and lust, then this mythology is one of the first things we will need to unlearn. We need to unlearn the belief, and, even more difficult, we need to unlearn the behaviors that our culture has taught us are the right and natural expressions of that belief.

Simply *knowing* that there is a difference between shame and love gives us the opportunity to make a choice, but it doesn't make the choice for us. If we were to ask our hearts if we wanted our relationships to be built upon love or shame, our hearts would surely say *love*. In the real world, however, it is often our bodies that make decisions for us without our consent. In the world of physical sensation, the choice is experienced as being between *intimacy* and *intensity*.

Intensity

In the long run, intimacy—and the love that makes it possible—is the more rewarding and healthy choice to make, but in a moment of passion, intensity makes a pretty convincing argument.

This chapter is my attempt to explain the difference between intimacy and intensity, show why they are mutually exclusive, and offer arguments for why you should let your mind and heart override the impulses of your body so that you can have long-term healthy, loving and intimate relationships.

Strong negative emotions, such as fear, shame and anger cause your body to release adrenaline and other stimulating hormones that create a state of physical arousal that I am calling intensity. It is a form of "fight or flight" response, which means that your senses are put on high-alert and your body is given extra energy to respond. Your heart beats faster, your palms sweat, you may feel weak in the knees, and your whole body seems to "buzz."

With your body in a state of hyper-sensitivity, sexual activity can be ecstatic, overpowering and exhausting. When movies depict wild passionate sex, this is the experience they are trying to capture.

This kind of sex might feel powerful and overwhelming, but does it feel *loving?* Jumping out of an airplane, riding a wave or skiing down a mountain may be exhilarating, but they have nothing to do with being attracted to a person's spiritual qualities.

If all of these powerful sensations are the byproduct of fear, shame or anger, then how can they be used as the foundation of a loving relationship?

The fact is, they can't. Fear, shame and anger are the opposite of trust, love and intimacy.

Fear is a sensation that tells us that the person we are with is dangerous. Shame is a flash of awareness that tells us that we are moving away from the qualities that we love. Anger tells us that we are being treated unfairly. It is impossible to feel fear, shame and anger at the same time as we experience attraction, trust, openness, intimacy, safety and well-being.

❀

Intimacy

If we want to enjoy having sex with a safe, loving, supportive and appropriate partner, we will need to replace our fascination with intensity with an appreciation for intimacy.

Fear, shame and anger generate sensations because they warn us of the *absence* of the virtues of safety, nobility and justice.

Intimacy is a virtue that is built upon the *presence* of these virtues, so it also generates a sensation. It feels safe, warm and affirming, and it increases in strength over time.

If we think of intense sex as a shot of whiskey, we could describe intimate sex as a warm cup of hot chocolate.

Whiskey goes down quick. It burns. It creates a buzz and it helps you forget whatever it is you are trying to forget. It is very intense, but not necessarily pleasant, and if you want the sensation to last, you will have to keep throwing back those shots.

Hot chocolate is warm and soothing comfort food. It is sweet, it has chocolate to release pleasure endorphins, yet it also has some protein, calcium and carbohydrates to nourish you. Just the smell of it—the *thought* of it, you might say—can bring a smile to your lips. You wrap your hands around it, sip it slowly, feel its warmth for hours, and remember every moment of it. You can also drink it every night without becoming addicted or ill.

We teach ourselves to drink whiskey; to find that whisper of sweetness underneath the overpowering burn of the alcohol so that we can experience the buzz and the forgetting that goes with it. We are told that intense sex is the best sex there is.

Or, we can teach ourselves to become connoisseurs of the sweeter things of life. We can *choose* to make the deeper, sweeter, more enduring sensations of intimacy the ones we strive for. We just can't do both at the same time.

Love is a light that never dwelleth in a heart possessed by fear.
— Bahá'u'lláh

⠗

This Is the Choice

Because they are mutually exclusive, you can choose a fear and shame-based relationship with the drug-like power of intense sex, or you can choose a love and virtues-based relationship that offers the sweet, satisfying and life-affirming power of intimate sex. But you can't have both at the same time.

If you were to decide that what you really wanted was intensity, then you would want to concentrate on those qualities and behaviors that help boost your adrenaline before engaging in sex. Fear, shame, anger and physical exertion are the four easiest ways to do this. You might go see a scary movie, engage in risky, dangerous or illegal activity, or choose a partner who is likely to hurt, shame or abuse you. Fighting gets the juices flowing too. Exploring the tingle of shame might also offer some interesting options— you could cross-dress, have sex in a public space, or have your partner spank you, for example. You could also try drugs or alcohol to alter the experience and make it more varied and intense.

Oh, there is just one word of caution: If you were to make this choice, no matter what you did, you would have to do something a little more frightening, violent or shameful the next time in order to achieve the same level of intensity. As with other drugs, your body gets used to adrenaline and requires more each time, which means that it is psychologically addictive. Even relatively safe activities eventually evolve into more risky behaviors when their goal is to increase intensity rather than intimacy. But boy, would your sex life be exciting …while it lasted.

Of course, if you don't really want to end up dead, burned-out or disillusioned before your time, you could avoid the addictive spiral of intensity and choose intimacy instead.

Good old boring intimacy.

Morally upright intimacy.

Spiritually uplifting intimacy.

Sexually stimulating intimacy.

Eternally improving intimacy.

Safe, warm, comforting, satisfying, transformative intimacy.
Intellectually and emotionally stimulating intimacy.
Spiritually uplifting intimacy.
Life-enhancing intimacy.

Once Chosen, How Do We Create Intimacy?

Intimacy involves a feeling of knowing and being known; of caring and being cared for, and of physical, mental and spiritual closeness. Intimacy involves sharing—not just sharing physical pleasure, but sharing time, thoughts, dreams, personal goals and spiritual priorities. The pleasure that comes from having sex with someone who knows who you really are—both the good and the bad—and loves you anyway, is more satisfying and long-lasting than the pleasure of intensity.

The foundation of intimacy is trust. Without trust, none of the other aspects of intimacy can be allowed to develop. So let's consider some of the elements of a relationship that will create the trust necessary to foster intimacy.

Honesty is the first. You must know that what a person says is true and that his or her words and actions agree with each other.

On a material level, this may be easy. But on an emotional level, honesty also requires us to know ourselves in order to be true to ourselves. A person who does not know his or her own feelings is incapable of being honest about them. This *inner* honesty is what I wrote about in *4 Tools of Emotional Healing*. Honesty implies a certain level of spiritual and emotional maturity.

Safety is the second essential element for building trust. You must feel physically safe from violence, disease and financial irresponsibility; emotionally safe from betrayal, abuse and abandonment; spiritually safe from self-centeredness, apathy and decadence.

Good character is the third requirement. Becoming intimate is a process in which people share their inner lives. There is a metaphoric "mingling of spirit," so to speak. If a person does not have a good character—if they are not kind, loving, generous, patient, etc.—then what they share will reflect their lack of these qualities and become a source of suffering and even spiritual degradation for their partner. Just as having physical intimacy with a person who is physically unclean can cause disease and even death, so too, emotional and spiritual intimacy with an unhealthy soul can cause spiritual and emotional illness.

Finally, commitment is of paramount importance. Every action has a consequence. Love, sex, intimacy—these all have the potential for long-term physical, emotional and spiritual consequences. It is not safe, it is not honest, and it lacks character to pretend that they only exist "in the moment."

Along with commitment goes perseverance. While it is possible to quickly recognize that you *want* to get to know someone, the process of actually getting to know that person always takes time. When we try to short-circuit the process, we often end up projecting our hopes on someone rather than discovering their reality. We fall in love with the person we want them to be rather than the person they really are.

Taking Time

The simple fact is that everything worth having is worth working for. "Work" involves both time and effort. Playing an instrument, playing a sport, learning to dance, learning to cook, building a house, building a career, learning to listen, learning to care— all of these goals require time and perseverance. Isn't it reasonable, then, to acknowledge that something as important and transformative as love, intimacy and great sex requires (and is worth) the same kind of effort? Think about it.

Spiritual and emotional intimacy develop in stages. We go from strangers to acquaintances, to activities partners, to friends, to close friends, to intimate friends.

"Instant spiritual intimacy" is a fallacy. It is a popular myth because it is very easy to project our fantasies on people rather than wait to see if a person's inner reality matches his or her outer appearance. "We have so much in common ... we think so much alike ... it was love at first sight."

No matter how much we want these things to be true, we can't know that they *are* until we spend some time together. If they are true, then the time we spend confirming our initial impressions will be a source of great pleasure and fond memories. But our initial attraction might just as easily be the result of unfinished business. Unless we have the help of an objective outsider, it will take time for us to work out what that unfinished business is. When we do, we will be grateful that we took the time to explore the source of our emotional connection before muddying our perception with sexual attraction.

Physical intimacy also develops in stages, and these stages should follow rather than precede their spiritual counterparts. "Instant physical intimacy" is really a form of exposure. There is an adrenaline rush that comes from laying ourselves out naked on the table (emotionally or physically) that has nothing to do with knowing, caring or moving closer, but a great deal to do with our deep longing to be known and accepted. If we do not establish our emotional safety first, then the vulnerability inherent in exposing this longing will only increase our fear and decrease our true intimacy

Sometimes our desire for great sex has to take a back seat to our larger goals. Sometimes sex has to wait until we deepen our connection with God, develop our virtues and meet some of our social obligations.

Responsible sex always has to wait until we are materially, emotionally and spiritually capable of making a permanent commitment. Waiting shows our partner and the world that we are ready to create a safe environment for nurturing intimacy.

So, are you mature enough to postpone sex until you are physically, emotionally, materially and spiritually ready for it? If not, then you can forget about having great intimate sex because no matter what your age, you won't be bringing to the relationship the qualities that make intimacy possible.

Having Your Cake...

I know what you're thinking—why not have *intense* sex now and worry about *intimate* sex somewhere down the road?

Because it doesn't work that way.

Why?

Because you are not a computer, and life is not a game. You can't push a "reset" button and start all over.

Because patterns and habits are hard to change.

Because getting used by different lovers makes you feel jaded and disillusioned.

Because using other people is a sign of irresponsibility and untrustworthiness.

Because you should not put yourself in a situation in which you are defined by your sexual behavior.

Because maintaining intensity requires increasing levels of risk, shame or substance abuse.

Because adrenaline is addictive.

Because risky behavior is addictive.

Because shame is addictive.

Because drugs and alcohol are addictive.

Because sex with people you don't really know only makes you desperate and lonely.

Because the people who are willing to have sex with you without really knowing you are desperate and lonely and not very nurturing.

Because other people will see your actions and begin to believe things about your character that will make it difficult for them to like and trust you.

Because you will observe your own behavior and begin to believe things about your character that will make it difficult for you to like and trust yourself.

Because it is hard to have a healthy relationship with God when you don't like or trust yourself.

Because the person you are looking for is not out there.

Because the person you are looking for is inside of you.

Because making babies is too sacred to do for a cheap thrill.

Because dying of AIDS is too painful to risk.

Because it can waste a lot of precious time.

Because it can waste a lot of precious years.

Because when sex *precedes* commitment, sex *replaces* commitment as the glue that holds a relationship together.

Because lust will blind you to a lover's faults.

Because shame can blind you to a lover's virtues.

Because it will deprive you of the joy of experiencing sex and intimacy for the first time with the person you truly love.

Because it will give you a variety of experiences that no single mate will be able to live up to, and will foster disappointment, jealousy and infidelity.

Because you deserve the best.

Now, while all of the preceding is true, it is also true that nothing in life is black or white. God is forgiving. You will not be damned to hell or addicted to a downward spiral of sexual promiscuity after your first sexual encounter outside of marriage.

But there *are* consequences to our actions. You *can* get pregnant, catch diseases, and start habits after only one sexual experience. Every time we behave in an unhealthy manner, it makes it harder to respond in a healthier way the next time. So why start (or continue) in a direction that will take you somewhere you don't want to go? What would you lose by making the right choice *right now?*

Contrary to popular belief, getting to know someone sexually will *not* increase your chances of making the relationship work. Many studies have indicated that living together, for example, actually *decreases* a couple's odds of having a successful marriage. Many couples remain married for a much shorter time than they managed to live together.

While some would suggest that this means that marriage is bad for a relationship, it really means that *people do not know how to make the transition from a relationship based on intensity to one based on intimacy.* Is it not wiser, then, to begin where you want to end up—with loving, honest, committed, trustworthy, safe intimacy?

What Do We Do in the Meantime?

If intimate sex is the best sex, and it requires time, maturity, commitment, character and the right partner, what do we do in the meantime? Freud would say that we would have to sublimate our sexual urges. I would say that we need to *elevate* them. After all, our desire for sex is a physical expression of our desire for love, and our search for love is a human expression of our longing for God. There are a myriad ways to express our longing for God— many of which are very pleasurable.

In its simplest form, sexual intensity is about physical sensations. Physical sensations are very important. They are the tools by which we prove to ourselves that we are physically alive and unique.

It is very important, then, that we not associate delaying sexual interaction with any kind of sensory deprivation. I mean, who would want to delay doing something that makes them feel more alive and unique? If that is how you think of the trade-off between intensity and intimacy, then your subconscious mind will rightfully sabotage your best intentions at every opportunity.

So what is the alternative? Remember, it doesn't work to *stop* doing something. Instead, we need to *replace it* with something better. But replace it with what?

The answer, I believe, is to simply take the next step. Our culture glorifies intense sex, but what we would rather have is *intimate* sex. The next step is to realize that what we are truly longing for is not the sex at all, but the *intimacy*. While we are waiting for the right time and right relationship to have intimate sex, we can enjoy an unlimited number of intimate *friendships*. Not only will they generate their own host of positive spiritual sensations, they will also help us practice the skills we need in order to be successful in the right romantic relationship when we find it.

Disclaimer:

When my editor read the preceding page, she wrote in the margins: "Ha! The spiritual sensations of a friendship could never be as much fun as great sex!"

This reminds me of the joke: "Aside from *that* Mrs. Lincoln, how did you enjoy the play?"

In most aspects of our lives, we judge an experience in its totality, not in isolated pieces. If you were to drink a glass of water and discovered dead cockroaches at the bottom of the glass, would you say "that was a great glass of water, except for the last inch?" Or would you say "that was disgusting!" When people talk about how great casual sex is, they are choosing to ignore the feelings of emptiness, shame, fear of disease or pregnancy and guilt that may haunt them for days or years after the few hours of intense physical sensation is a distant memory.

Is sex great? Yes...*when* you know you are safe, responsible, loved and committed. Otherwise, not so much.

Intimate friendship may not have the thrilling intensity of three minutes of orgasm, but it really is fun. Getting caught up in stimulating conversations, supporting each other, being of service together, these activities create opportunities to practice virtues that feel wonderful. Meanwhile, the hours, weeks and years of positive interaction they can bring have little or no down side. *Taken as a whole*, healthy friendships are much more fun than loveless sex.

Other Sensations We Mistake for Love

When we choose intimacy over intensity, we are choosing to base our relationships on true love rather than fleeting sensations.

True love is the recognition of, admiration for and attraction to the attributes of God in another person. There are, however, many emotional sensations that can masquerade as love. I have already talked about fear and shame. Others include need, pity, lust and attachment, along with many subtle variations of love itself.

We have been taught to call these sensations love, and we have learned to respond to them as though they were love. When we learn to identify them *accurately*, then we can choose to respond to them appropriately. Some of them we will want to avoid. Others we can enjoy, but enjoy for what they really are—interesting messengers, not the foundations for romantic relationships.

An exploration of the many emotions that we mistake for love will increase our awareness of the subtle differences between them. This exercise in emotional semantics will help us fine-tune our emotional senses, making us better able to identify our distinct emotional states and the virtues they signal.

Feeling Loved Is Not the Same as Feeling Love

Feeling loved is the sensation of being acceptable in our entirety. There is a sense of elation that comes from feeling good enough, and feeling of relaxation that comes from knowing we don't have to pretend to be something or someone we are not. Someone has looked in our hearts and seen a piece of God inside.

There is a confidence that comes from having our strengths confirmed and our weaknesses ignored. It is a wonderful feeling, but it has very little relationship to feeling love. It is entirely possible to be loved by someone for whom we feel little love. This is OK. We are not obligated to pretend to see qualities in a person if they are not there.

The problem is when we mistake feeling *loved* for feeling *love*.

It feels so good to feel loved that it is hard to walk away from it. Why would anyone want to burst the euphoria and come down to earth by admitting that they are not attracted to the qualities of the person who sees so much good in them?

Through a combination of guilt and denial, many of us go into relationships with people we are not attracted to, in whom we see very few admirable qualities, simply because we feel loved. Walking away from love is one of the hardest things a human can do. All of the songs, the movies, the books—and certainly, the people we are leaving—are telling us that if one person feels really strongly, then the other person just *has* to feel the same way or there is something wrong with them.

If you *do* walk away, the loss of euphoria combined with a feeling of guilt can cause a real crash in confidence and self-esteem. No wonder many people choose to stay in relationships they are not happy with.

Likewise, it is entirely possible to love people, i.e. see the qualities of God in them, without their being able to see the qualities of God in us. True love does not require reciprocity. Does a painting have to love us in order for us to see the qualities of beauty, harmony and balance in it? Loving someone who is incapable of seeing the good in you is painful, but that doesn't mean there is something wrong with either of you. You may have all of the wonderful qualities they want, but they just can't see them because something in their life has created a veil. Perhaps you remind them of someone who hurt them. Let them have their perceptions. Yours can be different.

When specific people do not appreciate your virtues as you would like them to, rather than getting defensive or depressed, it is helpful to focus less on feeling love and loved, and more on feeling loving and lovable in general.

❀

Feeling Loving and Lovable

While the feelings of *love* and being *loved* are specific to a person or quality, the sensations of feeling loving and lovable are more universal.

Feeling *love* has an object. It is a warm feeling in the heart that increases with the presence or thought of a particular person. It is like a spotlight, illuminating the qualities that we see in a person, and helping us discover even more hidden qualities by its light.

Feeling *loving*, on the other hand, is like sunshine. It makes us want to throw our arms open wide to the world and see the light of God in everyone and everything. As we learn to love more and more individuals, we begin to see their good qualities reflected in the world as a whole. Likewise, as we learn to see the qualities of God in the faces of strangers around us, we become better at loving the individuals in our lives.

When we love, we are looking for the attributes of God in the people and things around us. We feel *lovable* when we look *inside of ourselves* and see just how much we have to offer. Feeling lovable is a lot like feeling loved except, like loving, it is less person-specific. We can feel lovable when we are all alone. Feeling lovable comes with an inner calm, a general awareness that we are acceptable to the universe, no matter what individual people around us may say or do. While loving is a sensation of *radiating* sunlight, when we feel lovable, it feels like we are *basking* in that same light.

When we feel lovable, we are less likely to need to get into relationships in which we are idolized. Having a clear picture of ourselves, we can tell whether a person is seeing the qualities of God we *have*, or simply the ones they *wish* we had. We are attracted to people who see us for the children of God that we actually are. Feeling lovable also makes us less needy and less likely to use pity or guilt to attract other's affections.

Worship Is Not Love

Overwhelming love is not love. It is worship that is passing for love. There is a big difference between seeing the qualities of God in someone and making them your god. When love crosses the line from admiration to idolization it becomes impossible for mature love to exist. Human love must remain between two humans.

The person being idolized may enjoy feeling loved or resent being isolated on a pedestal, but in either case, it becomes impossible for him or her to admire the qualities of a person who has defined themselves as "less than."

Beware of any "love" that tries to make anyone "special." True love is about recognition of our humanity. Humans are humans. Every human is special. No human is more special than any other. If we use love as a way to feel better than other people, then that love is doomed.

It is one thing to say, "You are special to me" and another to say, "I love you because you are better than everyone else." These are subtle distinctions, but they are distinctions that make the difference between successful relationships and failures. They can also mark the difference between healthy love and dangerous obsession.

Love is about connections between people. Needing to be "better" than your partner or, conversely, needing to find a partner "better" than you creates a separation between the two of you. You can't truly love a person you have separated yourself from.

Love between non-equals is different. It *is* possible, for example, between parents and children or students and teachers. This love acknowledges that there is a separation or distinction in role or capacity. But this kind of love is inappropriate between spouses.

There are two kinds of relationship based on being "special" that are particularly sticky. One is when the person who loves you is the kind who tends to dislike everyone else.

I've had female friends who made a big point of letting me know that I was one of the few men that they could stand to be around. On one hand, this felt like a compliment and was a real ego boost. But it also meant that I was constantly walking the razor's edge. Would the next thing I said be the one to prove that I was just like all of the others? The constant fear of losing my special status meant that my adrenaline was always pumping and I felt energized.

The trade-off for this energy was that I was expected to accept a constant bombardment of negative statements about men in general without taking offense. If I expressed my dismay, it would just prove that I was not special after all. Feeling energized, admired and insulted all at the same time made this particular kind of "love" a deadly poison. This kind of "I hate everyone except you" approach to relationships is not limited to any one group of people. The critical and cynical are good at finding people whose self-esteem is susceptible to this kind of praise.

The other variation involves people who absolutely ooze love for all of their good friends. Their friends can do nothing wrong and everyone else on the planet pales in comparison. Their love is a brilliant heat lamp. The temptation to do whatever it takes to climb under it can be overwhelming.

I found myself on the edge of such a love one time and sacrificed one relationship to slide under its influence. I ignored dishonesty, irresponsibility, impropriety and a host of other flagrant problems so that I could hear this person tell me how wonderful and talented and creative I was. I stayed "perfect" for about two weeks. When I made one mistake, I didn't just fall off of my pedestal; I fell into the fiery pit. I could suddenly do no right. I was tossed into the cold and vilified among my friends for the next decade.

But that was OK because, standing outside of the blinding light of "love", I could finally see all of the things I had been willing to ignore before. My therapist explained that the "love" I had experienced was never really for me at all. It was a form of self-love called "Idealizing Narcissism." Having a name for it helped.

I learned the hard way what I should have realized long before: Feeling loved is not the same as loving, and *loving the feeling* of feeling loved is one of the most addictive drugs on the market. Recognize it. Avoid it. Warn your friends.

The ideal, of course, is to both love someone and feel loved by them. But if we are looking for absolute unconditional love all of the time, then the only place we can hope to find it is from God. Every other source of love is human and subject to change.

Pity Is Not Love

It feels good to care about other people, but there is a difference between loving someone and wanting to take care of them. We care for what we love, but we don't always love what we care for. The act of caring *itself* generates a sensation because it is expressing a virtue. Because it is a positive sensation, it is easy to confuse with love.

A friend of mine knew a boy in high school who was hospitalized after an accident. She didn't know him well, but she went to visit him anyway, just to be kind. She was the only one from her school who did. He was so grateful that she felt obligated to keep coming back. By the time he recovered, they were well on their way to being engaged. It was only after several years of marriage that she looked back and realized that she never *loved* him—was never attracted to his character. She felt sorry for him, and it made her feel good to feel needed. It is called the *Florence Nightingale Syndrome* but it can surface in any relationship in which pity is mistaken for love.

The flip side of mistaking our pity for love is to mistake someone else's pity for *us* as love. That is what my friend's husband did. She was there for him, so he felt loved. He didn't realize that pity and a sense of obligation are not the same as love and respect.

There are a lot of people who make this mistake. They try to get people to love them by constantly complaining about how awful their lives are, or by arranging their lives to be in a constant state of catastrophe. They believe that if people pity them, they will feel obligated to stay around and take care of them. This is the Jewish Mother Syndrome, but you don't have to be Jewish or a mother to use it on people—as my friend discovered.

Need Is Not Love

Need is closely related to pity, but it is more existential in nature. When people do not feel whole or complete or adequate as human beings, they often feel that they *need* someone else to make them complete. Two needy people can find each other and project onto one another the qualities that they think they need to be whole, but these imagined qualities rarely have anything to do with the other person's actual virtues.

Other times, a needy person can latch onto a *savior* or *rescuer* who believes him or herself to possess the right combination of qualities to fix the other person's life. In that case, one person mistakes *need* for love, and the other mistakes being *needed* for love.

Ultimately, we must make a distinction between two people supporting one another as independent human beings, and two people needing each other in order to feel good about themselves. A relationship between two needy people is like two half-people trying to become whole through their partner. It will not survive. A relationship between a needy person and a *rescuer* who believes himself to be a person-and-a-half is based on an impossibility.

If we think in terms of what the other person will do for us or allow us to do, then we *need* them—we don't *love* them. If we think in terms of how much better we will make another person's life and how useful and competent we will feel when we take care of them, then we feel needed, not love.

Lust and Attachment Are Not Love

Love is an attraction to a person's spiritual qualities while lust is an attraction to a person's body. Love is not limited to people of the opposite sex, to pretty people, to people of our age or race. Think about the person you are attracted to. Think about the virtues you have seen this person demonstrate. Think of a specific action that exemplifies this quality... then imagine that same action being done by someone physically unattractive to you. Is that action still charming? Attractive? Inspiring? Appropriate? If not, then it might not be the person's spiritual qualities that you are responding to.

If you are having sex with someone, what you are feeling might not be lust, but it might not be love, either. We call sex "making love," but of course sex cannot create love where love does not already exist. What it can do is generate physical attraction and emotional attachments.

This aspect of sex can help keep good relationships from falling apart when they hit temporary challenges. That makes it a useful survival tool for new marriages. It can also hold bad relationships together just long enough to convince people to get married. That makes it one of the biggest reasons why new marriages fail.

To get a feel for the difference between love and attachment, imagine magnets versus Velcro®. Magnets are attracted to each other, even from a distance. When they come together they stick, but you can pull them apart and the attraction remains. They will always return to each other. With Velcro®, there is no attraction, but once the two parts come together (i.e. have sex) then it becomes very difficult to separate them. Yet even in the throes of this attachment, there is this undercurrent that says, "If I ever let go, I'll never see you again." Pull Velcro® apart, and there is no invisible connection working to bring the parts back together.

How many couples have ended their relationships, only to discover that they were never really even friends?

Playing What If?

Perhaps one of the simplest ways to get a sense of what emotion our relationships are based on is to take a few moments and imagine what it would feel like if the relationship were to end, either by the other person's choice or our own.

Relationships based on pity will generate guilt when we contemplate ending them ourselves. If we worry about how guilty we would feel for breaking up with a person, and how bad *they* would feel, then we feel pity and obligation, not love. Likewise, if imagining them breaking up with us gives us a feeling of freedom or relief, then we know that we don't really love them.

On the other hand, if we find ourselves thinking that we cannot live without the other person and that life would be ruined if they were to leave us, then we feel need, not love.

Assuming that a relationship is still fairly new, the thought of saying good-bye to someone we love should generate a sense of deep sadness and loss, but not overwhelming grief, guilt, relief, hopelessness, worthlessness, abandonment, shame or sexual arousal. We should be able to sincerely wish them well and hope that they choose to return, but be able to continue with our own lives if they don't. A relationship can only work if it works for *both* people. A person can't be *your* one-and-only true love unless you are *theirs*.

Avoiding Abusive Relationships

It is impossible to go out looking for a healthy relationship without running the risk of getting sucked into a nightmare. Life is like that. There are excellent resources online for helping you avoid or get out of abusive relationships but they do little good if you don't recognize any of the major warning signs in advance. No one expects to find themselves in an abusive relationship and most people don't even realize that they are in one until some line is crossed. By then, they often feel it is too late to get out.

So the first thing you need to know about abusive relationships is that they can happen to YOU. I know a woman who wrote a PhD. dissertation on domestic violence in the Hispanic community and only realized afterward that what she had written described her marriage. Abuse crosses all economic, racial, religious, national and gender lines. You are not immune, but you can be inoculated if you pay attention.

Earlier I talked about the difference between need and love, and the difference between being worshipped or made special and true love between equals. One of the most common traps that good, loving people fall into is to become attracted to a wounded soul who has incredible talent, intelligence and potential, but who desperately *needs* someone who is equally special to rescue them from themselves. What starts out as "I need you and can't live without you because you are so loving and special," slowly devolves into the blackmail of, "If you were to leave me, I would do something horrible to myself or someone else." Finally it becomes, "If you threaten to leave me, I will kill you." The heady ego rush of believing that you can save someone who could do great things for the world blinds you to the pathology of the neediness and abuse.

Along this downward spiral, abusers also carefully isolate their victims from family and friends—both physically and emotionally. They will move to isolated areas, create friction with family and alienate friends. Abusers will try to make you feel helplessness and incompetent while at the same time sucking away your financial and emotional resources.

These are just a few of the external warning signs of an abusive relationship, but the most important signs are inside of you. If the thought of leaving generates sensations of either terror or relief instead of loss, then get help right away.

Filling the Emptiness

In the space between realizing that your old patterns and habits might not work anymore and the development of the skills needed to do it differently, there is a lot of room for panic. That's OK.

It is nice to think about learning how to identify emotions accurately and become attracted to the attributes of God reflected in the hearts of the people around you. Yet I have just listed about a dozen ways of relating to people based on shame, fear, need, pity, attachment, etc. that I claimed are not healthy. If, in reading my descriptions and reviewing your life you come to believe that many, if not most of your relationships are based on something other than love, you may be feeling a bit lost at sea.

So let me offer you three additional observations:

First, no relationship is either all good or all bad. You can need someone and love many of their noble qualities at the same time. You can be sexually attracted and emotionally attracted at the same time. Even the most dysfunctional relationship you have ever had has also had some spark of truth and beauty to it. Everyone reflects the qualities of the Divine, and every relationship is held together, in part, by that spark.

Second and third, it is likely that while you are in transition you will be visited by two uncomfortable sensations: loneliness and anxiety. In this next section, I would like to help you make friends with them.

Overcoming Loneliness

One of the many nice things about developing intimate friendships is that when we have friends, we are less likely to enter into unhealthy romantic relationships simply to avoid feeling lonely. Of all of the sensations that are mistaken for love, perhaps "not lonely" is the most common, and the most empty.

In order to understand loneliness, we need to understand why it is we feel the need to be around people in the first place. For me, there are two reasons. The first is that I need other people to mirror back to me who I am.

If I am creative, or of service to the world and I have no one to share it with, how do I know if I am really creative or not? How do I know I've been of service? God does not generally whisper in my ear or pat me on the back, so I have come to rely on other people to tell me when I am doing well. In a sense, I make other people the mediators of God's approval. I subconsciously try to please God by impressing the people around me.

The second reason I need to be with people is closely related to the first. I have a deep longing to exercise my spiritual capacity; to practice the virtues that God gave me. But most human virtues have to do with how we interact with other souls. I cannot be kind in isolation. It is difficult to be of service while hiding in my room. Generosity, forgiveness, compassion, patience, respect, cooperation, these all involve other people.

So we need human contact, not just to receive positive feedback, but to develop our spiritual potential through the process of giving of ourselves.

Without that human contact, many of us become anxious because we fear we may simply disappear. We fear that without human mediators, we will become invisible to God, and without opportunities to *give* of ourselves we will slowly cease to *be* ourselves.

When we understand the dynamics of our discomfort, we can approach loneliness from three different directions.

First we can forgive ourselves for needing other people. It is not a weakness. It is part of being human.

Second, even though it is natural to seek positive feedback, it is not good to get *all* of our feelings of value from other people. We need to find a higher source for validation—either ourselves or a higher power.

Third, when we *have* to be alone, we can focus on the many virtues that do *not* require the presence of other people. This makes us feel alive and present instead of invisible.

Let me explain these points more fully.

#1: Forgiving Ourselves

Our culture values rugged individualism. We are not supposed to need anyone else. We should be brave and confident and not care a hoot what anyone else thinks about us.

Right.

That may sound noble, but in reality it just makes us feel guilty when our natural need for human support surfaces. Remember, *no man is an island.*

One night, as I was struggling with this conflict between my need for human feedback and my desire for independence, I flashed on an image of myself as the filament in a light bulb. Here I was putting out all of this light, but insisting that I didn't need any mirrors to reflect back to me how I was doing. Well, if a light bulb doesn't have anything to bounce its light off of, not only is the light pretty useless, but from the filament's point of view, it can't see any light at all. All it knows is that it is standing in the middle of a vacuum and its heart is on fire.

We all need to see the effect of our efforts, and for most of us, that means we need to see at least some of the people whose lives we touch. We are told not to hide our light under a bushel. Neither should we burn ourselves out in a vacuum.

So it is OK to need to be around people who give us positive feedback about who we are and how we are doing.

#2: Finding a Higher Source of Validation

It is good to be able to get at least *some* of your self-esteem from inside yourself. If you depend completely on other people to make you feel good about yourself, then you may find yourself doing things that you don't want to do just to make them happy. You need to know who you are and what you stand for, even when no one else does.

Early in my recovery, I became best friends with a woman who had spent several weeks in a rehabilitation center for codependency. She told me that one of the exercises they had her do was to wear a sign that said, "No male contact." This sounded very difficult to me. I said, "It must have been hard to go a week without touching or hugging a single man." She snorted and said, "You don't understand. I was not allowed *any* contact: no verbal contact, no eye contact, no interaction whatsoever with any male resident or staff."

I remember it clearly. We were driving down a desert highway in New Mexico when she said these words, and as their meaning registered, a panic descended upon me. I felt as though the earth had opened up a bottomless pit in front of me and a howling wind was trying to suck me into it. Just the thought of not having at least one woman look at me every single day felt like soul-death to me. I couldn't imagine surviving it.

So, of course, I knew I had to try it.

It took several weeks for me to build up my courage and arrange my affairs so that I could cut myself off from all human contact for a week, but I did it. No calling friends, no flirting with store clerks or waitresses, no dancing. Just reading, praying and working in my apartment.

I discovered that I really didn't need anyone else to mediate my relationship with God. Even with no one looking at me, I did not disappear or have an anxiety attack. I was who I was, even when I remained by myself for an extended period of time. By seeing myself through my own eyes, I began to get the sense that God *also* saw me through a different set of eyes than the people around me—eyes that were a lot less judgmental than my own or anyone else's. It is good to have self-esteem. But it is even better to know that you have the esteem of the One Who created you.

If you feel the need to constantly surround yourself with people, as I did, then you might find the experience useful.

#3 Finding Virtues We Can Practice Alone

One of the insights that would have helped me get through that week is the realization that part of my need to be around people comes from my need to practice virtues. What I know now is that there are many virtues that do *not* require the direct presence of other people. When I am feeling lonely now, I focus on virtues like creativity, curiosity, knowledge, faith, perseverance, gratitude and many others.

My first therapist gave me an assignment of spending one hour a night doing something creative. Since I'm an artist and writer, you might think this would be something I did all the time anyway. It is strange, though, how, when we are lonely and depressed, we tend to avoid doing the very things that we know make us happy. Creativity is a virtue, and also one of the core attributes of God, so allowing ourselves to express our creativity helps fill the void we feel when our longing for people overshadows our longing for God.

There are also virtues that can be expressed towards people, but at a distance. Research has shown, for example, that writing a letter of gratitude to someone in our past can improve our mood for months, even if we don't deliver it to them face-to-face. This is because practicing a virtue draws us closer to God, even if no one ever knows about it.

Overcoming Anxiety

Loneliness and anxiety often appear together and both can cause a level of desperation in our search for healthy relationships. I'd like to explain the connection and offer some remedies.

When I describe shame, I compare it to the sensation of unexpectedly stepping off of a curb. It is the uncomfortable feeling that you are suddenly falling away from God, virtue and your highest potential. We feel it when we have just done or are contemplating doing something that is not in harmony with our longing for God. If we think about it for a moment, we can name exactly what behavior we are ashamed of.

Anxiety, on the other hand, is the result of a long, slow drift away from God and our spiritual potential. There is no single action or activity that has severed our feeling of connection with God. Rather, we simply wake up in the morning and sense that something is not quite right, that we are heading in the wrong direction; that something bad is going on, but we can't quite put our finger on it.

Psychologists accurately characterize anxiety as a low-grade fear response. What they haven't quite grasped is *what* it is that we are afraid of. Many people feel anxious when there is no rational reason to be afraid. Their material needs are met, their jobs are lucrative, their family is fine, their health is good, and yet they are still anxious.

This is because the fear at the root of anxiety is not about our physical well-being, but our spiritual progress. Anxiety is the subconscious awareness that our longing for God is not being attended to. If we neglect our relationship with God, then we run the risk of drifting farther and farther away from our spiritual reality. We lose contact with the Foundation of our identity and the Source of our virtues. There is nothing in life more terrifying than this. This fear will set the heart trembling and the limbs quaking. I'm not exaggerating. This is the sensation I experienced when I contemplated spending a week alone. I felt anxious because I subconsciously associated being alone with losing my connection with God.

So loneliness is one thing that can cause us to feel disconnected from God, but it is far from the only thing. The fact is, we can be surrounded by people and still have our minds so focused on our material pursuits that our souls feel completely adrift.

While our souls are created with a longing for God, our bodies are born with a need for food, shelter and a host of other material requirements. There is nothing wrong with putting forth a lot of effort to meet those needs. But if that is the *only* thing we focus on as we go through our daily routines, then over time we will feel more and more connected to the material world and less and less connected to our spiritual reality. If we don't focus at least a little bit of attention on our spiritual needs, then even if we do everything *right* in a material sense, we will subconsciously sense that something is wrong.

There are three simple ways to keep ourselves focused on our connection with God. The first is to set aside some time each day to pray and meditate. Consciously turning towards the Transcendent is a good reminder that there is more to life than pursuing our material needs.

The second is to remember to work on developing the virtues that I described in *4 Tools of Emotional Healing*.

The third way is to continue doing many of the material things you are currently doing, but find a way to put them into a spiritual context. You see, the things we do, in and of themselves, do not draw us closer or farther from our spiritual reality. It is the *motivation* behind what we do that makes the real difference.

If, for example, you pray in the hope of getting rich, then prayer, for you, is a material pursuit. On the other hand, if you go to work each day in order to serve humanity, then your material work becomes a form of worship and is a spiritual pursuit.

When you look at your daily routine in the light of your longing for God, there are some things that you will want to *stop* doing, some things you will want to *start* doing, and a whole lot of things that you will have to *continue* doing. For each of these, try to discover a spiritual benefit or deeper meaning behind it.

If we work to be of service, eat in order to nourish the Human Temple, play in order to connect with our family and friends, read in order to increase our knowledge or deepen our understanding of the human condition, listen to music in order to uplift our hearts, and do all of the other things we do each day as an expression of our love of God, then we will not find ourselves drifting into anxiety. From the outside, our lives might not change much at all, but from the inside, we will be strengthening our connection to the world of the Spirit and letting go of our attachment to the world of dust.

Of course in practice, few people can maintain a spiritual focus every moment of the day. It helps, though, if even once or twice a day you think to yourself, *"Why am I doing this?"* When you can relate your actions to the expression of a virtue, you will forge a link between your material actions and your higher spiritual goals. Without this link, life can lose its meaning.

When we approach our commitments and responsibilities with an aspiration to bring compassion to the world around us, any action, no matter how small or seemingly insignificant can be meaningful.
        — *His Holiness the 17th Karmapa*

There Are No Deadlines

One of the sources of unnecessary anxiety is our culture's insistence that if you aren't in a romance, then you are drifting farther and farther away from your God-given destiny; that if you don't find your true love by the time you are thirty, then all of your dreams will crumble to dust.

But there are no deadlines for love.

It is much better to spend the next ten years living a life of personal growth and discovery than to get married to the wrong person and then spend years trying to correct the damage you caused.

When I was in my twenties, I was desperate to be married so I could have children before I turned thirty. This desperation led me to get married at 26, only to be divorced at 33. In my thirties, I was desperate to be married again so my wife could have children before we turned forty. I was fortunate to find the *right* person at 38, and my wife had two healthy children *after* she turned forty. Now, at 56, I have adult stepchildren, two teenage kids, a grandchild and enough maturity to deal with all of them. If I live as long as my mother did, I have another 30 good years ahead of me—enough to see my kids through college and probably lots of grandchildren.

But what if I hadn't gotten married at 38? What if I got too old to have the biological children that I dreamed of? Think about this: do you really want to get the family and children you planned for, but screw them all up because neither you nor your spouse is emotionally healthy or spiritually suited for each other? If you were forced to choose, wouldn't you rather change your plans and build a different dream?

If your biological clock really does run down, or some other twist of fate means that your life goals get postponed or set aside for twenty or thirty years, it really isn't the end of the world. History is full of people who made their contributions to the world late in life. If you can't have the children you want, you can still adopt or find other ways to contribute love to the planet.

Life is long.

Take your time.

It is important to become the kind of person who can lovingly parent children *before* you look for someone to have sex with.

It is better to spend the last few years of your life with someone you really love than to spend fifty years with someone you pity, need or despise.

HOW TO FIND LOVE

OK, you are working on being attracted to virtues, you are aware of the many sensations that can masquerade as love, you have dealt with loneliness and anxiety, and you are not desperate. You are beginning to like yourself, you are dealing with old family patterns, and you think you are becoming the kind of person that can attract an emotionally healthy person. Now what?

First of all, congratulate yourself. You are already dealing with the most important issues and are far ahead of most people who are desperately looking for love.

Second, appreciate the fact that knowing that real love is a response to a person's virtues will change everything about the way you look for love. Knowing that the sensations that you associate with love are often misleading or inaccurate protects you from wasting time on unhealthy relationships. Nothing else I can tell you will make as big a difference in your future relationships as these two insights.

What I can offer from here on out are secondary observations that apply these two ideas to the process of looking for a life partner.

My first piece of advice is practical, not psychological: get out of the house. Find something interesting to do at least three nights a week—even if it is with people who are not the right age. Not only can you learn about virtues from them, but they all have friends, relatives and coworkers. If you impress them with your maturity and character, they will introduce you to someone else who has impressed them.

Signs, Signs, Everywhere a Sign

My second piece of advice is psychological, but Carl Jung would not approve: *Don't* look for "signs."

If you are a pragmatic person, you probably don't know what I'm talking about, but if you are the kind who is waiting for God to send you your one true love, then you know exactly what I mean.

On my path to finding the "right" woman, I dated one because she had the same vanity plate on her car that I had tried to get. I dated one who had a similar first name and birthday as mine. I dated one who had a similar *last* name as mine. I dated at least four who had had dreams that we were to marry. I dated one who made my knees weak, and another who made my fingers tingle. I dated four Susan's in a row and five variations of Kathy in a row. I dated one woman because we both liked The Beatles. I dated another because we both used the made-up word "fantabulous" *and* had the same Transcendental Meditation mantra. (I was young.) I dated one redhead whose hugs were so soft and warm that I just wanted to melt into her arms—until I realized I was really in love with her down jacket.

In short, I took anything and everything as a sign that God wanted me to try to make a relationship work—that the feelings I was feeling must be true love, not lust or confusion or wishful thinking. Yet none of these relationships worked out.

It wasn't until I stopped looking for signs and started using my head and heart in harmony that I found/created a relationship that worked, and is still working.

Forget "Soul Mates"

One of the reasons why we look for signs is that we believe that there is "one special person" who we are destined to meet and fall in love with. We think that if we miss the signs, then we doom ourselves to loneliness and misery. It was Aristotle who said, *"Love is composed of a single soul inhabiting two bodies."* People have been looking for their other half ever since. Of course, if you review his record, Aristotle was wrong about just about everything—including this.

It takes two whole people to enter into a healthy relationship. If we *think* we have found our soul mate, then we have probably found one of our parents in disguise.

Everyone has the capacity to reflect the attributes of God, so we can love anyone. On a planet with almost seven billion people, the search for the "right one" is hopeless. Just trying will make us anxious and desperate. But when we realize that that same seven billion includes *millions* that would be perfectly compatible if we put forth the effort, then we can relax and enjoy the search.

Get an Outside Perspective

I encourage you to do the one thing that people who *think* they are in love are loath to do: get a third (fourth and fifth) opinion. For this, I encourage you to consider a professional therapist, as well as parents, siblings and trustworthy friends.

By "getting a person's opinion" I don't mean you should ambush them with the news that you are in love and ask for their blessing. I mean you should ask someone you respect to share their opinion about your partner's character; what they think the strengths and weaknesses of the person (and a potential relationship) might be. If they say good things, ask for examples. If they say bad things, ask for examples. If they say nothing ... well, you know what that means.

To be honest, I did not ask my friends' opinions. Instead I made an agreement with my therapist. I had been dating women non-stop for four years. At the end of my next-to-last relationship, my therapist asked me if I might have been able to predict the outcome earlier.

I had to admit that I was fully aware of all of the reasons why the relationship was doomed even before I entered it, yet the "signs" and my own wishful thinking had led me into it anyway.

So my therapist and I made a deal: I would not consider another woman romantically unless I could describe her to my therapist and answer probing questions about her *before* I got romantically involved.

As it turned out, I did not need my therapist's brilliant insights and probing questions to figure out that the next several women I thought about dating were not a good idea. All I had to do was imagine myself describing them to my therapist. I already knew exactly what the fatal flaws in the relationships were before I even started them.

After having gone from one relationship to another for four years, it was six months before I dated again. When I finally brought a name to my therapist, I didn't even really need her approval (though I got it). I knew that this person was different from the rest because I had entered into the friendship differently. This was the woman I decided to marry, and we are still together eighteen years later.

Make Lists

If you don't know what you want, you will waste a lot of time and heartache chasing something else. When I encourage you to make a list, I don't mean that you should decide what your ideal partner will look like or any of the incidentals. Your list should include your bottom-line requirements. It is OK to have a second-ary list of "wouldn't it be nice if..." but if you go for that and ignore your non-negotiables, you will be doing yourself and your relationships a disservice.

Here is my list. It included four lifestyle requirements and four values requirements, but yours may not be the same. That is for you to decide, though I hope that this book has given you some valuable insights into what you want to spend your life with.

Willing to join my religion.
Willing and able to have children.
Willing to participate in couple's therapy.
Non-smoker.
Both intelligent and sweet.
Honest.
Responsible with money.
Single, female.

At the time, I had not developed my thoughts on honesty, for-giveness, compassion and faith, but I suspect my understanding of "sweet" included elements of compassion and forgiveness. "Join my religion" certainly included an openness to faith, so in many ways my old list included the same qualities I would look for today.

Though there are only eight things on this list, the "join my religion" requirement quickly eliminated almost everyone on the planet. My fear that there would be no one in the world who both met my minimum requirements and would be willing to commit to me drove me to compromise on one or more of these require-ments in relationship after relationship.

As a result, I wasted years of time and lost a great deal of integ-rity by pursuing inappropriate and ill-fated relationships. I can't guarantee you that sticking to your minimum requirements will magically make your perfect match appear, but I *can* guarantee you that *pretending* to be willing to compromise (just so you won't be alone) will *not* bring you what you want. It will anger those you have misled and call into question your integrity.

The last few pages may not seem like much in terms of guid-ance for finding someone to spend your life with, but combined with the insights of the rest of the book, it is much more than most of us ever dreamed of having when we set out to find true love. Remember to focus on virtues, and continue to question the hidden meaning of the emotional sensations you experience, and you will figure out anything else you need to know.

From Love to Commitment

For many years, my beliefs about love were entangled with my thoughts on marriage. I tried to keep myself from loving anyone I couldn't marry. I received a great gift when I fell in love with a married woman. I realized then that if I could love a person I *couldn't* marry, then I could also allow myself to love people I didn't *want* to marry.

I now know that love and marriage are completely different things. Love is like going to school. Marriage is like choosing a career. When you go to school, you can study anything that interests you—science, art, literature, history—you can find something to love in any subject.

That is how love should be. Everyone you meet has an interesting story and reflects a unique constellation of virtues. If you look hard enough, you can find something about them to love.

But marriage is like choosing a career. You balance what you enjoy against what helps you achieve your long-term life goals. You should never choose a career that you hate, but that doesn't mean that you will choose the career that you find the most stimulating. Some relationships are like French Poetry. They may express virtues that you enjoy experiencing, but that doesn't mean you can build a life around them.

As in choosing a career, it is not enough to know what you love. You also have to know what you want out of life. Do you want children? Do you need financial security? What country do you want to live in? Are you a city or country person? Do you smoke? These goals represent other virtues that you love. Some of these goals are non-negotiable and will eliminate a large number of perfectly wonderful people from your list of potential mates. That is okay. It is not a crime to balance your immediate passions with your long-term loves.

If you truly understand the difference between love, sex and marriage, then you can continue to love and enjoy a wide range of people after you commit yourself to be faithful to and build a life with your marriage partner. After all, we all have hobbies outside of our careers. You wouldn't, however, choose a hobby that would destroy your career.

A surgeon doesn't take up boxing as a hobby. A married person doesn't hang out with sex addicts. Trust is as easily broken as hands.

Building a Healthy Relationship

Once you have made a commitment, the work of *keeping* your commitments begins. Ultimately, the surest way to avoid temptation and remain faithful is to keep your current relationship as strong, honest and secure as possible.

While this is not a marriage manual, I do have a couple of insights that you might find helpful, starting with a reminder that there is a difference between the *sensations* that love generates, and love itself.

We all know that love feels good. When we discover the signs of God in another person—courage, wisdom, kindness, responsibility—then it is helpful that our hearts respond with a positive sensation that attracts us to this person and those qualities. The sensation is a message that says, "Look this way! Notice this person! Learn from these qualities!" The sensation makes us enjoy spending time with this person and lets us know that we have found someone worth investing time and attention in.

But a message is just a message. Once the message has been delivered, there is no need for it to stand around whispering in your ear. The sensations of love need not last forever.

Think of love as a fragrance. When you step into a person's life, you smell the fragrance and it pleases you. But in time, your ability to smell that particular fragrance fades. It is not that the fragrance has gone away, but your need to smell it, and therefore your *ability* to smell it has disappeared.

Now, if a completely *different* fragrance enters the room, then *that* is what you will notice. Perhaps the person you love smells like kindness, responsibility and patience, but now someone who smells like creativity and courage steps into your life. If you believe that the most important thing about love is its ability to generate sensations, then you will believe that you no longer love the first person and now only love the second.

The truth is, you may love them both. The question is, which have you made a commitment to? When you understand how love, sensations and virtues relate to one another, then you know that commitment trumps sensation almost every time.

Knowing that sensations fade over time, we can:
- Minimize the importance we give to sensations.
- Never lose interest in our partners. If we keep growing and keep exploring one another's character, then we will continue to discover new virtues and capacities that will awaken new sensations of appreciation and attraction.
- Shift our focus from love to happiness.

The sensations we associate with love come from being *attracted* to a person's virtues. The sensation of happiness, on the other hand, comes from *appreciating* those virtues. It come from an attitude of gratitude.

Think of the sensation of love as the scent of a rose, while the sensation of happiness is the beauty of the rose. Our sense of smell can become so accustomed to a scent that it disappears, no matter how hard we try to sense it. Our eyes, on the other hand, are never blinded by the beauty of the rose, even if we sometimes forget to look at it. We are happy when we are surrounded by virtues. Our partners are like a garden of flowers. We may not always feel the strong pull of attraction, but we can always choose to look for and appreciate the virtues they exhibit.

Please note that I am not telling you that you should try to *be* a happy person. Nor am I suggesting that you try to *make your partner happy*. I am asking you to focus on *being happy with the person you have committed to*. This is much easier than either of the other two.

Being a happy person involves learning to like yourself. That is a lifelong process. You will spend years discovering and struggling with your inner demons. That's your job. When you learn to appreciate your partner, you only have to deal with his or her *outer demons*. That's a lot less work. It is almost always easier to forgive other people's faults than it is to forgive our own. If we make a conscious choice to focus on our partner's virtues and strengths, it will be easy to be happy with them.

On the other hand, trying to make your partner happy is impossible. They have their own inner demons to deal with. We are not responsible for anyone else's feelings. Trying to predict and control someone else's emotional state "for his own sake" is the codependent's misguided path to happiness. You can't make them happy. They can't make you happy. But you can both choose to be happy with each other.

One step in the process of becoming happy with the one you are with will undoubtedly involve adjusting your expectations. We enter relationships expecting our new partners to fill our empty spaces and meet all of our needs. If our happiness depends on this, then we entered into our commitment under false pretenses. We enter into relationships with human beings, not solutions to our problems. The fact is, you may *never* receive from your partner more than a fraction of what you hoped to get. That is because, *whatever* it is you want, it isn't anyone else's job to give it to you. We long for God, yet we look to other humans to give us things that symbolize the things that only God possesses.

Here's the distinction you need to be able to make: There is a difference between a spouse who cannot or will not give you what you need, and a spouse who actively tries to take from you what you try to generate yourself. If a spouse is abusive; if they rob you of your dignity, self-esteem, security and identity; if their untrustworthiness undermines your well-being, then you need to go elsewhere. These are the abusive relationships that I mentioned earlier. There are online checklists you can find to help you identify these relationships, both before and after you get caught in one.

But...if they are unable to give you *more* of these things than you can generate for yourself, then they are simply human. Look to God for *these* things, and much, much *more*, and be happy with your spouse for being willing to walk the path towards God with you. That's really all that any of us can ask from another person.

The people who live in our fantasies are just that: fantasies. Even if we put a name and face and body to the fantasy, until we live with them day in and day out, we can't know if they would be any more able to meet our needs than the one we are with. Until we accept and love and support our current spouses on their path towards God, we can't know the heights that our present relationships might achieve.

Being Sexually Content

Often, the problem we *think* we have with our spouse is really a problem caused by our inability to make the transition from a relationship based on intensity to one based on intimacy.

As I've explained, a relationship based on love and trust and security generates a *completely different range of sensations* than one based on intensity. Many of us *start* our relationships with a sex-life based on intensity. Sex outside of marriage, though socially acceptable for many people, still carries the excitement, titillation and shame aspects of the forbidden fruit. Once a relationship is sanctioned by the church and state, much of that extra energy starts to wear off. If we expect sex to maintain that intense edge after marriage, then we begin to think something is wrong—with us, with our partner, or with our marriage. If it doesn't wear off after marriage, it often does after a first child is born and couples start seeing each other as parents rather than sex partners.

If we have a long history of sexual activity based on intensity, how do we change our habits and adjust our expectations?

The unfortunate answer is that once a set of habits has formed, it can take an incredible amount of conscious effort to re-educate our unconscious responses.

While I firmly believe that we can re-train both our physical and our spiritual attractions, re-training our *spiritual* attractions is certainly the easier of the two. Changing our expectations concerning the physical experience of sex is difficult. If we are young and our partner is understanding, then it can be just one more process of discovery that can be explored in the years ahead. If we are old and our expectations, habits and preferences are deeply ingrained, then it might be too much to ask of our partners to struggle through our process of transformation.

If one partner is drawn to excitement and shame, while the other only responds to security and affection, then there may be no happy compromise between these two needs. Or, if one is drawn to shame and the other is repelled by it, then even communication between the two may be impossible.

Most often, however, both partners were originally attracted to the forbidden fruit of passionate sex, and now that the relationship is sanctioned by God and consummated with children, there is no fear, shame or excitement left to inspire passion.

In this case, you have to decide which is worse: having a sexually tepid marriage, or having a marriage that is subconsciously conspiring to generate fear and shame in order to recapture the sexual tension of the pre-marital pseudo-romantic period.

If the thought of a tepid sexual relationship with your partner sends you into the kind of bottomless pit of panic that the thought of being alone gave me, then you may need to think about what that means for you. If you and your partner are both young, with only a few years of patterns to break, then reorienting your sex life around love and intimacy may be very easy. If you are older, with lots of patterns, expectations and habits, then it might take a lot of effort to change. How many hours, days or years of your life do you want to devote to this? If your partner is not as driven as you are to develop new ways of interacting, then it might be impossible to restart your sexual relationship on a more spiritual foundation. That doesn't mean that you can't build a more intimate spiritual relationship. It just means that it might never be as sexually satisfying as you fantasize.

Building Spiritual Relationships

Ultimately, our sexual relationship with our spouse is only a tiny sliver of our over-all relationship. It is only as important as we make it.

Our spiritual relationship, on the other hand, can support us in our individual striving after God, and can last on into the next world. If we apply the virtues of honesty, forgiveness, compassion and faith to our most important human relationship, then it can't help but improve over time. As our primary relationship improves, our temptations, obsessions, addictions and shame will become less of a distraction on our path towards God. Our spiritual relationship with our partner will help us heal our spiritual relationship with God.

Avoiding Globalizing

When we love someone, we are not just attached to them sexually. We are spiritually attracted to a whole host of interconnected virtues. One of the benefits of seeing our partners as this constellation of positive qualities is that it helps us to avoid globalizing.

I mentioned globalizing in the section on forgiveness when I said that we should not label an entire person based on one negative quality or action. The reverse is also true. When we fall in love with a person, we tend to globalize their positive qualities, which can then be used to mask a person's flaws.

There is an expectation in our culture that if you are going to love someone, you must love them *warts and all*. But that is not really healthy. We don't need to pretend to *love* a person's faults in order to *accept* their faults as a part of who they are. Trying to love *all* of a person is the kind of *all or nothing thinking* that led to perfectionism when we applied it to ourselves. When we try to use the same kind of black-and-white thinking in our relationships, it causes us to see our partners as either wonderful and loving, or the source of all of our problems.

If, instead, we see people as a constellation of virtues—some of which are well-developed and some of which are weak—then we can realistically adjust our response to each character trait individually.

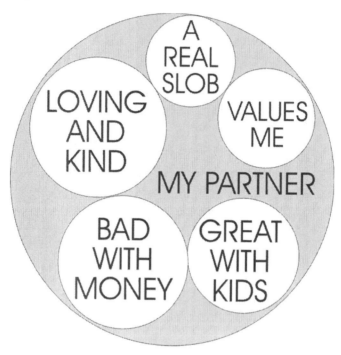

When we globalize, we only see one quality at a time. We alternate between seeing only good and only bad. When we see people as a constellation of virtues, we see all of their qualities at once, and relate to them as a whole person with strengths and weaknesses.

Dealing With Temptation

No matter how wonderful our relationships are, we will still face temptations that can undermine trust and intimacy. In many ways, dealing with *these* temptations is no different from any other temptation. From infidelity and pornography to overeating and smoking, there are many actions we feel compelled to engage in even though we know they are not spiritually, emotionally or physically healthy.

The best way to deal with temptation, of course, is to avoid it. In Part One, I shared this parody of our compulsive behaviors:

Find a cookie.
Tell yourself that eating the cookie is a bad idea.
Eat the cookie anyway.
Regret eating the cookie.
Deal with guilt by looking for more cookies.

The first step is always finding a cookie. If you don't go looking for a cookie, you are much less likely to be tempted by it. In other words, avoid people, places and things that send your mind or your body in a direction that you know is unhealthy for you. For example, if you hope to find or maintain a healthy, committed relationship, then avoid sex addicts, bars, massage therapists, adult bookstores and movie theaters, swimming pools, co-ed fitness clubs, web-surfing alone at night and anything or anyone that gets your hormones pumping.

Sometimes, though, the world throws cookies in our laps. Seriously. Unless we lock ourselves in a tower with no contact with the outside world, we *will* face temptation. So what do we do then?

For most people, the standard response is to "tell yourself not to eat the cookie." That is, throw shame and guilt at ourselves as a punishment for even *thinking* about eating the cookie.

This is counter-productive. First of all, if we are going to punish ourselves *before we even take a bite*, then we might as well go ahead and do what we feel guilty for. Second, the unhealthy actions—flirting, sex, pornography, cookies—are usually ones that generate a sensation strong enough to temporarily turn off the guilt and shame. So our desire to numb guilt and shame actually pushes us *towards* the behaviors they are warning us about.

Our first step, then, is to remind ourselves that it is normal to want the cookie. *Of course* we want a cookie. We are human. This helps defuse the shame.

After this, there are several alternative responses. We can distract ourselves, devise a long-term reward for refusing temptation, devise a short-term reward or consequence, or explore the deeper longing.

Distraction is certainly the easiest, but like most alternatives, it requires forethought. Often temptation springs out of nowhere and hijacks our rational minds with unexpected and intense sensations. Thrown into such a situation, it is difficult to focus on anything except the tempting opportunity in front of us. Whether we encounter it by walking past a bakery or walking past an adult video store, having a list of alternative activities or points of focus can be a real life-saver.

These could include:
Saying a prayer or affirmation.
Going to a 12-step meeting or calling a sponsor.
Calling a close friend to talk.
Working on a creative project.
Going for a walk or jog.
Taking a shower.
Getting a haircut.
Downloading a new song to listen to.
Singing a song to yourself.
Reading a book.
Thinking about your children or other loved ones.
Counting backwards from 100.

This last one might seem way too short to be of any use, but the fact is that most sensations only last a few minutes if we don't feed them with shame or fantasy. If we can get ourselves around the metaphoric corner, then we are halfway home.

Long-term rewards work for some people. The promise of going to heaven, finishing school and starting a career, having a happy and healthy family—these have successfully motivated many people to walk away from temptation and make healthy choices.

If those motivations worked for you and me, however, we probably wouldn't have lived the lives we have. That is why researchers in the science of self-control recommend coming up with short-term rewards and punishments (*other* than guilt and shame) to help us overcome our tendency to settle for immediate gratification. It is also why AA has a coin to celebrate 24 hours of sobriety as well as one week, one-month and one-year coins.

Depending on the temptation you are trying to escape, coming up with a way to reward yourself after one day, one week or one month of success is a great way to change your focus when temptation knocks.

Gentle punishments can also help pull us away from actions that are unhealthy—but be careful that your feelings of unworthiness don't cause you to slip up so that you can dish out the punishment you already think you deserve. Instead, be creative.

For example, I heard a story about two sisters. One smoked and the other didn't. The one who didn't vowed to donate $1,000 to the Ku Klux Klan if the other sister ever smoked another cigarette. The sister quit smoking cold-turkey rather than allow money to be given to an organization she despised.

You might try something a little less extreme, like giving $50 to a cause you dislike, or scrubbing your toilet, or doubling the number of 12-step meetings you go to, or confessing your slip to your sponsor or therapist.

Ultimately, though, I believe that staring temptation in the face and asking it to explain itself to us may be the best way to get it to back down. When we respond to temptation with, "Oh, I'm such a horrible person, I'm so guilty, I'm so ashamed," we are really being self-indulgent. We are wallowing in our own low self-esteem instead of looking at our actions objectively and considering how they affect the world around us.

☒

Dealing with Inappropriate Attractions

My friend Phyllis Peterson, author of **Remaining Faithful** and *Assisting the Traumatized Soul*, asked me to address a very concrete challenge that many of us face. She asked:

One facet of the challenge we face is learning to work together, associate together without sexuality becoming our focus. How do we act with maturity? How do we overcome an adolescent response to someone who may take our breath away?

My answer is that we *pay attention*. We look our uncomfortable sensations in the eye and try to name them accurately. We shine a light on every response that appears to draw us away from our highest good.

We remember that sensations are messengers, and that once the message has been accurately received, the sensation often evaporates. We keep no secrets. And in the meantime, we take appropriate action to protect ourselves and others from rash and foolish actions.

That doesn't sound like very concrete advice, so let me give you an example from my own life.

I was attending a workshop on the Authenticity Project. This is a very intense workshop that deals with the most profound levels of human interaction. The conversations between breaks were refreshing and stimulating.

There was one young lady whose comments were particularly stimulating. She was stunningly beautiful, had a French accent and was so full of life and energy that she was a joy to talk to. I was immediately drawn to her and joined her circle of conversation every chance I got. The problem was that every time I was near her, my heart would race and my whole body would go on high alert. It was embarrassing. I was a married man, and she was twenty years younger than I was.

I went to bed that night with my mind in an uproar. Why was my body reacting this way? Was I really that lecherous that I couldn't talk to a young woman without getting aroused?

If I hadn't already been aware of the difference between love and lust, I could have easily convinced myself that I was in love and that I should leave my wife and run off with this woman. Fortunately, I knew that sensations don't always mean what we think they do.

So I sat myself down and had a little conversation with myself. Did I want to have sex with this young woman? I took a serious look around my heart and concluded that I really didn't.

This reaction wasn't about desire at all. But if the sensation wasn't about sex, then it was probably that *other* sensation—shame. But why would I feel shame if I weren't already thinking about having sex with her? What was I ashamed of? Was I afraid I was going to be unfaithful to my wife? No. Did I enjoy talking with her? Yes. Was she intelligent? Yes. Was I going out of my way to talk with her? Yes. But if she was intelligent and fun to talk with, why shouldn't I go out of my way to do so?

Because it looked bad.

Oh.

I wasn't embarrassed because I wanted to have sex with her. I was embarrassed because I was afraid that she would *think* that I wanted to have sex with her. I was afraid of looking like a dirty old man, when all I wanted to do was have an intelligent conversation with someone who just happened to be young and beautiful.

Some of you are probably thinking, *"Who does this guy think he's fooling?"*

But I know that this was the source of my feelings because the next morning, I did the unthinkable: I told her.

I went up to her and said, "I need to tell you that I've been feeling uncomfortable around you because you are so young and beautiful, I was afraid that you would think that I was trying to flirt with you when I'm not. I just really enjoy talking with you."

She said, "Oh, don't worry. I didn't think that at all. I enjoy talking with you, too."

And suddenly, *poof!* All of those strange sensations evaporated. She became a normal human being. We spoke many times over the course of the weekend, and that was the end of that. No romance. No riding off into the sunset. No clandestine rendezvous, and no more shame.

Knowing What Love Doesn't *Feel Like*

I was fortunate that I could tell that what I was feeling was *not* love. That allowed me to go pounding on internal doors until I figured out what the feeling really was.

Knowing what it *isn't* is a valuable first step. If your heart is going pitter-patter, or your knees get weak, or your fingers tingle, or any of the dozens of Hollywood stereotypical sensations hit you over the head, then you can rest assured that what you are feeling is *not* love. That means that you can safely explore all of the other options without getting distracted.

If it's not love, you don't have to worry about leaving your spouse and destroying your marriage. If it's not love, then sex is clearly inappropriate. If it's not love, then it's not your one-and-only chance at happiness. If it's not love, then you don't have to *do* anything about it until such time as you figure out what it *is*.

If it's not love, you can honestly describe it as a *strange* or *uncomfortable* physical sensation. If you describe it to yourself in this way, it may help you name it.

You can also tell your spouse, *"I experience a strange and uncomfortable sensation when I'm near that person. Do they cause you to react in any way?"* This is so much better than, "I think I'm in love with the new person I just met. May I run off with them, please?"

Other possible causes for the sensations we feel around attractive people can include:

- Fear that we will be rejected by them if we approach them in friendship.
- Fear that they will accept us at first, then abandon us.
- Fear that they will treat us the way the family member they remind us of would.
- Embarrassment because they are prettier, richer, taller, stronger, younger, more talented, etc., than we are.
- Fear that they will be able to identify some fatal flaw in our lives.
- Embarrassment that they appear to be inappropriately attracted to us.

- Fear of authority figures.
- Subconscious recognition of the fact that they are predatory, abusive, sex addicts, dishonest or violent.

Remember, our emotions tell us about our spiritual environment by sending us signals—both physical and spiritual. If you are experiencing Unidentified Feeling Obsessions (UFO's), then there is probably something going on spiritually that you need to figure out. When you do, it will become a CSI—a Clear Spiritual Insight, and the sensation will fade.

❀

Can Men and Women be Friends?

Absolutely.

Can every man stay friends with every woman? No.

This is a question that requires a supreme amount of self-knowledge, perception and sensitivity.

In the future, I think this will be much easier, but right now, our culture is so focused on sex that it is difficult for two single people to maintain friendships, and those between a married and a single person can be difficult.

What I have found helpful is to remind myself that my soul and my body function in two completely different ways. As long as I don't let my soul be confused by what my body tells me, then I'm safe.

To be specific: In any interaction between a healthy male and a healthy female, there will come a moment in which their bodies will become aware of their sexual reality. It might be at first sight, it might be months into the friendship.

At that point, the soul has a choice. It can say, "Oh, my God, I'm sexually attracted to this person. What will I do? What does this mean? Is this the end of our friendship?"

Or, the soul can say, "Hmm. Interesting. My body just noticed the obvious. That is what the body is supposed to do. But it doesn't mean anything. Physical attraction is like a cloud in the sky. If you don't seed it with fantasy, it will simply blow over."

If you try to ignore the attraction, as I've said before, you just give it the power of secrecy and shame. If you look it straight in the eye and say, "Thank you for reminding me that I am alive, but I'm not interested in moving in that direction," then the attraction will usually kiss you on the cheek and walk away.

I have many, many female friends, including some of my previous girlfriends. I work with women, hang out with women, e-mail women, even dance with women. I stay aware of which ones I might be tempted by and avoid dangerous situations. I tell my wife about everyone I correspond with, and introduce her to as many of my female friends as I can.

She tells me which women she considers dangerous and I agree to not spend time alone with them.

My wife, in turn, has male friends.

Dealing with Compulsive Behaviors

What do we do if we find ourselves sexually aroused by shoes, cross-dressing, children, nuns, dolls, exhibitionism or anything or anyone that our religion or moral compass considers inappropriate?

The sexual arousal we associate with fetishes and compulsive behaviors are similar to the fight-or-flight response I described on page 193, but in this case they are caused more by the sex-related shame spirals I described way back on page 31.

After reading these two-hundred plus pages, you *know* that true spiritual attraction is not the same thing as fear or shame. So when fear or shame causes your body to react inappropriately, you have a choice. You can define yourself by the way your body reacts, or you can define yourself by the way you *want* to react and then make a conscious decision to behave accordingly. Even though you may not be able to change what you fear or escape your subconscious shame triggers, you *can* change how you respond to them.

We all have free will. We can choose to walk *away* from shame-based sensations rather than running *towards* them. If we find a *different* sensation to call attraction—a *warm and loving* sensation, then we can change *what* we respond to and *who* we choose to become lovingly intimate with.

In our culture, we call fear and shame love, and then insist that we can't change who we love. But if that were true, then women who are "attracted" to abusive men would be doomed to only be with abusive men.

That is crazy.

When we understand the true source of the sensations that we define as attraction, we can change our definitions. We can call spiritual attraction *love*, and shame-based attraction *arousal, lust, fear, shame* or *desire*. When we name them accurately, it is easier to choose between them.

⊗

We Are Not Defined by Our Desires

If I defined myself by my lusts, I would not be defined as a very spiritual being. During the years between my divorce and my second marriage, I came to realize that my desire for almost every single woman that I had ever thought I was in love with was based on some deeply-seated dysfunction. Because my older sister was mentally ill and sexually abused, and my mother was afraid of men, the women I was physically and emotionally attracted to were, without exception, some combination of:

Mentally ill.
Sexually abused as children.
Angry or fearful of men.

Because my father left my mother with a house full of children when I was just developing my identity, I also found myself desiring women who were considering divorce, or had just gotten divorced and had children at home under the age of seven. I could literally sit in a bar and point to women from across the room and tell you what their dysfunction was, based on my physical response to them. The soul is amazingly perceptive.

So, if I were to define myself by my "natural" desires, then I could call myself a:

Schizosexual.
Abusexual.
FearSexual.
And/or Divorsexual.

If this sounds like an absurd way to identify oneself, then you can see the fallacy in someone identifying themselves primarily by their emotional or physical desires. We are all humans, and we each happen to respond physiologically to different types of stimuli.

Big deal.

In Part One, I said that being able to accurately name and de-fine our emotions gives us a certain amount of power over them. This power of words applies to *us* as well. Defining ourselves by our emotional desires, especially if those desires are fear- or shame-based, gives those desires an excessive amount of control over our lives.

When we see ourselves as spiritual souls on a path to God, then it becomes obvious that *we* have the capacity to be in control of our attractions and our desires, rather than the other way around.

If I were to assume that my attractions are set at birth and are unchangeable, then I would be foolish to try to fall in love with or marry someone who is not crazy, abused, afraid and divorced.

If, however, spiritual attractions and physical desires are both the result of life experiences and are subject to transformation, then I can consciously *choose* the kind of person I want to marry and raise a family with. I can then train myself to recognize and become attracted to this kind of person.

I can also make a conscious distinction between spiritual at-traction and shame-based physical desire, and choose to prioritize the sensations of love over the sensations of shame. After all, which is more important—the buzz my body experiences when a person generates a jolt of adrenaline in my presence, or the warm feeling I get when a person demonstrates kindness and responsibility in my presence?

I can't stop myself from reacting to the presence of people who remind me of my past, but I can stop calling that reaction attrac-tion. I can name the sensations I feel *fear, shame, pity,* or simply *confusion,* and behave accordingly. I can also learn to recognize true attraction to the spiritual qualities of the people I meet, and respond appropriately to them.

If I can do it, so can a person who is aroused by abusers, or alcoholics, or children, or high-heeled shoes, or cross-dressing, or pornography, or any partner that is not spiritually and emotion-ally healthy.

Don't Feed the Shame

Instead of telling ourselves how horrible we are for doing something, we could be asking ourselves why in the world we would want to do it in the first place.

I've talked a lot about how different experiences generate sensations and how easy it is to misinterpret those sensations. What I haven't addressed is just how *unsatisfying* those sensations really are. After all, they are generally *substitute* sensations—ones generated by the third-cousin once-removed of the spiritual quality we are really seeking.

What we long for is God. When we recognize the spiritual need that is at the root of our obsessions, we begin to see the chasm between what we are doing and what we really want and need. Suddenly the temptation is not so tempting. It becomes a farce, a charade, a ludicrous pastime that wastes the precious hours of our day that could be spent doing something real and true and life-affirming.

Nowhere is this gap more obvious than in the temptation of pornography.

Pornography

Let me start by shocking some and angering others in saying that pornography (assuming it involves consenting adults), is not that big of a deal. Many married couples watch pornography together. If you don't have one partner hiding, sneaking or lying to the other, it doesn't do much harm.

Of course, it is also not all that much fun anymore. If you take away the guilt, the shame and the adolescent titillation, pornography is generally about as interesting as watching two people churning butter. The music is awful, the acting is worse, the plots are absurd, and the production quality looks like it was filmed in someone's garage. Oh, right—they usually are.

So if pornography is so poorly made, why do people find it so exciting? Here is what a pornography addict wrote to me once:

In many ways I feel so alive when watching pornography, and yet, I am so .... sexually charged. I am afraid I will not stop at just pornography or sexual chatting online......

This was my answer to him:

Our souls have experiences that generate physical sensations. These sensations are signals, or messages from our souls to our bodies. Our minds then try to interpret what those sensations mean. It is our interpretations, not the sensations themselves, that guide our actions. If we interpret wrong, then we will respond incorrectly to the messages we are receiving.

If I were to throw you overboard into icy arctic water, you would suddenly feel very much "alive." Every cell in your body would react in an attempt to KEEP you alive as you recognized the imminent threat of death. The same systems that would respond slightly if you stepped outside without a jacket in winter would go into high alert to warn you that something was wrong.

You are not feeling "alive" and "sexually charged." You are feeling *shame*.

Your soul is warning you that your relationship to your wife and family may be at risk. Shame is a signal that we have just done, or are about to do, something imperfect. It reminds us that we are human and can make mistakes.

It is a helpful signal. When we feel a little bit of shame, we flush and feel a slight tingle in our face and hands. When we are about to do something that can cause irreparable harm to our spiritual lives, then the signal gets louder. Sometimes a LOT louder. *So* loud that it becomes a wake-up call.

But when we feel asleep, or even dead, sometimes that warning signal—the tingling in our arms and legs, the racing of our hearts, the hyper-alertness of our senses—feels more like a pleasant gift than a warning.

When this happens, the sensations that were designed to make us STOP, TURN AROUND, GO BACK, THINK IT OVER are interpreted as: "LOVE, LIFE & EXCITEMENT –THIS WAY!!"

Unfortunately, just like the sensations of being thrown into ice water, if you revel in them, they will lead to your (spiritual) death. They will not bring you love. They will not give you a better life. They will only lead to the kind of excitement that leads to more shame. Take the warning, and change direction.

At the same time, recognize the fact that this wake-up call only felt good because you were already feeling asleep and dead. Start there. Find people and activities that make you feel awake and alive, instead of shame. You will be able to tell the difference both in the way your body feels and in your ability to share the details of them with your wife and family.

No spouse can meet all of a person's mental, physical, social and spiritual needs, but they can take pleasure in hearing the stories of how they were legitimately met elsewhere. Service organizations, clubs, work, community activities, writing, reading, prayer, singing, exercise, hobbies, gardening—there are many ways to feel spiritually alive.

* * *

What we are looking for is love, affection, connection, a sense of belonging and a belief in our own worthiness. But the physical sensation associated with self-stimulation leaves us feeling *less* loved, *less* connected and *less* worthy of affection.

So the first step in letting go of pornography is to look at it in the light of day and admit that it isn't helping us feel what we *want* to feel. It is only making us feel *something*. *Something* is better than *nothing*, but not by much.

Next, let go of the shame. It only feeds the addiction. Pornography is simply the pure distillation of what our sex-obsessed culture throws at us every single day. Yikes! The cover of that magazine has a nearly-naked woman on it! Yikes! The woman who walked by was wearing her underwear on the outside. Yikes! That thirteen-year-old is wearing a "foxy lady" tank top! Yikes! Aunt Fritzi has awfully big breasts!

Getting embarrassed by our response to the images we are bombarded with and the people we are surrounded by only gives them more power. If we feel guilty or embarrassed for noticing the obvious, we will try to *fight* the obvious, which will just keep us focused on it that much longer.

It helps to realize that *all* men are hard-wired to have a hard response to visual images of women, especially young, beautiful women. If the hip-to-waist ratio is right, a healthy adult male will respond instinctively.

Visual stimulation does not affect women in the same way, which makes it difficult for them to understand its allure for men. Women don't understand that, for a man, walking down a crowded street in springtime is like walking past rows of bakeries and chocolate shops. The sight of attractive women is just as stimulating as the scent of donuts and chocolate. It cannot be controlled any more than we can stop our mouths from salivating at the scent of a croissant.

Women, of course, are not exempt from the lures of pornography, they just call it by a different name. Just as the internet has revolutionized the availability of visual sexual images for men, the e-book revolution has made erotic romance the fastest growing category of downloadable books. Women can become just as aroused by the written descriptions of sex as men are by pictures, and those written descriptions have just as much potential to involve shame, violence and fetishes as a video. (Witness the runaway sales and the social acceptability of *Fifty Shades of Gray*.) The difference is that a woman can read an erotic e-book in a crowded room and no one will even notice.

It is also easier to ambush men with visual images than to trick women into reading erotic literature, so men find themselves being constantly tempted.

Men are also hard-wired to get an erection several times a day for no discernable reason whatsoever. It doesn't mean we are horny. It means we are healthy.

When we expect men to be able to control their passing thoughts *and their autonomic nervous systems*, we set them up for continual failure and shame. What we *can* control is how we respond to the ways our bodies react.

When we experience a flash of arousal, it is tempting to focus our attention on it. After all, it feels *good* to have your groin tingle for a moment. Since these sensations tend to be fleeting, it is tempting to do something to try to prolong them, like grab a magazine or pop open a web site.

If, however, we let the thought or the sensation have its moment and then let it go without focusing on it or fighting it, then
it will fade. If we consciously choose to shift our focus *away* from
the sensation, then pornography will have less allure. We can't
stop thoughts from coming to us, but we can keep them from
hanging around and affecting our behavior.

This is equally true of thoughts we might consider disturbing
or inappropriate. If they are passing thoughts, let them pass. If
they are reoccurring thoughts, let them pass for now, but try to
explore their source in a safe therapeutic environment. Don't assume that you have some dark evil nature just waiting to burst
into action. Assume that you have *been* disturbed by a thought,
not that you *are* disturbed for having it.

If you have experienced abuse as a child, *of course* you will
have disturbing thoughts caused by memories or fears. You can
accept the memories as part of your past without reenacting the
behaviors as part of your future.

One of the darker sides of pornography is that it often includes
disturbing or inappropriate images. If you can't escape the pull of
pornography completely, try to choose images that at least pretend to be more about relationships than about shame or violence. Set a goal of finding "uplifting" pornography, about love
and passion, then slowly wean yourself onto love stories that don't
involve nude sex.

Finally, practice honesty, forgiveness, compassion and faith.
Be honest with yourself and (if possible*) your significant other
about your addiction and your efforts to let it go. Forgive yourself
for your behavior. Forgive others for encouraging it, or shaming it,
or introducing you to it, or whatever you need to forgive.

Try to experience compassion by humanizing the women in
the pictures that you fantasize about. Try to imagine what kind of
pain they must be in to be willing to debase themselves in this
public way. Imagine their stories, from broken homes to abusive
parents and vile boyfriends. See their anger. See their pain. See
their search for identity. See their attempt to wrestle power from
the chains of shame. Feel compassion for them, and the passion
of lust will evaporate. They are participants in your drama. You
victimize each other. Forgive them and yourself.

Have faith that you can take a different path. If you are a porn addict, you are still a child of the universe. You are still better known to the angels in heaven than you are to your own self. You were still loved by God before you were even created. The breath of the Holy Spirit was breathed into you, and you were created out of the clay of God's love. Nothing you have done or will do can ever change that.

The internet age has made it very difficult to escape pornography. The 24/7 availability of pictures and videos and the infinite variety of types of stimulation are unlike anything the world has seen before. If you continue to struggle with a porn addiction, or even if you are just curious about why internet porn is so much more addictive than magazines, then I encourage you to visit the website www.yourbrainonporn.com. It explains the science behind the effect of over stimulation on the brain and has pages and pages of great advice and support.

The M Word

Since I am on a roll, let me shock and anger some additional people by saying that masturbation is also not as big a deal as the ultra-religious would like us to believe. At the same time, it is not as completely harmless as the rest of the world would have us think.

Here's why: The *best* sex, as I explained earlier, is between two committed people who love each other and are expressing affection, intimacy, security, curiosity and a desire to please one another and grow closer together. Ideally, every association we have with sex will be connected to our loved one and be positive and ecstatic in nature, rather than being associated with shame, forbidden fruit, guilt or sin.

In an ideal world, people would enter marriage with knowledge, but with no sexual experience, and absolutely no negative thoughts, emotions, sensations or expectations around their sexuality, their private parts or their bodies in general.

Did you notice the word "ideal" at the beginning of that sentence? Unfortunately, we have ALL grown up with sex and shame intertwined more closely than any other two sensations. Because of this, the chance of a woman entering a marriage without any sexual experiences or associations is significantly reduced, and for a man, this may well seem to be impossible. (I'll explain the difference shortly.)

So, the question with masturbation is whether it increases or decreases the unhealthy relationship between sex and shame. The more experiences we have in which we associate sex, arousal and orgasm with shame or fear rather than affection, the more difficult it will be for us to turn off that association and replace it with something healthy.

This observation raises a host of additional questions that you will have to answer for yourself. No one else knows your history, your fantasies, your goals, your current relationship, or your desire or ability to transform your sex life.

For example, if you are currently one of the few people who associate sex with love and affection, and you associate masturbation with shame and secrecy, then masturbating will increase your association between sex and shame.

If, on the other hand, you associate sex with shame and sin, but you associate masturbation with self-care and have fantasies about love and affection, then masturbation might help change your attitude towards sex with your spouse and improve your love life.

If, like many, both sex and masturbation are associated with shame, and your sexual fantasies are fear, shame or intensity-based, then masturbation will just make it that much harder to develop an intimacy-based love life. On the other hand, if you can consciously change the nature of your fantasies, then you might be able to change the kind of sexual contact you are attracted to. After all, if we can change our spiritual attractions, we can change our fantasy attractions, too.

If this sound like a great excuse to continue masturbating, let me throw in this one word of caution: If your fantasies are too wonderful, then no real-life person will ever be able to match them. No one can compete with your imagination.

The *ideal*, then, is to have your fantasies and your reality, your expectations and your experience all be at the same time with the same person. But for many, the ideal is not even remotely possible. As they say, "That train left the station a long time ago."

For them, masturbation may well have a valid place as a tool for self-care. I really don't know. What I *think* I know is that actions are rarely moral or immoral. It is our motivation behind them and what we do with them that gives them meaning.

It's important to dispassionately consider how masturbation combined with a personal fantasy life might affect your current relationship, any potential future relationships, your feelings about yourself, your feelings about your religion, and the relationship between your heart, your mind and your body. Then make your peace with masturbation.

Whatever you decide to do, just don't shame yourself for the decision. Hold out for the ideal, or make do with what you can offer yourself. Then pay attention and remain open to change.

Why This Issue Is More Difficult for Men

Earlier I suggested that there is a difference between men and women in this area. People often disparage men for their constant interest in sex. One reason, as I mentioned, is that men respond more to visual stimulation, of which there is an abundance in our culture.

But there is another reason that is rarely talked about. A woman can go her entire lifetime and never experience an orgasm, but a man will start having an orgasm about once a month once he reaches puberty, whether he wants to or not. It is hard to miss something you've never had, but once you've experienced something pleasurable, it is difficult to ignore it.

Just as a woman ovulates every month, a man builds up a supply of semen that has to be released. If he doesn't release it through masturbation, it will be released in his sleep as a nocturnal emission (a wet dream). Because the body must be aroused to ejaculate, a male will usually wake up from a vivid dream in the throes of an orgasm. That dream, more often than not, will be of a sexual nature.

In other words, a healthy male will have a sexual fantasy resulting in an orgasm about once a month, whether he wants to or not. It is not surprising, then, that many men choose to assist the process consciously.

Wet dreams, like ovulation, are beyond a person's control and can therefore become a great source of confusion and shame. Like any dream, they are unpredictable. Sometimes they are about love and affection, but often they are about something intense, embarrassing or confusing. They are always messy. For boys, masturbating can be a way to take control of the experience, the feelings and the evidence. Like any pleasurable habit, it can be hard to break.

Women face a different challenge. If women were to have an orgasm every time they inserted a tampon, they would think about sex a lot more than they do. Instead, women who masturbate (and most do) get to take control of their sexuality in a way that men can't. It is a conscious choice, not an alternate to the unpredictable. It is a process of discovery rather than a required release.

Consequently, women tend to fantasize more about romance rather than sexual acts. If these fantasies help a woman learn about her body so that she can share more knowledgably with her spouse, then it may be a real blessing. If these fantasies are a way to escape intimacy with the person she ought to be closest to, then it can become a real problem. Only you know how you are using your intimate moments.

TOOLS OF PERSONAL GROWTH

This section offers a few tools and resources to help you be successful in your efforts at transformation.

Affirmations

Some of you may already love affirmations, while others may be wondering, "Why should I sit around talking to myself?"

The answer is that we all sit around talking to ourselves all the time. We have a constant background voice, sometimes referred to as the inner critic, who often sounds remarkably like our mothers. Many of us give ourselves thousands of negative messages every single day. If we want to retrain our inner critic so that its comments reflect our more mature, enlightened understanding of ourselves, then we will have to take active steps to do so.

One of the most effective tools I have found is the use of affirmations. An affirmation is simply a positive statement that is specifically chosen to counteract or contradict a previously held negative belief about oneself or the world. This positive statement is repeated over and over, either out loud or silently to oneself, to try to change the way we think about ourselves.

Note that I said *positive* statement. Affirmations should be phrased as a positive rather than negative statement. So, for example, if a part of you feels *worthless*, instead of saying, "I am *not* worthless," you would say, "I am *valuable*," or "I am *precious*."

In order to choose the right phrase to use for an affirmation, you need to get in touch with the inner voices you are trying to counteract. This is where the techniques I described in The Secret of Emotions, such as internal consultation, cocktail-partying, journaling, focusing and the help of a good therapist can really come in handy.

There are, of course, generic affirmations that lots of people have found helpful. Many people say an entire list of affirmations every day. That is one way to start, but I encourage you to pick a few to say more frequently. You can always switch from one affirmation to another, but finding just the right affirmation for *you* can have a more powerful effect than saying a few random affirmations every day.

During one powerful exercise, I discovered that I felt broken, worthless and uncomfortable with my male energy. The affirmation I wrote for myself included the words *whole, man* and *precious*. I said it 100 times every day for a year. It was much more effective than the ones I had borrowed from my recovery worksheets.

On the other hand, having already used popular affirmations for more than a year had given me a good feel for what worked for me.

There follows here a short list of just a few affirmations I found online. You can find thousands more, along with detailed explanations of how and why to use them by typing in "recovery affirmations" in a search engine.

You'll see that they counteract a wide range of negative thoughts, some subtle, some not. I encourage you to read through this series of affirmations, slowly and out loud. Do any make your heart twitch or your throat tighten? Do any seem completely ridiculous? Those are the ones to take a second look at.

- I am blessed.
- I am good enough just as I am.
- I am willing to change and grow.
- What I do makes a difference.
- I release all fear and know that I'm always protected.
- I trust myself.
- I know the Truth of who I am.
- I am exactly where I need to be at all times.
- I am surrounded by love.
- I have faith in the goodness of life.
- This too shall pass.
- In my heart, I'm always at home.
- Serenity and calm are my birthright.
- Self-abuse has no place in my life.

- All things in their right time.
- I am surrounded by peace.
- I surrender to my good.
- I remember the truth of who I am.

Affirmations are not magic, but they are effective. They are used a great deal in the Recovery community but are also a part of many standard therapy techniques.

There are also many religious traditions that use prayer as a form of repetitive affirmation. If you are a member of a religion that uses written prayers or scripture, I would like to share a particularly powerful way to combine the power of affirmations with the power of prayer.

I call this tool "power prayer." I take just a phrase from a prayer that resonates deeply in my soul and repeat it over and over all day long. This is different from the more focused personal affirmation that I just described. This spiritual affirmation combines the power of prayer with the power of affirmations to help rewrite the negative self-talk that we all live with. Phrases like *"The Lord is my Shepherd"* or *"Create in me a pure heart, O my God,"* or *"all things work together for good to them that love God,"* or *"Noble have I created thee"* make good power prayers.

Once you feel really comfortable with a power prayer, you can use it like a shower to wash away negative self-talk. You can take a specific negative thought, like, "I am unworthy" and hold it in one corner of your mind while you shower it with a positive prayer like, *"I knew My love for thee."*

With a regular affirmation, your negative beliefs can sometimes be stronger than the positive affirmation. This is particularly true if that negative belief was taught to you by a powerful source of authority. By using Scripture, the positive belief has the added power of faith in God. Instead of being overwhelmed by negative thoughts, scripture-based affirmations can actually transform these thoughts by holding them up to the light of a higher authority.

Affirmations can also be helpful starting points for the Internal Consultation technique I described earlier. If an affirmation brings up feelings—either comfortable or uncomfortable—it is helpful to explore where those feelings come from.

A Final Plug for Twelve-Step Groups

Surfing the web looking for recovery affirmations reminded me once again just how much I *love* the recovery community. Everywhere you go, there are people talking about their Higher Power, and personal growth, and overcoming challenges, and being kind to themselves and others, and taking responsibility for their own actions. I don't hear that kind of conversation many other places.

The recovery community is the only place I've seen where people talk about God without having any ulterior motive. I say that, knowing full well that many of the people reading this book will be offended by the statement. But it is true. They aren't trying to save your soul or save the world.

People in recovery talk about God, and they couldn't care less what name you have given your Higher Power, where you worship, what your politics are, or if you think they are going to heaven. Theirs is not an Institutional god. They talk about their *personal* relationship with God, not what God is doing in the world and how we should be following His guidance to fix everyone else's problems.

Yet, if more people worried more about *their* personal relationship with God and *less* about *everyone else's*, then the world would be a much more loving and spiritually healthy place.

So give it a try. Go online and visit the sites for some of the recovery organizations. Read what they have to say.

If you feel too shy or embarrassed to go to an actual meeting, just explore the concepts they present. Many of these organizations even have on-line meetings. They aren't the same as talking face-to-face, but I'm sure they will be enlightening. I've put the ones of particular interest to people dealing with sex and relationship issues in **bold**.

Al-Anon/Alateen, for friends and family members of alcoholics
AA - Alcoholics Anonymous
ACA - Adult Children of Alcoholics
CA - Cocaine Anonymous
CLA - Clutterers Anonymous
CMA - Crystal Meth Anonymous
CoDA - Co-Dependents Anonymous, for people working to
end patterns of dysfunctional relationships and develop
functional and healthy relationships
Co-Anon, for friends and family of addicts
COSA - Codependents of Sex Addicts
COSLAA - CoSex and Love Addicts Anonymous
DA - Debtors Anonymous
EA - Emotions Anonymous, for mental and emotional illness
EHA - Emotional Health Anonymous, for mental and
emotional illness
FA - Families Anonymous, for relatives and friends of addicts
FA - Food Addicts in Recovery Anonymous
FAA - Food Addicts Anonymous
GA - Gamblers Anonymous
Gam-Anon/Gam-A-Teen, for friends and family members
of problem gamblers
MA - Marijuana Anonymous
NA - Narcotics Anonymous
NAIL - Neurotics Anonymous, for mental/emotional illness
Nar-Anon, for friends and family members of addicts
NicA - Nicotine Anonymous
PA - Pills Anonymous, for prescription pill addiction.
OA - Overeaters Anonymous
OLGA - Online Gamers Anonymous
SA - Smokers Anonymous
SA - Sexaholics Anonymous
SAA - Sex Addicts Anonymous
SCA - Sexual Compulsives Anonymous
SLAA - Sex and Love Addicts Anonymous
SIA - Survivors of Incest Anonymous
WA - Workaholics Anonymous

Which of this staggering list of organizations should you explore? Well, the fact is that most people have multiple issues. Start with the biggest problem you are willing to admit to and work from there.

Since you are reading this book, you might want to consider SA, SAA, SCA or SLAA. SLAA is more about relationship addiction, while the others are more about problems of sexually acting out.

CoDA is an excellent catch-all group for people dealing with all types of relationship challenges, not just sex and romance issues. ACA is for people whose parents were alcoholic. Many of the other family and friend support groups don't require an active addiction, but are good sources of support for relationship problems.

In the process of dealing with what you *think* you know, you may discover that you need to visit SIA, or OA, or WA, or any number of other support groups. That's not a bad thing. It is a sign that you are learning about yourself and taking care of the things you discover. Remember, *it will all work to the good in the end.*

Asking for Help

I'm sorry. No matter how many times you read this book, how many affirmations you say or how many twelve-step meetings you attend, it will not be a substitute for a good therapist. I know that this will be disappointing to many of you, and absolutely terrifying for others. But if your life is not going as well as you would like, then finding an objective, compassionate person to consult with about it will do you a lot of good. It doesn't replace prayer and meditation, but then prayer and meditation don't replace consultation, either.

Having a real, live person look into your eyes and say, "You have a right to feel that way" can break through more layers of denial and fear than a hundred books, so give it a try.

Before I visited my first therapist, I was terrified. I was sure that she was going to call in the guys with the white coats and drag me away. Assuming that your fears are a little more rational than mine, let me start by relieving you of three of the most common.

First, there is the fear of stigma. If people know you are seeing a therapist, won't they think there is something wrong with you?

No. Not anyone worth paying any attention to, anyway. After all, if you don't think someone will be supportive of your efforts to improve your life, why would you bother to tell them you are in therapy? Your therapist won't tell them.

But you may be worried for nothing. If you have educated friends, then the chances are good that they, or one of their family members, have also seen a therapist at some point. We live in a stressful world. Between addictions and depression and work stress and family problems and ... well, there are thousands of good reasons to see a therapist. If you are ashamed of the *reason* why you need a therapist, then keep that part of it to yourself. That's your right.

The second fear is that it won't work. In the movies we see psychiatrists charging $200 an hour, week after week, while the client never seems to make any progress. First, forget everything you've ever seen about a therapist in any movie or TV show. They are *entertainment* and real, successful therapy sessions are not entertaining to watch. Real therapists would lose their licenses for doing what you see in the movies.

Consider therapy a kind of consultation on how to improve your life, the way you would bring a contractor in to help remodel your home. If you don't feel you are making progress after half a dozen sessions, *change therapists.* Don't give up. If a plumber did a bad job on your kitchen, you would get a new plumber, not order take-out for the rest of your life. If one therapist doesn't work well with you, there will be others to try. You deserve the best life possible, and finding the right "consultant" will help you do that.

Finally, people are afraid that therapy costs too much. Again, forget the movie version. Many therapists use a sliding scale based on what you can pay. Some take insurance (but don't decide how long to stay in therapy based on your insurance limit).

Also, if money is a big concern for you, then there is a good chance that your inner demons are sabotaging more than just your love life. The same shame and dysfunctional relationship patterns that are interfering with your serenity and psychological well-being are probably also interfering with your self-esteem and relationships at work. People who are psychologically and spiritually healthy are more successful in *every* aspect of their lives.

The year I started therapy was also the year I had to declare bankruptcy. I was living on about $12,000 a year, and considered buying a toothbrush a luxury. Therapy helped me change my relationship with money and wealth so that I was no longer ashamed *or afraid* to take care of myself materially. Of course, I can't *guarantee* that spending money on a therapist will pay for itself, but *can* pretty much guarantee that if you find a *good* therapist and *you do the work* you need to do, you will consider your money well spent.

Finding a Good Therapist

A "good" therapist is not the one that charges the most money, or the one with the most letters behind his or her name.

Good therapists hold healthy beliefs themselves and can confirm for you that they are true, not just in general, but *for you in specific.*

Here is a list of healthy beliefs that a good therapist will help you internalize:

- I am safe—though my body may be frail and vulnerable, my soul is strong and eternal.
- I am valuable—I matter to God and to the world. I make a difference.
- I am lovable—I am created in the image of God and reflect spiritual virtues.
- I am loving—I am attracted to the signs of God reflected in the people around me.
- I have capacities—I am not a helpless pawn of the universe. I can make choices and accomplish goals.
- I can grow—I am not static. I can learn and develop new skills and virtues.

A good therapist will also support your efforts at developing honesty, forgiveness, compassion and faith.

Before you walk into a therapist's office, you need to determine whether the therapist wants to focus on developing your spiritual capacity, or to simply change your brain chemistry and send you home. Does he or she believe the things I listed above? If therapists don't believe these things themselves, they may not have the tools needed to help you counteract your own unhealthy beliefs.

If you believe in God, Free Will and the importance of spiritual growth, then you need a therapist who can do more than smile condescendingly at you while writing a prescription. In short, you need a therapist who understands that you were born with an innate longing for God, and who shares that longing.

Fortunately, there are thousands of spiritually-minded therapists who, if given the opportunity, will be happy to support a process of healing that includes respect for your spiritual development. I have found that non-denominational Pastoral Counselors are the most open to an integrated psychological *and* spiritual approach to healing, but there are also spiritually-minded social workers, psychologists, psychiatrists and a dozen different forms of certified therapists. Many therapists and treatment programs use a twelve-step recovery approach to personal issues. Their focus on a "Higher Power" offers a non-denominational yet spiritual approach to healing. While counselors' training is valuable, it is their ability to make the personal connection that will make the healing possible.

Of course some types of training are more conducive to a spiritual approach to emotional healing than others. If you find someone who practices *Cognitive Therapy* or *Behavioral Therapy*, ask them up front if they believe in a Higher Power and if they are supportive of participation in a twelve-step program. If not, then they will probably not be supportive of the approach I've presented here.

If you are hesitant to ask friends and family for recommendations, then you can still find out a lot about a prospective therapist before seeing them. These days you can go online and research a therapist's training and philosophy. Look at their photographs. Read what they have to say about themselves and their style. Notice the words they use. Listen to your intuition, then e-mail or call for a trial appointment.

Summary of Part Three

I am hoping I can end this book with a bang, but that is really up to you.

- In Part One, *The Secret of Emotions*, I explain that our emotions tell us about the presence or absence of virtues in our lives.
- In Part Two, *4 Tools of Emotional Healing*, I explain the value of developing honesty, forgiveness, compassion and faith.
- In Part Three, *Longing for Love*, I define love not as a sensation, but as an attraction to the attributes of God reflected in the hearts of the people around us.
- I explain that healthy relationships are the result of falling in love with virtues, and then letting that love lead you to people who are of good character.
- I offer hope that each of us is capable of retraining our hearts to become attracted to the qualities that create healthy relationships.
- I point towards the means of identifying virtues and becoming attracted to them.
- I describe the many emotions that masquerade as love.
- I explain the difference between intensity and intimacy and argue that they are mutually exclusive.
- I give reasons why you should choose intimacy over intensity.
- I offer insights into how to deal with feelings of loneliness and anxiety.
- I point out some love myths—like signs and soul mates—that create chaos.
- I encourage you to be happy with the one you love.
- I shine a light on temptation in order to increase clarity and reduce shame.

- I remind you that you are defined by your relationship to God, not your sexual attractions.
- I explain the value and power of affirmations
- I introduce you to the 12-step recovery community.
- I encourage you to accept professional help and support.

Any one of these pieces of insight would have saved me years of heartache and shame if it had been offered to me when I was younger. Whether it can be of any use to you is entirely in your hands.

Good luck.

APPENDIX

An Alternate View of Salvation

In Part One, I describe how belief in Original Sin makes it very difficult to feel good about ourselves or humanity in general. It is difficult to believe in Original Sin and still believe you are a noble, worthy human being.

In Part Two I refer to research that suggests that belief in an angry or judgmental God is associated with a host of mental illnesses. From this you might have gotten the impression that I was anti-religion, or at least anti-Christianity. Nothing could be further from the truth. I revere the Founders of every major religion, but I believe that Their teachings have sometimes gotten turned around and misunderstood.

I believe that it is possible to believe in Jesus Christ as your personal Savior *without* believing that He is saving you from being sent to Hell because you are too evil to go to heaven without His blood sacrifice. If He is not saving you from Hell, though, *what* is He saving you from? That is the subject of this appendix. I hope to offer you an understanding of salvation that is ennobling and uplifting rather than damning.

This section is more overtly religious than anything else in this book, but you don't have to be overtly religious yourself to have struggled with our culture's obsession with sin and punishment.

In order to understand the real meaning of salvation, we need to answer four simple questions.

What am I being saved from?
Why do I need to be saved?
Why can't I save myself?
What do I have to do to be saved?

What am I being saved from?

God wants to save me—but *not* from some outside force (the devil) or some external punishment (hell), and not even from my own supposedly innate sinfulness. God's great desire for me is to save me from my complete and utter ignorance of my own true self – what God created me to be, and the sacred trust he placed within me and my life.

God's goal is to help me redefine *who* I am, *why* I was created, and *how* I can achieve my fullest potential. God wants me to learn, grow, love and be happy.

If we see a plant that does not grow, we call it dead. Likewise a human soul that does not grow and learn and become what God meant for it to be is *spiritually* dead. There is no worse "punishment" than this.

Why Do I Need to Be Saved?

The usual answer to this question is that we are sinful—that because of original sin we deserve punishment and are unworthy of God's grace.

But if we replace the word "sinful" with the word "ignorant," then we can easily recognize our innate need for education without feeling any shame for not being perfect to begin with. We are all born ignorant, but with an immense capacity to learn and grow. We are born not knowing who we really are, and not having lived up to our full potential. This is obvious.

Why do I need help to be saved?

What is not so obvious is why we are in need of Jesus—or any other Messenger of God—as an outside source of guidance. Why can't we "save ourselves"? That is, why can't we figure out who we are on our own? Plants don't need teachers in order to grow and blossom. Why do we?

We need God to send us Divine Educators for the simple fact that people learn primarily through example. We study and observe the people and things around us and come to conclusions about how things work and how we should behave.

If humans were simply animals, then we could learn everything we need to know by observing other animals. But we aren't.

Humans have souls. We are infused with the Holy Spirit. Our souls operate under a different set of laws and are guided by a different set of principles than animal instinct. In order to learn how to behave like humans, we need spiritual examples. This spiritual example *has to* come from outside the normal worldly plane.

If people followed the example of animals, we would live by the law of the jungle, but God wants us to follow the Golden Rule. When we explore the example of the *physical* world, we find that it is limited and prone to chaos. When we explore our *spiritual* reality, we find that we are unlimited, creative and full of love.

This does not mean that the material world is *evil*. It simply means that the material world is an inadequate example for us to follow when we are trying to explore our uniquely human potential.

With all of the examples of limited physical reality that surround us, it is *essential* that God save us from a material perspective by providing us with spiritual examples. We cannot create these examples or discover these truths on our own. That is why God sent us Jesus Christ. That is how He saved us. The example of the life and teachings of Jesus Christ *saves us* from the degradation of a purely material, animal existence. That is how *all* of God's spiritual Teachers save us from ignorance of our true spiritual selves.

Because these Divine Messengers have been providing positive examples since the beginning of time, we might try to convince ourselves that we don't really need them. But if we try to imagine a world in which there never were any spiritual examples, it becomes clear that we would not have "discovered" the Golden Rule (let alone "turn the other cheek") by observing nature alone.

What do I have to do to be saved?

The two competing answers to this question that we hear from most Christians are that we are either saved by faith or saved by works.

Both are required.

First, I have to have *faith* that God knows more about me than I know about myself, and that He will guide me to healthy behavior. As an expression of this faith, I also have to be willing to recognize, believe in and love God's Teachers when He sends them.

This is no small task.

But salvation is not a one-time event. It is a process of discovery and growth. So, in addition to these initial acts of *faith*, salvation also requires a lifetime of effort, action and determination on my part to live up to my full capacity. Believing in God's teachings requires faith. Living up to them requires works.

Becoming My True Self

Becoming my true self involves loving God and obeying God. It involves loving God's virtues, and *living* those virtues in my daily life. We are all created in the "image of God." We "reflect" the qualities of that image when we develop our God-given virtues such as love, compassion, honesty, reverence and courage.

Loving, learning, growing, living, reflecting virtues, being human, being obedient—these are not separate processes. They are different ways of looking at the same thing. When we embrace the process, then we are assured of eternal life and growth, and when we resist the process, we begin to wither and die.

I hope that this simple explanation of what God is saving you from, why, and how, makes sense to you. If it does, you will be able to retain your love and faith in God, while letting go of the religious misunderstandings that feed your guilt, shame and self-loathing.

ABOUT THE AUTHOR

Justice Saint Rain is the author of several books that blend psychology with spiritual insights. He is both a writer and an artist, and has been producing a line of spiritually-oriented material for over 30 years. He currently lives with his family on a farm in Southern Indiana.

He does not do life-coaching or consultations by phone or e-mail, but he does have a FaceBook page called *Love, Lust and the Longing for God*, an author's page at GoodReads.com and a writer's blog.

He will be happy to try to answer questions and respond to comments posted at any of these sites.

Join the conversation at:
www.justicesaintrain.com

Love Lust and the Longing for God is available as three separate gift books, or as a single volume for personal use:
The Secret of Emotions
4 Tools of Emotional Healing
Longing for Love
Love, Lust and the Longing for God

Available in print and Kindle editions from:
SecretofEmotions.com and Amazon.com

Made in the USA
Lexington, KY
07 February 2014